SPEECH AND MORALITY

SPEECH

AND

MORALITY

ON THE METAETHICAL
IMPLICATIONS OF SPEAKING

TERENCE CUNEO

OXFORD
UNIVERSITY PRESS

OXFORD
UNIVERSITY PRESS

Great Clarendon Street, Oxford, OX2 6DP,
United Kingdom

Oxford University Press is a department of the University of Oxford.
It furthers the University's objective of excellence in research, scholarship,
and education by publishing worldwide. Oxford is a registered trade mark of
Oxford University Press in the UK and in certain other countries

First Edition published in 2014

Published in the United States of America by Oxford University Press
198 Madison Avenue, New York, NY 10016, United States of America

British Library Cataloguing in Publication Data
Data available

Library of Congress Control Number: 2014930366

ISBN 978–0–19–871272–5

For Niko, who is learning to speak

Preface

A prominent philosopher once expressed to me his view that philosophers should, every five years or so, distance themselves from their area of specialty to develop a new one. The idea behind this approach, apparently, is that it protects philosophers' work from becoming stale. Were it followed, there would be much less temptation to repeat oneself or to get stuck in a theoretical rut. In the ideal case, we philosophers would have new things to say about fresh topics.

For all I know, this might be excellent advice. But I have failed egregiously to follow it. Whether that is because I am a creature of habit or because of the magnetism of the ideas about which I find myself thinking, I cannot tell. However that may be, this book is not an attempt to say new things about fresh topics.

But it is an attempt to say some new things about a familiar topic. For my project in this book is to offer an unfamiliar argument for a familiar position, namely, moral realism. When I say that moral realism is a familiar position, I mean two things. Moral realism is, in the first place, long familiar to the philosophical tradition (although, of course, it has not always had a name or been called "moral realism"). It is also a position with which I am well familiar, having developed an argument for it in a previous book.[1] In the Introduction, I lay out my reasons for thinking that it is worth developing another argument for moral realism. Here I would like to emphasize that while this book and its predecessor develop different arguments for moral realism, they are animated by a common conviction. Both books press the case that morality is ubiquitous, showing up in and having implications for areas that many philosophers have not supposed it would.

---

1. Cuneo (2007).

The main idea I develop in this book is that one such area is speech. Speech, I maintain, is a thoroughly normative phenomenon: one performs speech acts such as asserting, promising, and commanding, I claim, by altering one's normative position with regard to one's audience, acquiring rights, responsibilities, and obligations of various sorts. Reflection reveals, I further claim, that some of these rights, responsibilities, and obligations, are moral. Indeed, I argue, they are as moral realists say. Although I have relatively few Kantian tendencies, the main argument I develop could be described as being transcendental, as it implies that a necessary condition for the possibility of speech is that there be moral facts of certain kinds.

I do not believe that this argument itself vindicates moral realism in the sense that one cannot reasonably reject one or more of its premises. It is better viewed as part of a larger, overarching case to be made in realism's favor. On this occasion I have not attempted to lay out this more general case, choosing instead to focus on one argument that, in my judgment, presents both an interesting case for realism and a challenge to rival antirealist positions. In most instances, I should note, I do not find these rival antirealist positions to be obviously false, especially in their most nuanced and sophisticated forms. But I do find most of them unsatisfactory—and some of them deeply unsatisfactory—in important respects. Part of my aim here is to try to highlight some of the respects in which these views are unsatisfactory. I am especially inclined to put pressure on a line of thought that I encounter rather frequently, which is that the rejection of moral facts is relatively innocuous, as it would not have widespread theoretical or practical implications. I believe that this line of thought is mistaken. In my judgment, if there were no moral facts then we would not be able to speak.

I remain fully aware, of course, that moral realism is a deeply contested position that many excellent philosophers reject. I call attention to this fact not because it distinguishes realism from other philosophical positions; most other substantive philosophical views are also hotly debated and rejected by some excellent philosophers. Rather, what distinguishes realism from most of these other views is that, unlike advocates of these other contested philosophical positions, realists ordinarily believe that it matters a great deal whether their view is true. It is important, realists hold, that our ethical choices and appraisals can be mistaken or improved because they fail to answer to moral standards not of our own devising. And it is important that our ethical disputes can be decided by not the exercise of power or whim but by the apprehension of how things are morally. If realists are right about this, then the awareness of moral reality should make a difference to how we live and view our lives and evaluate the lives of others. At any rate, it is in this regard that many realists believe that their view is different from other highly controversial philosophical positions, such as four-dimensionalism or presentism, which bear only a very indirect relation to how we should view and live our lives and evaluate the lives of others.[2]

Although realists ordinarily believe this, they do not have the luxury of recommending their position on prudential grounds, citing the ways in which its acceptance will bring meaning or fulfillment to one's life. Nor can they plausibly suggest that there is a set of ascetic disciplines or "experiments in living" that will place one in a better position to see its truth, as the ancient Stoics believed about their views. The best that can be done is to develop a wide-ranging and fairly abstract case in its favor. My project in this book is to contribute to such a case.

I have tried my best to streamline the book's discussion so as to keep its main line of argument firmly in view. This has meant that, although I have attempted to address important alternatives and objections to what I say, there are many alternatives and objections, which other philosophers might find interesting, that I fail to consider. Some might complain, for example, that the discussion takes too much for granted. At various points, after all, the argument leans on the assumption (for which I offer no argument) that there are prosaic practice-based normative features such as the rights, responsibilities, and obligations that attach to Major League Baseball players, US postal workers, and officers of the law. Although I myself cannot think of compelling reasons to be skeptical of this assumption, those who are will find much of what I say unpersuasive.

---

2. Moral fictionalists, such as Joyce (2001) and (2006), disagree, pressing the point that, as a practical matter, it would not matter much if there were moral standards or whether we genuinely believed they exist. Cuneo and Christy (2011), Olson (2011a), and Enoch (2011), ch. 5, offer responses to the fictionalists. Bloomfield (2009) is a valuable discussion of the practical implications of metaethical views.

Others might complain that, even if the main argument of the book goes through, it establishes too little. For suppose we distinguish, following Derek Parfit, two conceptions of normativity: the *reason-involving* conception (which refers to reasons or apparent reasons) and the *rule-involving* conception (which refers to requirements or rules that distinguish between what is correct and incorrect or what is allowed and disallowed).[3] It might be pointed out that this book defends the claim that moral features exist in only the ruling-involving sense. And that, it might also be said, is not terribly interesting. What would be important and interesting is if the argument were to establish that moral facts exist in the reason-involving sense. (The sense of "reason" in question is the irreducibly normative one in which reasons are considerations that favor responses of various sorts.)

I disagree. Defending a view according to which moral facts exist in something close to the rule-involving sense can be both interesting and important. Imagine, for example, one were to accept a non-Humean account of reasons, according to which, necessarily, moral considerations imply reasons to behave in certain ways regardless of our desires or goals. It might be much easier to defend such a view if we had excellent reasons to believe that moral facts exist in at least something close to the rule-involving sense.[4] (In Chapter 7, I gesture at why this might be.) Or suppose, somewhat differently, one were to embrace a Humean account of reasons, according to which moral considerations do not necessarily imply reasons to behave in certain ways, since they depend on the contingent desires or goals of human agents. If this view were true, establishing that moral facts exist in something close to the rule-involving sense would imply that they are the sorts of considerations that could be (the constituents of) reasons in the only available sense. Both conclusions, as I say, might be both interesting and important.

Books take a long time to write, and I have accumulated debts of gratitude to many. In 2007, Calvin College provided a teaching

---

3. Parfit (2011), Vol. I, p. 144. In Chapter 5, I introduce a similar distinction between *lean* and *robust* normativity.
4. In Chapter 4, I maintain that many reasons appear to be non-Humean. If they do appear to be non-Humean, then the view I defend is one according to which there are, according to Parfit's taxonomy, normative considerations in the reason-involving sense.

release that allowed me to complete a first draft of this manuscript. My former colleagues at Calvin also provided helpful feedback on a version of the paper that laid out the book's main argument and an early version of Chapter 4. Audiences at the American Philosophical Association, Boston University, Purdue University, the University of Edinburgh, Wake Forest University, and Washington University St Louis all provided perceptive comments on various parts of the manuscript.

I am especially grateful to several groups of philosophers who read substantial chunks of the manuscript. A group of my colleagues at the University of Vermont—Sin yee Chan, Louis deRosset, Don Loeb, Mark Moyer, and Matt Weiner—met with me weekly in Spring 2009, providing extremely helpful comments on an early draft of the manuscript. The feedback that this group provided changed the manuscript more than any other. Over the last four years I have also subjected members of the University of Vermont Ethics Reading Group—Lorraine Besser-Jones, Sin yee Chan, Tyler Doggett, Randall Harp, Arthur Kuflik, Crystal L'Hote, Don Loeb, and Andrew Reisner—to versions of Chapters 1, 3, 6, and 7. Predictably, the result has been to send me back to the drawing board multiple times. Finally, in 2012, a small group of philosophers at Washington University St Louis that included Eric Brown, Charlie Kurch, and Martin Turner read the manuscript and invited me to discuss it with them, which eventuated in stimulating discussion and more changes. In addition to these three groups, Paul Bloomfield, Sean Christy, David Enoch, Chris Eberle, Bill FitzPatrick, Guy Fletcher, Dan Hooley, David Liebesman, Christian Miller, Luke Maring, Mark Murphy, Jonas Olson, Anne Poortenga, Andrew Reisner, Patrick Rysiew, Russ Shafer-Landau, Daniel Star, Sarah Stroud, Christine Tappolet, Mark van Roojen, René van Woudenberg, Jeff Wisdom, and Nick Wolterstorff all provided comments on or discussed with me sections of the manuscript. In addition to two anonymous referees for Oxford University Press, Matti Eklund, Charlie Kurch, and John Mumm were kind enough to offer me written comments on a draft of the entire manuscript.

My greatest philosophical debts are, however, to several of my colleagues at the University of Vermont—Louis deRosset, Tyler Doggett, and Mark Moyer—and Nick Wolterstorff. In characteristic fashion, Tyler offered me copious written comments on drafts of

Chapters 1, 3, 6, and 7. Sometimes it took me days to see that a seemingly minor comment of his was actually very important, requiring me to rethink and reorganize sections of the book. Louis and Mark read not only one but nearly two entire versions of the manuscript, sacrificing a great deal of their time to do so. They provided so much input that at a certain point it became intolerably distracting to note in the text where I owe an objection or insight to them. Suffice it to say that both Louis' and Mark's comments required me to extensively revise the book and that their influence on it is extensive. To Nick Wolterstorff I owe a different sort of debt. It was Nick who first introduced me to both speech act theory and the normative theory of speech. Those familiar with his work on this topic will see its influence. More importantly, Nick has been to me not simply a mentor but also a dear friend.

Finally, I owe thanks to Peter Momtchiloff at Oxford University Press, who expressed interest in the project from the outset, for his sure-handed guidance, and to Luke Reinsma, who volunteered his considerable copy-editing skills, for his efforts.

Authors frequently speak of their books as if they were their own children. Sometimes, however, the lives of books are in fact intertwined with the lives of one's actual children. This is one such book. It sprang to life at roughly the same time that my son, Niko, was born. In the roughly seven years that have passed since their respective beginnings, Niko has developed in ways that are much more impressive and interesting than this book. Among other things, he began to speak. And, as any parent knows, that is like watching magic happen right before one's very eyes.

Contents

1
Clarke's Insight

In the *Leviathan*, Hobbes asks us to imagine a state of nature in which human agents live in a pre-civilized condition. Agents in the state of nature, Hobbes maintains, have a variety of practical reasons to act—reasons to protect themselves and their kin from harm, for example. But while agents in the state of nature have practical reasons to act, none of these reasons, Hobbes claims, is *moral* in character. Only when the people make a compact with one another to cede their natural freedoms to a ruling body, the Leviathan, do moral reasons emerge, these reasons being the product of the Leviathan's directives to the citizenry. To this tale about human behavior in the state of nature, Hobbes adds an important qualification: the story is not a piece of philosophical fantasy. In its main lines, it is the best explanation we have of the emergence of moral norms.[1]

Hobbes' early critics, such as Samuel Clarke, complained that they could not coherently imagine how this story would go. Clarke writes that in order "to make these compacts obligatory," Hobbes

> is forced...to recur to an antecedent *law of nature*: and this destroys all that he had before said. For the same law of nature which obliges men to fidelity, *after* having made a compact; will unavoidably, upon all the same accounts, be found to oblige them, *before* all compacts...That compacts ought to be faithfully performed, and obedience to be duly paid to civil powers: the obligation of *these things* [Hobbes] is forced to deduce entirely from the internal reason and fitness of things themselves.[2]

---

1. Or so goes a popular interpretation of Hobbes, accepted by many of his contemporaries. I make no claims about its accuracy.
2. Clarke in Raphael (1991), 219, 221; cf. also 222. Korsgaard (1996), 28, brought this feature of Clarke's view to my attention.

Under a natural interpretation, Clarke's point is that if agents in the state of nature are to make a compact with one another—if they are genuinely to *promise* certain things to one another—moral obligations must already exist. To illustrate his point, Clarke adverts to the obligation that promises be faithfully performed. An obligation of this sort, Clarke intimates, is not generated by promising but is a condition of performing a promise in the first place. Accordingly, Clarke maintains, Hobbes' contractualism does not explain the emergence of moral norms. Rather, it presupposes their existence.

When suitably qualified, I believe that Clarke's claim is correct. Suppose that, in standard conditions, I utter the sentence "I promise to lend you my vintage Les Paul." According to an ordinary understanding of promising, I have thereby acquired the obligation to lend you my vintage guitar—the uttering of this sentence being what (in part) generates this particular obligation. But in addition to this obligation, I also have the obligation, in Clarke's words, to "faithfully perform" what I have promised, where this means that, when promising, I at least intend to do what I say. This latter obligation, however, is not generated by my promising anything. Rather, it is a normative condition thereof. In ordinary conditions, when promising to act in a certain way, an agent ought to intend to act as he says he will.

Let us call Clarke's claim that normative conditions of this sort attach to the performance of speech acts such as promising "Clarke's Insight." In this book I contend that Clarke's Insight generalizes: normative conditions attach not only to the act of promising, but also to the whole range of speech acts, including asserting, requesting, and commanding. Indeed, I contend that we take a step beyond Clarke, maintaining that normative conditions not only attach to the performance of speech acts, but also account (in part) for their performance. These two claims, I argue, are of metaethical significance.

The details of the argument come later, but at a first approximation the proposal I defend is this: suppose we think of the normative conditions that attach to speech broadly, so that they include not only obligations, but also rights and responsibilities of various sorts. If so, we can say that an agent can perform a speech act only if and because he has rights, responsibilities, and obligations of certain kinds *vis-à-vis* his audience—these rights, responsibilities, and obligations constituting what I call a *normative standing*. An agent's having a normative standing of this kind, I argue, implies not only that he possesses rights, responsibilities, and obligations of certain kinds, but also that some of these rights, responsibilities, and obligations are themselves moral. And these moral features, I further claim, are best understood along realist lines. On the assumption that agents perform speech acts, it follows that moral facts, realistically understood, exist. The argument I am going to present, then, is an argument for moral realism from the nature of speech.

"An ambitious argument!" one might think. Like most arguments for philosophically interesting conclusions, the argument I wish to develop is indeed both ambitious and controversial, mostly because it rests upon a contested version of speech act theory. Still, I think the argument is worth airing for the following reasons.

First, moral realists are frequently accused of accepting a position that is purely defensive in nature. Rather than offer good positive reasons for accepting their view, realists—it is said—typically offer defenses of their position against antirealist attacks, coupled with counterattacks on these antirealist positions themselves. And, this, it is further claimed, is unsatisfactory. Realism is, after all, a highly controversial metaethical position. Given its controversial status, it is not enough to be given a laundry list of the problems from which its rivals suffer. We want to know why we should accept realism in the first place.[3]

There is, I believe, more than a grain of truth to this charge. Rather often realists have assumed that theirs is the default metaethical position, proceeding as if their primary task is to engage in defensive maneuvers designed to protect their view from objections. In my estimation, this way of conducting the debate between realism and its rivals is unfortunate. This is not because I deny that realism is the position to beat. In fact, I suspect it is. Rather, it is because "playing defense" can obscure from view the positive case that can be made in realism's favor.

---

3. Of realism's critics, Christine Korsgaard has pressed the point most emphatically. See Korsgaard (1996), 39–40, and (2008), ch. 10; as well as Loeb (2007).

Theoretical modesty requires, I think, that we not overestimate the force of this positive case. Philosophy is, after all, typically a holistic enterprise in which we gauge the strength of a given position by comparing it with rival views along multiple dimensions. In metaethics, things ordinarily run as follows: we first identify a certain range of data that we want to explain, such as that we appear to have significant stretches of moral knowledge. We then ascertain whether a given position smoothly accommodates these data by, among other things, determining how well they comport with other deeply entrenched commitments we have, such as our leading accounts of knowledge. If successful, an argument for a given position will establish that our favored position more smoothly accommodates the data than its rivals, say, because its rivals imply that moral judgments do not even purport to represent moral reality and, hence, cannot be candidates for knowledge. But even when a position has the virtue of better accommodating a range of data, this will typically not be enough to vindicate it. For ordinarily there are other data that we want to explain, and it may be that our favored position does not account for them very well. A metaethical position might, for example, nicely explain how we could gain moral knowledge but have little to say about why such states of knowledge are so closely tied to motivational states in which we are moved to action.

In light of this dynamic, it is best, I believe, to view the particular arguments offered for realism as considerations that do not themselves purport to vindicate realism. Rather, it is better to view them as only part of a series of considerations which, in various ways, boost realism's credentials, typically by driving up the cost of accepting rival positions. When combined with other factors, then, the positive case for realism is only one component of an overarching argument whose purpose is to tip the balance of reasons in realism's favor. At any rate, offering positive arguments for realism, such as I do here, can help to present the view in its strongest form, as a position that is not primarily reactive in character, but one for which there is a constructive case to be made.

The second reason it is worth developing the present argument for moral realism is that it should have wide appeal, recommending itself to realists of various sorts. I emphasize this feature of the argument because, in recent years, realism has enjoyed an increasing number of defenses. These defenses, however, have typically been highly partisan, endeavoring to defend either a version of naturalistic realism, according to which moral facts are ordinary natural facts, or non-naturalistic realism, according to which moral facts are not natural.[4] I prefer, by contrast, to present a positive case for a more generic form of realism. This way of proceeding defends core claims upon which most realists agree, such as there being a realm of moral facts, leaving more controversial issues about which they disagree, such as the nature of moral reasons, for a later "in house" discussion.

In my view, this strategy has the advantage of focusing upon the most powerful challenges to realist views, which typically come not from rival realist positions, but from views that reject realism altogether. Moreover, the particular argument I develop has the virtue of addressing concerns that some realists have about other members of their family.

Consider, in this regard, the following worry about moral non-naturalism. Non-naturalists are suspicious of views which claim that moral facts behave like ordinary natural facts, playing causal explanatory roles that form the subject matter of the natural sciences. This suspicion stems from the non-naturalists' conviction that ethics is not an inchoate science; it is not involved in the task of predicting or verifying empirical claims about how people actually act. Rather, ethical thinking is fundamentally practical in orientation, being concerned with how we should live. As such, non-naturalists claim, the findings of the natural sciences have relatively little bearing upon the fundamental ethical questions. Were biology to reveal, for example, that human beings are naturally aggressive, this—according to non-naturalists—would settle no ethical issues. It would simply become input for substantive ethical deliberation in which we ask ourselves whether we ought to act upon our naturally aggressive tendencies.[5] According to critics, however, these commitments leave non-naturalists vulnerable to the charge that their view is suspect because it implies that moral facts would play no interesting explanatory

---

4. Defenses of naturalistic realism include Railton (1986); Boyd (1988); Brink (1989); Jackson (1998); and Bloomfield (2001). Defenses of non-naturalism include Shafer-Landau (2003); FitzPatrick (2008); Enoch (2011); Parfit (2011).
5. FitzPatrick (2008) develops this theme.

roles were they to exist. And this—so claim the critics—is a serious liability, as it offends against the deeply seated conviction that entities should earn their keep in our theoretical schemes by doing sufficient explanatory work.

If the argument I develop is on the mark, however, non-naturalists have a principled response to charges of this sort: they can maintain that moral facts play the indispensible explanatory role of generating speech. This explanatory role, as I will indicate in a moment, is not causal. So, the argument I shall offer allows non-naturalists to remain faithful to their view while addressing legitimate concerns about it. Indeed, if one is a non-naturalist, one conclusion to draw from this discussion is that the contemporary debate about moral explanation has been misconceived, since it rests on the widespread assumption that were moral facts to play an important explanatory role, then this role would have to be causal.[6] In light of what I argue here, non-naturalists might conclude that participants in this debate were correct to assume that moral facts should play explanatory roles of important kinds. But they were wrong to assume that these roles would have to be causal. I should emphasize, however, that while naturalists have ordinarily wished to defend the claim that moral facts play causal explanatory roles, they need not also maintain that all legitimate explanations are causal. Indeed, when defending the claim that moral facts belong to the natural world, some naturalists, such as Judith Jarvis Thomson, have appealed to the fact that moral facts enter into non-causal explanatory relations.[7]

Let me now adduce a third reason for philosophers to take interest in the argument I develop. There have been developments in moral philosophy in which philosophers claim that moral facts exist, but deny that this implies moral realism of any sort. One such development is the recent wave of deflationary positions in moral

---

6. I am thinking here of the debate spawned by Harman (1977), ch. 1; and Sturgeon (1984).

7. See Thomson (1996). Railton (1986) may be another example, as he defends the claim that moral facts enter into nomic explanations but does not claim that they are causal. As for myself, I reject the claim that we have sufficient reason to believe that moral facts exist only if they play one or another explanatory role that philosophers find important, such as causal roles. I do hold, however, that were we to have strong evidence that moral facts do play such a role, this would provide reason to believe that they exist.

philosophy. Of course, "deflationism" means different things in the mouths of different philosophers. And it is not always easy to discern what position these philosophers mean to defend, for they frequently appeal to metaphors, telling us that moral facts are mere "shadows" that come "for free" with the assertoric form of moral discourse.[8] In Chapter 6, I will have more to say about how we should understand these metaphors. For present purposes, it is enough to note that deflationists about morality maintain that moral facts exist but are explanatorily idle, as they do not explain anything of interest. They exist, as deflationists sometimes put it, simply because they are the semantic values of moral locutions that themselves primarily play expressive or quantificational roles. Be that as it may, one can see how providing an argument for the claim that moral facts play a robust explanatory role such as generating speech is a way to vindicate a distinctively non-deflationist account of moral facts.

In principle, then, realists have much to gain by furnishing an argument for the claim that moral facts do important explanatory work: it allows them to respond to worries about both the defensive character of their view and whether moral facts realistically understood deserve a place in our best picture of the world. Still, it is natural to raise questions about the line of argument that I wish to develop. For I said that my overarching aim is to argue for the thesis that an agent can perform speech acts only if and because she has a normative standing of a certain kind, which (in a wide range of cases) is itself constituted by moral facts. I further claimed that these facts should be understood along moral realist lines. Claims such as these might lead one to ask: How should we understand moral realism? And what is the best way to think of the character of speech acts? Finally, how ought we to think about normative standings, which I said play a role in generating speech acts? My project in this chapter is to address these three questions. Doing so will place us in a better position to explicitly formulate what I call the Speech Act Argument for moral realism.

---

8. See Wright (1992), 181; and Blackburn (1998), 80. Gibbard (2003), ch. 8, seems to accept something like this view as well.

I The first issue: moral realism

Nearly everyone believes that there are prosaic descriptive facts such as

that the average annual rainfall for Seattle is thirty-eight inches

and

that the number 2 is the smallest prime.

Moreover, it is not terribly controversial to hold that there are prosaic normative facts such as

that every citizen of the US has a legal right to a fair trial

and

that Major League managers are prohibited from ejecting umpires.

Some philosophers, however, believe that there are facts that fall into neither of these categories. These philosophers hold that, in addition to the prosaic descriptive and normative facts, there are moral facts such as

that Himmler exhibited great wickedness

and

that it is wrong to torture someone simply because she has inconvenienced you.[9]

Call those who maintain that there are facts of these last types the *moral realists*. Moral realists hold that not only are there moral facts such as these, but also that they are objective in a way that the prosaic normative facts mentioned above are not.

Let me fill out this brief description of moral realism, beginning with the notion of a moral fact. For present purposes I shall assume that we have a clear enough idea of what a moral fact is. A moral fact is simply that which is reported by true predicative moral sentences

9. In addition to normative facts, there are also anthropological facts, which are best understood to be facts about normative systems. Facts of this sort would include *according to the rules of baseball, Major League managers are prohibited from ejecting umpires* and *according to the norms of morality, it is wrong to torture someone simply because she has inconvenienced you.* When speaking of normative facts—moral or otherwise—I will not have facts of these sorts in mind, as they are not normative facts as I think of them.

such as "Himmler exhibited great wickedness" or (a certain range of) true generalizations such as "It is wrong to torture someone simply because she has inconvenienced you." Given certain additional assumptions about the relation between moral sentences and facts, we can say that moral facts are those which are represented by true moral sentences such as these (if any true sentences of these sorts there be). Accordingly, if there is any moral knowledge, moral facts are the objects of such knowledge.[10]

The sense in which moral facts thus understood are objective is more difficult to articulate. But we can make progress on the issue by focusing our attention on the examples of prosaic normative facts offered above. Consider, once again, the fact *that Major League managers are prohibited from ejecting umpires.* The first thing to notice about this fact is that it is deeply contingent; we could easily imagine the rules of baseball being such that they allow managers to eject umpires. The second thing to notice is that this contingency has a particular explanation; it is rooted in the fact that some agent with the relevant authority—what we can call a "conferring agent"—declared that managers and umpires would have certain powers and be subject to certain prohibitions (but could have easily declared otherwise). Suppose we use the term "recognitional stance" to stand for a host of attitudes or actions that a conferring agent could take toward something, such as taking it to be F, wanting it to be F, valuing (or disvaluing) it as F, declaring it to be F, or the like. We could then say that prosaic normative facts have the following pair of features: they are both *recognition-variant* and *recognition-dependent.* The fact *that*

10. Let me add to this a pair of qualifications: first, this account is intended to be largely neutral regarding various accounts of the nature of facts—with this exception: I assume that the reporting relation to which the gloss above refers implies that there is a robust representation or "aboutness" relation between some true moral sentences and facts. It is because of this that the view I defend is incompatible with deflationism about moral facts, for, according to deflationary views, moral facts do not "answer to" the contents of moral sentences. See Blackburn (1999), 216, and (2001), 25. Second, the view I defend is that moral facts are that which are reported by true moral sentences such as those I offer above. This qualification is important, since it both identifies focal examples of moral facts and places constraints on the sort of thing that could count as a moral fact. According to the view I favor, nothing could count as a reasonably comprehensive and consistent moral system (for beings like us in a world similar to ours) and fail to include principles such as *that it is wrong to torture someone simply because she has inconvenienced you.* Cuneo and Shafer-Landau (2014) develop this position. I also touch upon it in Chapter 7.

Major League managers are prohibited from ejecting umpires is recognition-variant insofar as baseball managers could easily have had powers different from those they in fact possess, since a conferring agent might have declared it so. A fact such as this is recognition-dependent insofar as baseball managers are subject to the prohibition against ejecting umpires simply because a conferring agent has declared that anyone who occupies that role is subject to that prohibition (but could easily have declared otherwise).

Moral realism—at least of the sort under consideration here—tells us that moral facts are different. According to realists, at least some moral facts are neither recognition-variant nor recognition-dependent. To see how realists are thinking, consider the two examples of moral facts offered above, namely,

> *that Himmler exhibited great wickedness*

and

> *that it is wrong to torture someone simply because she has inconvenienced you.*

According to realists, neither of these facts is recognition-variant. Given Himmler's actions, it is impossible (in a world similar to ours) that he was anything but wicked. Similarly, given the nature of torture, it is impossible (in a world similar to ours) that having been inconvenienced by someone is sufficient grounds for torturing her. It follows that even if most of us found torture delicious, this would make no difference regarding its moral status. Moreover, realists claim, neither of these facts is recognition-dependent. In this case, realists deny not only that the moral status of torture is determined by the recognitional stance that conferring agents actually have toward it. They also deny that its wrongness is determined by any recognitional stance that a conferring agent (or agents) would have toward it, even under idealized conditions. It follows that, according to realists, even if a perfectly rational agent would disapprove of torture, this is not what renders torture wrong; it is wrong independent of any such disapproval.[11] So, while realists would agree that there are important

---

11. I use the term "agent" broadly enough so that an agent could be a collective of individual agents but not so broadly that it could refer to God, since moral realists have not ordinarily supposed that moral facts would have to be relevantly independent of God's attitudes.

differences between moral facts and prosaic descriptive facts such as *that the number 2 is the smallest prime,* they would also hold that they have this much in common: facts of both kinds are mind-independent in an important sense, for facts of neither sort are recognition-variant or recognition-dependent.

It is this last claim that distinguishes moral realism from that family of positions commonly labeled "constructivism." For constructivists hold that moral facts are akin to what I have called prosaic normative facts, claiming that they are recognition-dependent.[12] In Chapter 6, I will explore constructivism in more detail. But it may be worth stating more exactly what it is that realists and constructivists disagree about.

The reason is that, strictly speaking, realists need not deny that some moral facts are recognition-dependent. T. M. Scanlon, for example, has argued that actions are wrong simply because they are disallowed by some principle that no one could reasonably reject—where "reasonable" is understood in terms of moral reasons.[13] In principle, realists could accept such a position. For it might be that those moral features that (partially) account for an action's being wrong—namely, the moral reasons—are as realists understand them. Similarly, constructivists need not deny that some moral facts are recognition-independent. Constructivists could, for example, hold that agents are virtuous not because of some stance that a conferring agent takes (or would take) toward them, but because they are reliably disposed to respond well to moral reasons. For it might be that the moral features that account for someone's being virtuous—namely, the moral reasons—are as constructivists understand them. But if this is so, how can we more sharply distinguish the two positions?

Here is one way do so. Suppose we assume that moral properties of certain kinds are explanatorily basic. That is, suppose we assume that there are moral properties of some types such that there is a range of conditions that if something exemplifies them, then there is no other moral property that accounts for this. Take the property

---

12. More exactly, all constructivists claim that some moral facts are recognition-dependent, while only some maintain that they are recognition-variant. Shafer-Landau (2003), Enoch (2009a), and Street (2010) offer somewhat different accounts of constructivism from the one I present.
13. See Scanlon (1998).

being wrong, for example. This property is explanatorily basic just in case there is a range of circumstances such that there is no other type of moral feature that accounts for the fact that actions are wrong. Actions are wrong, according to this view, not because we have most moral reason not to perform them or they are morally un-fitting. (This last claim, it is worth noting, does not imply that nothing determines whether an action is wrong. Rather, it implies only that it is not determined by other moral properties. Most realists would agree that an action's being wrong is determined by other non-moral properties, such as its causing gratuitous pain.)

Suppose, now, that facts are simply things having properties. Then we can say that a moral fact F is explanatorily basic if and only if it is not the case that there is some moral fact F* such that F* accounts (in part) for F. According to this way of thinking, what distinguishes realism from constructivism is that realists hold that there are ex-planatorily basic moral facts that are not recognition-dependent. Constructivists deny this. They claim that at least some explanatorily basic moral facts are recognition-dependent.

Moral realism (at least of the variety I defend), then, is incompatible with constructivism. Given what I have said so far, it might be tempting to label the position for which I will argue a version of "robust" moral realism.[14] I am going to resist doing so, however, because there are two important senses in which the view I defend is fairly minimalist.

In the first place, the type of realism I defend here does not imply that moral facts are or give rise to categorical reasons—reasons that apply to an agent regardless of her goals or desires or her commit-ments to social institutions of various kinds. My own view is that real-ists should defend the categoricity of moral reasons and that paradigmatic realist views are committed to their existence.[15] But de-fending this claim is not something that will occupy me on this occa-sion. That said, I think defending a realist position that is compatible with the thesis that all moral reasons are non-categorical or Humean is worthwhile. As a colleague once put the point, it is always instructive

---

14. Both FitzPatrick (2008) and (2011) and Enoch (2011) describe their versions of non-naturalism as being cases of robust moral realism.
15. For the argument, see Cuneo (2007), chs. 1 and 7. Shafer-Landau (2009) offers a defense of this position with which I have considerable sympathy. I return to this issue in Chapter 7.

to think about what metaethical view one would accept were one to become convinced that one's favored view is false. In my own case, if I were to become convinced that paradigmatic realism is false, I would accept a version of realism according to which there are moral reasons, albeit only of the Humean variety.[16] Even philosophers need contingency plans!

The second reason why the view I defend is not robust is that it does not suppose that moral facts are *sui generis*, belonging to a non-natural order of things. Although I believe that such views merit careful consideration, the type of realism for which I wish to argue is generic in nature, being compatible with various versions of so-called naturalist, non-naturalist, theistic, and non-theistic realism. That said, it may bear mentioning that some of the most prominent naturalist views defended by contemporary philosophers, such as those championed by Frank Jackson and David Lewis, are naturally interpreted to be versions of constructivism, at least as I have described it.[17] So, the argument in this book develops a line of thought that proponents of certain kinds of naturalist position will not find attractive. I should also point out that the view I defend is inhospitable to certain kinds of theistic views. Divine command theories, for example, ordinarily maintain that all moral obligations are generated by God's contingently issued speech acts. If the argument I develop is sound, however, this could not be so. Speech itself cannot generate moral features of these kinds. Rather, Clarke's Insight tells us that a condition of an agent's performing speech acts in the first place is that he has the rights, responsibilities, and obligations of being a speaker.

II The second issue: speech acts

A few paragraphs back, I said that my central aim is to defend the claim that the performance of speech acts requires the existence of

---

16. This might invite the suspicion that the form of realism I defend is very weak. After all, if the view is compatible with there being no categorical moral reasons, what is to distinguish it from a view according to which moral reasons are merely conventional, akin to those generated by the social practices of chess and baseball? I address this issue in Chapter 3.
17. See Lewis (1989) and Jackson (1998), 156–7.

moral facts of certain kinds. I now need to turn to our second issue, which concerns the nature of speech.

In what follows, when I use the term "speech" I refer to the performance of *speech acts* of various sorts. And speech acts themselves, I will assume, are best understood along the lines suggested by J. L. Austin in his classic *How to Do Things with Words*.[18]

Suppose on some occasion that I utter the sentence "Hume is the greatest modern philosopher," thereby delighting my colleagues, who are deeply sympathetic with Hume's positions. How many act-tokens have I performed? According to the dominant, Austinian tradition in speech act theory, at least three: in the first place, I have performed the action of uttering a sentence, namely, that "Hume is the greatest modern philosopher." Second, in uttering this sentence I have thereby asserted *that Hume is the greatest modern philosopher*. And third, by asserting this sentence I have delighted my colleagues.

To say that I have performed three different act-tokens when I utter the sentence "Hume is the greatest modern philosopher" might seem excessive, as if we were multiplying actions beyond necessity. But I think reflection on the case supports the claim that I have actually performed multiple act-tokens.

Begin with the following observations. It is possible for me to utter the sentence "Hume is the greatest modern philosopher" and not assert anything. For example, I might utter the sentence simply to test whether a microphone is working or to offer you an example of a well-formed English sentence. In such a case, no one would rightly hold me to the view that Hume is the greatest modern philosopher because I uttered this sentence. Likewise, it is possible for me to assert that Hume is the greatest modern philosopher without uttering the sentence "Hume is the greatest modern philosopher" (or any sentence for that matter). If I am competent with sign language, for example, I can assert this proposition about Hume simply by moving my hands in certain ways. And finally, I can perform the action of delighting my colleagues by doing many things other than uttering sentences about Hume. I might compliment

18. See Austin (1963). Alston (2000), ch. 1, notes that Austin's way of thinking about speech acts is, in some respects, idiosyncratic. I present what is, I believe, the core framework of his view, absent its idiosyncrasies.

them by praising their own work, for example, intimating that it is worthy of Hume himself.

Of course, these observations do not themselves imply that I have performed multiple act-tokens when I utter the sentence "Hume is the greatest modern philosopher." We need to supply a principle of act-individuation to secure that result. To that end, suppose we accept the following pair of principles. First, an act-type Φ is identical with an act-type Ψ only if it is impossible to perform Φ and not perform Ψ (or *vice versa*). It follows from this principle that, in the case just described, I have performed (at least) three different act-types. Second, suppose that act-tokens are individuated by the act-types that they instantiate. And suppose, furthermore, that the phrases "being a sentence utterance," "being an assertion," and "being a case in which one delights one's audience" designate different act-types. (One might hold, in fact, that some are natural kinds, since they appear to play a fundamental explanatory role in the discipline of linguistics.) From these assumptions it follows that, in the case just described, I have performed three different act-tokens.

I myself favor this approach to act-individuation. But it is controversial, as philosophers divide into two camps on the issue. "Multipliers," such as myself, maintain that when I utter the sentence "Hume is the greatest modern philosopher" I have performed several act-tokens—in the case I offered, at least three. "Unifiers," such as those who follow Donald Davidson, maintain that when I utter this sentence I have performed only one act-token that falls under several different descriptions or act-types.[19] As I say, I shall conduct my discussion as if the multiplier view were true. But I am willing to be ecumenical on the issue of act-individuation. Nearly everything I say about speech acts, I believe, can be translated into the unifier idiom. So, I do not believe that rejecting the multiplier position affects the substance of my argument.

In fact, I am willing to accept the view, defended by Alvin Goldman, that we should countenance two metaphysical categories of events: one according to which events are individuated by the event-types they instantiate—such as *being an utterance of a sentence* or *being an assertion*—the other according to which events are individuated

19. See Davidson (1970).

by their spatio-temporal features—such as their taking place simultaneously at a given time and place. The first approach is embraced by the multipliers; the latter is defended by the unifiers. If Goldman is correct, however, we do not have to choose between these two positions.[20] Events of both types exist and are represented in different ways. According to this approach, we can accept what Austin says about speech. Typically, when speech occurs, agents perform multiple act-tokens, albeit of the type in which multipliers are interested.

With this in mind, let us return to the case in which I utter the sentence "Hume is the greatest modern philosopher." Following Austin's lead, I will call the event of uttering this sentence a *locutionary* act. As an initial approximation, locutionary acts are acts of uttering or inscribing sentences (or sentence surrogates). But it is worth emphasizing that the class of locutionary acts is actually much wider than this: sending smoke signals, tapping out patterns of noises, signing with one's hands, and sending flashes of light all count as locutionary acts as well. In keeping with Austin's terminology, I will call the act of asserting *that Hume is the greatest modern philosopher* an *illocutionary act*. Illocutionary acts are also a diverse lot; they include acts such as asserting, requesting, commanding, christening, adjourning, begging, promising, and so on. Later, I will have more to say about the character of these acts. But for present purposes, think of illocutionary acts as those acts one performs in performing some locutionary act. Finally, I will call the act of delighting my colleagues a *perlocutionary act*. Roughly speaking, acts of this type ordinarily consist in producing an effect on one's audience (usually a mental state) by way of the performance of an illocutionary act. Examples of such acts would be evoking delight, dismay, or puzzlement in one's audience.

Fundamental to my discussion is the assumption that acts of these types come in a hierarchy. One performs an illocutionary act *by way of* performing a locutionary act. Likewise, one typically performs a perlocutionary act by way of the performance of an illocutionary act. Although there is much to say about the relations that

---

20. See Goldman (2007). Goldman (1970), ch. 1, offers a defense of the multiplier position with which I sympathize.

the performance of these different act-types bear to one another, my attention will be focused almost exclusively on the phenomenon of performing an illocutionary act by way of performing a locutionary act.

We can better understand this by-way-of relation, I suggest, by having before us the notion of *count-generation.* Suppose we use the term "generate" to stand for the generic relation of *bringing something about* or *making something the case,* where this relation is not causal. Examples of such a relation are not difficult to find. When Socrates was executed—to use a standard case—Xanthippe simultaneously became a widow. But presumably Socrates' execution did not simultaneously cause Xanthippe to become a widow. There is no causal law, for example, which specifies that executions simultaneously cause people to become widows. If so, the execution of Socrates non-causally generated the state of affairs in which Xanthippe is a widow.[21]

Let us use the phrase "count as" to stand for the phenomenon of something's falling under a concept but not simply in virtue of its intrinsic or essential characteristics. For example, in the game of baseball, a hit ball that clears the outfield fence in fair territory—what we can call an *H-event*—counts as a home run. But H-events do not fall under the concept 'home run' simply in virtue of their intrinsic or essential characteristics. They count as home runs only (and also) because, at the time of their performance, certain rules of baseball are in effect. That these rules are in effect at the time of the performance of an H-event is, however, highly contingent. We can easily imagine a scenario in which an H-event occurs during a game, but the rules of that game specify that it is impossible to hit a home run by performing an H-event in that game. In a scenario such as this, the hitting does not count as a home run.

With these two pieces of terminology in hand, we can define the notion of count-generation (as it applies to actions) as follows: an agent's performing an action Φ *count-generates* his performing an action Ψ just in case his Φing generates his Ψing and his Φing counts

---

21. Kim (1993) offers an elaboration of this case. Audi (2012) offers examples of other non-causal explanations while explicating the notion of grounding.

as his Ψing (at least in part) in virtue of his Φing.[22] Following Nicholas
Wolterstorff, I will assume that this analysis of count-generation
helps us to understand what it is for an agent to perform an illocutionary act by way of performing a locutionary act. In short, an agent
performs an illocutionary act by way of performing a locutionary act
just in case his performance of that locutionary act count-generates
his performance of that illocutionary act.

To illustrate, return to our earlier example in which I assert *that
Hume is the greatest modern philosopher* by way of uttering the sentence "Hume is the greatest modern philosopher." According to
the view just presented, I succeed in doing this just in case my uttering the sentence "Hume is the greatest modern philosopher"
count-generates my having asserted *that Hume is the greatest modern
philosopher.* For in this case my uttering the sentence "Hume is the
greatest modern philosopher" not only generates my asserting *that
Hume is the greatest modern philosopher*, but also counts as my having
asserted this proposition.

As I understand the phenomenon of count-generation, then, it
is always acts (or events) that count-generate other acts (or events).
If you are driving in the United States, for example, flipping your
blinker to the down-position count-generates your signaling to take
a left-hand turn. Similarly, if you are speaking English, it is your uttering the sentence "Hume is the greatest modern philosopher" that
count-generates your having asserted *that Hume is the greatest modern
philosopher.* However, as I indicated earlier—and will defend later—

---

22. See Wolterstorff (1980), Part One, and (1995), ch. 5. Wolterstorff fashions the notion of count-generation in light of what Goldman (1970), ch. 2, says about conven-
tional-generation. The main difference between their two views is that Wolterstorff
denies Goldman's claim that the normative features that non-causally generate actions are mere conventions. David Liebesman has asked whether we could spell out
the by-way-of relation between locutionary and illocutionary acts entirely in terms of
one act's generating another, without making any use of the counting-as relation. I
suppose we could. Still, I find the conceptuality of counting-as illuminating. It helps
to remind the reader of the type of generation in question, which is loose in two respects. First, locutionary acts are not themselves sufficient for the production of illocutionary acts; something more is needed for them to generate speech. Moreover,
locutionary acts do not count as illocutionary acts simply in virtue of their intrinsic
or essential properties; they are, to use Hume's terminology, distinct existences.
Nevertheless, the relation is intimate insofar as people—even philosophers with
whom I have spoken—often tend to think of locutionary acts, such as sentence utterances of certain types, as being illocutionary acts, such as assertions.

when acts count-generate other acts (or events), they always do so in virtue of there being certain conditions that hold at the time of the performance of those acts. These conditions are what explain the "hook-up" between count-generating acts, on the one hand, and count-generated acts (or events), on the other. Central to the argument I offer is the thesis that these conditions include an agent's having the rights, responsibilities, and obligations that constitute a normative standing of a certain kind. Normative facts are among those conditions that bind locutionary and illocutionary acts together; they are, so to speak, "action-binders."

If this is right, normative facts do not themselves count-generate speech acts. Rather, they are among those features in virtue of which locutionary acts count-generate illocutionary acts. When speaking with precision, this is how I will talk about the relation between count-generation and normative facts. Often, however, I will speak of an agent's having rights, responsibilities, and obligations as *being ingredient* in the count-generation of speech. But by this I simply mean that having these rights, responsibilities, and obligations is (at least in part) that in virtue of which a locutionary act count-generates an illocutionary act.

Count-generation, then, is not itself a brute determination relation. To say it again, actions count-generate other actions (or events) in virtue of there being further conditions that hold—these conditions being that which determines or accounts for any count-generation that might occur. It would be nice to have an illuminating account of the nature of this determination or accounting for relation. But I have no such account. I can, however, furnish examples of it. I can, for example, direct your attention once again to that case in which, when driving, you flip your blinker to the down-position, thereby signaling a left turn. In this case, your flipping your blinker count-generates your signaling in virtue of there being certain conditions that hold, such as there being certain rules of the road that are in effect.

Reflection on cases of this sort might not reveal the character of the sort of determination relation in play. Still, it might help us to say what the relevant determination relation is not. The relation in question is not causal. That certain rules are in effect does not simultaneously cause the flipping of your blinker to count-generate the signaling. Nor is the relation in question mere modal covariance. This relation would not, after all, explain why the count-generation occurs. Nor, finally, is the relation part-whole composition. For the event of signaling does not have as one of its parts that the rules of the road are in effect. These observations could, I suppose, be supplemented in various ways by positive claims about some of the relation's formal properties. Reflection on our case reveals, for example, that the determination relation in question is asymmetric. That certain rules of the road are in effect determines whether you have signaled a left-hand turn, but that you have so signaled does not determine whether the rules themselves hold. Having narrowed conceptual space in this way, we might hazard that the determination relation in question is a species of the *constitution* relation.[23] And perhaps it is. Nothing hangs, however, on the label we use to designate the relation in question. What matters most for my purposes is to see that speech occurs because there are two sorts of non-causal explanatory relations that hold: the count-generation relation itself and the determination relation that certain conditions bear to the actions that count-generate speech.

III The third issue: normative standings

To this point, I have sketched the type of realist view for which I will argue and how I shall understand the character of speech acts. Central to the account of speech acts I have offered, however, is the thesis that an agent's having a normative standing is (at least in part) that in virtue of which the performance of a locutionary act count-generates the performance of an illocutionary act. Let me now explain what I understand a normative standing to be.

We human beings can have a variety of standings such as *being a mother, being the Prime Minister of France,* and *being the Postmaster General.* Some of these standings are normative. That is, some of these standings are such that agents have them in virtue of their having rights, responsibilities, and obligations of various kinds. Consider,

---

23. See Baker (2000), Johnston (2005), and Bengson (forthcoming); also see Audi (2012)'s discussion of grounding.

for example, the standing of being the Postmaster General. Presumably, a person enjoys this standing just in case she is entitled to certain privileges and has responsibilities of various kinds. Given the present arrangement in the United States, for example, she may hire and fire US Postal employees and must regularly report to the Governor of the US Postal Service.

According to the account of speech that plays a prominent role in the subsequent argument, agents perform speech acts by altering their normative status with regard to their audience, acquiring rights, responsibilities, and obligations. Upon altering their normative relations in this way, speakers acquire normative standings of certain kinds. Upon asserting a proposition p, for example, you acquire the normative standing *being an assertor of p*. Likewise, upon commanding someone to Φ, you acquire the normative standing *being a commander of Φing*. If this is right, every type of speech act Ψ is such that upon performing Ψ, an agent acquires a correlative normative standing— call it a "Ψ-correlate normative standing"—such that she performs Ψ only if and because she has the rights, responsibilities, and obligations constitutive of its Ψ-correlate normative standing. For ease of reference I will often refer to such a standing as simply the normative standing of *being a speaker*.[24] Agents, I claim, perform speech acts in virtue of having the rights, responsibilities, and obligations of being a speaker.

About normative standings let me offer several observations. First, unless I indicate otherwise, I assume that the rights, responsibilities, and obligations that constitute such a standing are *pro tanto* in character. (I use the term "*pro tanto*" in much the same way that others use the term "*prima facie*." *Pro tanto* obligations are, for example, considerations that, in the absence of countervailing considerations, yield all-things-considered duties.)

Second, when I say that normative standings are constituted by rights, responsibilities, and obligations, I take rights, responsibilities,

---

24. The locution "being a speaker," I realize, is multiply ambiguous. On some occasions of use, it designates a disjunction of various Ψ-correlate normative standings, including the asserting-correlate normative standing, the requesting-correlate normative standing, and so on. On other occasions, however, it designates only one such standing, such as the asserting-correlate normative standing. Where this ambiguity matters, I will mark it; when it does not, I will not.

and obligations to be distinct. Consider rights to begin with. Unless the context indicates otherwise, I will think of rights as claims or entitlements. More specifically, I will assume that for A to have a right against B is for A to have a claim against B to B's treating A in a certain way, such as not restricting A's freedom to move his body or to express his views. If this is correct, then rights are not identical with obligations. For obligations are not claims or entitlements; they are requirements. In fact, they are often requirements to honor rights. Or so I shall assume. I realize that assuming this is controversial, as some philosophers believe that while there are obligations, there are no rights. I am not, however, going to defend the theoretical respectability of rights on this occasion, as I believe that has been done elsewhere.[25] If you are averse to there being rights or using rights talk, I have no objection to your attempting to paraphrase my talk of them in terms of reasons and obligations.

Similarly, I assume that responsibilities are distinct from both rights and obligations. This may appear to be even more controversial than the claim that rights and obligations are distinct, but I believe it is not. For note that in ordinary English, the term "responsibility" has two distinct senses. In one sense, responsibilities are reasons or obligations for which one can be held accountable. This sense of "responsibility" has its natural home in phrases of the form *S has a responsibility to* Φ. For example, we might say that I have the responsibility to update the family's photograph album by adding new photographs to it periodically. If I have the responsibility to act this way, then I have a reason or obligation to act this way, and I can be held accountable if I fail to do so.

In another sense, however, responsibilities are not reasons or obligations but *liabilities*. This sense of "responsibility" is expressed in phrases of the form *S is responsible for* Φ*ing* or *S is responsible for having* Φ*ed*. To stay with the example just offered, we might say that I am responsible for having failed to update the family photograph album.

---

25. Similar misgivings, such as those advanced by Anscombe (1958), are occasionally raised about the intelligibility of moral obligation. My advice to those who are skeptical about moral obligation is the same as to those who are skeptical about rights. Wolterstorff (2008), Parts II and III, offers a response to those who are skeptical about rights, such as MacIntyre (1984). Important defenses of the legitimacy of rights also include Feinberg (1970) and Thomson (1990).

By this we mean that I am accountable or rightfully open to correction, reproach, blame, or the like for having failed to update the album. In what follows, I will regularly speak of agents having the responsibilities of being a speaker. Unless the context indicates otherwise, when I speak this way I will have in mind the second sense of "responsibility" just introduced. Agents, I will assume, have responsibilities in the sense of being liable or accountable. Understood in this way, I take responsibilities to be distinct from both rights and obligations, though I concede that they might be determined by rights or obligations.

Third, while I hold that some normative standings are constituted by moral rights, responsibilities, and obligations, I shall not think of moral rights, responsibilities, and obligations as themselves being moral facts. Rather, I shall think of them as being properties that agents can have or relations in which agents can stand. Still, these properties and relations, I will assume, form the constituents of moral facts. For example, I will assume that for any moral right R, if an agent A bears R against some other agent B, there is the correlative moral fact *that A bears R against B.* Similarly, I shall assume that for any moral obligation O to Ψ, if an agent A has an obligation O to Ψ, there is the correlative moral fact *that A is obligated to* Ψ. So, when I defend the claim that normative standings imply that moral facts exist, this should be interpreted as this claim: take any normative standing whatsoever. If an agent S's displaying that standing implies that she has a moral right R, then there is the correlative moral fact *that S has R.* Similarly, if an agent S's having that standing implies that she has a moral obligation to Ψ, then there is the correlative moral fact *that S is obligated to* Ψ. And so forth.

Finally, let me close this section by highlighting an assumption that I am making about the relation between normative standings and speech acts, which should prevent a misunderstanding of the argument I shall present. In what follows, I will regularly claim that an agent's having the rights, responsibilities, and obligations of being a speaker is ingredient in what count-generates his having performed one or another speech act. Speaking thus invites the supposition that a temporal sequence of events is involved in the performance of an illocutionary act. According to this supposition, an agent first performs a locutionary act, then at some later time acquires the rights, responsibilities, and obligations of being a speaker, and then (perhaps at some still later time) performs an illocutionary act of some sort. This, however, is not how I think of the matter. With an exception I shall note in Chapter 2, there is no temporal sequence of this sort. The three events of an agent's performing a locutionary act, his having the relevant normative standing, and his performing an illocutionary act, occur simultaneously.

IV The Speech Act Argument

The framework for the argument I wish to present is now in place. Keeping in mind that the phrase "being a speaker" is simply a convenient way to refer to what I have called a Ψ-correlate standing and that the term "moral facts" refers to moral facts realistically understood, the Speech Act Argument can be formulated as follows:

(1) Agents perform illocutionary acts such as asserting, promising, and commanding.

(2) Illocutionary acts are count-generated by locutionary acts. But locutionary acts are not sufficient for the count-generation to occur; there must be something else that explains why it occurs.

(3) It is an agent's having the rights, responsibilities, and obligations of being a speaker that explains (at least in part) why the count-generation of illocutionary acts occurs.

(4) So, agents have the rights, responsibilities, and obligations of being a speaker.

(5) If an agent has the rights, responsibilities, and obligations of being a speaker, then moral facts exist.

(6) So, moral facts exist.

Thus stated, this argument is intended to be broadly transcendental in character. It assumes that speech acts occur. How is their occurrence possible? The argument's claim is: in virtue of the fact that agents have the rights, responsibilities, and obligations of being a speaker. Since some of these rights, responsibilities, and obligations are moral, it follows that moral facts exist.

I am going to assume, at least initially, that the first two premises of the Speech Act Argument are not controversial. We do in fact perform such actions as asserting, commanding, and promising. Moreover, on the assumption that locutionary and illocutionary acts are different, then there must be something that explains the "hook-up" between the two actions. Accordingly, I am going to focus my attention on defending the argument's third and fifth premises. The defense I offer of these premises runs as follows.

Those familiar with the development of contemporary speech act theory know that philosophers working within this field have tended to divide into two camps. One group of philosophers—those inspired by the work of Paul Grice—have attempted to analyze speech acts in terms of the intentions of speakers to bring about various types of perlocutionary effects in their audience. This position I refer to as the *perlocutionary-intention view.* The other group of philosophers—those working within the research program initiated by William Alston and John Searle—have rejected the Gricean view, analyzing speech acts in terms not of perlocutionary intentions but of the normative standings that speakers acquire. This position I refer to as the *normative theory of speech.*

In the second chapter, "A Normative Theory of Speech," I side with the second group of philosophers. There I lay out the theory of speech that figures in the argument's third premise, highlighting some of its virtues and responding to objections. Central to my argument is the following trio of claims. First, it is an agent's having the rights, responsibilities, and obligations of being a speaker that is ingredient in what count-generates his having performed a speech act of a certain kind. Second, this thesis is not obviously incompatible with what is often presented as its main rival, the perlocutionary-intention view. Third, while it is possible to formulate a version of the perlocutionary-intention view that is incompatible with the normative theory, it is less satisfactory than the normative theory. This is largely because the normative theory yields a more unified account of speech.

The argument in Chapter 2 yields the conclusion that rights, responsibilities, and obligations are ingredient in the count-generation of speech. But it has no direct implications concerning what *sorts* of rights, responsibilities, and obligations they are. Might some be moral? Premise (5) of the Speech Act Argument answers this question in the affirmative, telling us that moral rights, responsibilities, and obligations are ingredient in the count-generation of speech.

This last claim receives an extended defense, as it is the topic of Chapters 3, 4, and 5. The first stage of the defense is developed in Chapter 3, "The Moral Dimensions of Speech." In this chapter, I contend that an illuminating and sufficiently nuanced account of some of the rights, responsibilities, and obligations ingredient in speech makes essential recourse to moral concepts. The best explanation of the fact that we categorize these normative features as moral is, I argue, that they are as they appear.

However, this line of argument has hope of succeeding only if we do not have good independent reason to believe that there are no moral features. So, in Chapters 4 and 5, "Against the Mixed View: Part I" and "Against the Mixed View: Part II," I engage in a rearguard action in which I develop an objection to what I call the *mixed view*. According to the mixed view, there are practice-based rights, responsibilities, and obligations such as those that belong to the practices of etiquette, baseball, law, and the discursive practices of giving and receiving promises, giving and receiving requests, performing and responding to assertions, and so forth. Defenders of the mixed view, however, maintain that these are not moral rights, responsibilities, or obligations, as we have sufficient independent reason to believe that moral facts do not exist. In Chapter 4, I maintain that this position is unstable, as it is subject to a dilemma. For the major arguments offered in favor of the mixed view, I contend, imply either that practice-based features of various kinds do not exist or arbitrarily weight some features of ordinary moral thought and practice while discounting others. Since neither of these conclusions is acceptable, the position should be rejected. Chapter 5 engages with expressivism, defending the claim—up to this point merely assumed—that moral concepts function descriptively.

If the argument up to Chapter 5 succeeds, we should accept not only that normative features are ingredient in the count-generation of speech, but also that some of these features are moral. So far, however, the argument does not imply that these facts are as realists say. Should we also accept this further claim? In Chapter 6, "Three

Antirealist Views," I address this question by drawing out the implication of the argument for three prominent types of antirealist position: the error theory, expressivism, and constructivism. In this case, I try to anticipate some of the maneuvers available to friends of these views, considering the resources upon which they might draw to account for the normative dimensions of speech or, alternatively, to deny that we speak at all. I conclude that we have compelling reasons to reject these views and to accept a realist understanding of moral facts. In the final chapter, "Epistemic Implications," I conclude by putting the Speech Act Argument to further work. I maintain that the argument can help realists to address some knotty issues regarding how we might grasp moral reality were moral facts to exist. Specifically, I claim that the Speech Act Argument can help non-naturalist realists to explain how we might apprehend moral reality and also reliably track it.

Much of what contemporary metaethicists discuss concerns the ways in which moral discourse functions. In this sense, metaethics is heir to the so-called linguistic turn that in the last century occurred in Anglo-American analytic philosophy. My concern in this book is broadly metaethical. And it concerns the nature of speech. But I am not primarily concerned to explore the character of moral discourse. Rather, I wish to focus on the issue of *what it is to speak*. My claim is that addressing this question has far-reaching metaethical implications. So, in a sense, this book is an attempt to get beneath much of what those working in metaethics discuss, to get at the workings of speech itself. For those already sympathetic with realism, the hope is to bolster its credentials, highlighting attractive dimensions of the view that have been largely unexplored. For those skeptical of realism, the aim is to invite you to take another look.

2

A Normative Theory
of Speech

Jake's Big Band has been on stage for two hours and is now performing a lively rendition of *Mack the Knife*. As he stands before the Big Band, bandleader Jake Stephens raises his right hand, showing four fingers. Four bars of music pass, and at the end of the fourth bar the Big Band abruptly ends its performance of the piece. About this series of events we want to know: In virtue of what does Jake's waving four fingers in the air count as his directing the Big Band to stop playing the piece they are presently performing at the end of exactly four bars? And, more generally, what does this counting-as relation consist in?

We can eliminate immediately three answers to our first question. First, Jake's raising his four fingers is not identical with his having issued a directive. For Jake could issue the same directive without raising four fingers in the air or, alternatively, raise four fingers in the air without issuing a directive. Second, Jake's raising his four fingers in the air does not logically imply that he has issued a directive. There are, after all, all sorts of cases in which an agent's raising four fingers counts as an entirely different speech act, such as asserting *that it is four o'clock*. Finally, Jake's raising four fingers in the air does not cause him to direct the band members to stop playing their instruments. For there is no causal law specifying that an agent's raising four fingers in the air simultaneously causes him to direct a group of people to cease to perform a musical piece. Nor, for that matter, is there some relation of constant conjunction specifying that whenever an agent raises four fingers in the air, he has thereby directed a group of people to cease to perform a musical piece. Take any plausible analysis you like of what it is for one thing to cause another. None will yield the result that Jake's action causes him to direct a group of people to stop performing a musical piece.[1]

But if so, what does explain the fact that when Jake raises his hand he has thereby performed the illocutionary act of directing the band members to stop playing the piece they are presently performing? The answer that I will defend in this chapter is that offered by proponents of the normative theory of speech. According to the normative theory, an agent's performing a locutionary act counts as his having performed an illocutionary act of a given type (at least in part) in virtue of his having the rights, responsibilities, and obligations of being a speaker.[2] This answer might strike some philosophers as getting off on the wrong foot. Is it not obvious, these philosophers will ask, that conventions lie at the core of speech? Take, for example, Jake's having raised four fingers in the air. Is it not evident that this act counts as his having directed the Big Band to continue playing only four more bars of music because there is a particular convention in effect—one which specifies that performing hand movements such as this counts as performing a directive of a certain kind?

---

1. Jake's raising four fingers in the air may, of course, play a causal role in getting them to stop playing their instruments. That, however, is a different issue from whether Jake's raising his four fingers causes *him* to perform the action of directing them to stop playing their instruments.

2. Those sympathetic with the normative theory include Searle (1969); Wolterstorff (1980), part IV, (1995), ch. 5, and (2008), Part III; Brandom (1994) and (2000); Alston (2000); Green (2007), ch. 2; and Kukla and Lance (2009). Habermas (1991) and Williamson (2000) also have much in common with these views. It may be helpful to say several things about how the view I shall develop compares to those defended by other normative theorists. First, my way of stating the normative view follows Wolterstorff's and Brandom's most closely inasmuch as it utilizes the concept of a normative standing. While Alston and Searle do not themselves fashion their views by explicitly employing this concept, to state their views by appeal to this concept is not, I believe, to misrepresent them. Second, Brandom develops his version of the normative theory in the context of defending an inferentialist semantics. Alston deploys his version of the view to develop an account of sentence meaning. Neither of these projects is a concern of mine. The normative theory, I assume, is of interest independent of these other projects. Third, Searle argues that speaking consists in performing acts according to systems of "constitutive rules," where these rules themselves constitute "institutional facts." According to this view, constitutive rules "involve" rights and obligations (186). While I have reservations about the constitutive rule approach—and Alston's "rule subjection" approach—I believe the position I defend is compatible with them.

This view regarding the role of conventions in speech is, in my estimation, only half right. Conventional arrangements, according to the normative theory, have a role to play in the explanation of speech. But they are not what lie deepest in such an explanation, as they are simply the vehicles by which we acquire the rights, responsibilities, and obligations of being a speaker. Later in this chapter and in the next, I will offer an explanation why. For now, I wish only to emphasize that, according to the normative theory, conventional arrangements have a role to play in the generation of speech, although this role may be different from and less fundamental than what some philosophers assume.[3]

With that noted, let us begin by having the main lines of the normative theory before us. Perhaps the best way to do so is to return to the case of Jake and his Big Band. Assume, for illustration's sake, that Jake performs three speech acts in his capacity as bandleader. First, suppose Jake knows that in the audience is a group of foreign music students interested in jazz. Accordingly:

> Immediately prior to performing *Mack the Knife*, Jake addresses the audience, uttering: "Ella Fitzgerald performed *Mack the Knife*."

Second, suppose that while the Big Band greatly enjoys performing *Mack the Knife*, Jake does not ordinarily include it on the set list. On this occasion, however:

> Jake says to the members of the Big Band prior to the performance: "I promise I will direct you to play *Mack the Knife* late in our first set."

Assume, third, that at the end of *Mack the Knife*,

> Jake holds up four fingers, thereby directing his band to play exactly four more bars of the piece they are presently performing.

Let us consider each of these speech acts from the perspective of the normative theory of speech.

---

3. One point of clarification might, however, be helpful. As will be apparent later in this chapter and the next, I work with a distinction between *conventional arrangements* (arrangements in effect by convention), on the one hand, and *conventional normative features* (rights, responsibilities, and obligations in effect by convention), on the other. The point I am making here concerns only conventional arrangements. In this chapter, I remain neutral regarding the issue of whether the rights, responsibilities, and obligations ingredient in the count-generation of speech are conventional.

In the first case, Jake utters the sentence "Ella Fitzgerald performed *Mack the Knife*," thereby altering his status *vis-à-vis* his audience, for he has now asserted something. Why do normative theorists hold that this alteration is a normative one? The answer that these philosophers offer is that by uttering the sentence specified in this case, Jake has thereby "stuck his neck out" and taken responsibility for the obtaining of a certain state of affairs: namely, *that Ella Fitzgerald performed "Mack the Knife"*—taking responsibility in this case being not a matter of Jake's having brought a state of affairs into existence, but rather laying himself open to appropriate correction, blame, or admonition were this state of affairs to not obtain.[4] For in this particular case, were it true that Fitzgerald never performed *Mack the Knife* (or that Jake does not himself believe that she did), then Jake's audience would have the right to correct, blame, or reproach him—all else being equal, of course.

Now consider the second case. By uttering the sentence "I promise I will direct you to play *Mack the Knife* late in our first set," Jake thereby alters his status with regard to the Big Band, for he has promised them something. Why believe, in this case, that the alteration is a normative one? Normative theorists answer that, by uttering the sentence in question, Jake has taken responsibility for both his having the authority to lay an obligation on himself and his actually having laid an obligation on himself. Were Jake not to have the authority or intention to lead them in such a performance, then Jake would rightly be subject to correction, admonition, and even blame for his behavior—once again, all else being equal.[5]

---

4. See Alston (2000), 54. Brandom (2000) speaks of this phenomenon in terms of a speaker's having *committed* himself to a certain state of affairs' obtaining. In what follows, I will use the phrase "takes responsibility for," so that it is roughly synonymous with "commits oneself to." I will not assume, incidentally, that either taking responsibility for or committing oneself is necessarily an intentional phenomenon. I will, then, leave open the possibility that one can take responsibility for or commit oneself to a state of affairs without intending to do so.

5. I realize that proponents of the so-called Humean theory of promising—who deny that promising involves laying an obligation on oneself—will not find the view I articulate above congenial. While I find the Humean view unsatisfactory, it is worth noting that, strictly speaking, one could combine the normative theory with a version of the Humean view. For one could hold that, in promising, an agent takes responsibility not for having the power to lay an obligation on herself but for creating the expectation in her audience that she will act in a certain way.

Turn, finally, to the third case. In this example, Jake has also altered his status with regard to his audience, for he has directed them to do something. Why hold, though, that the alteration is normative in this case too? The answer offered by normative theorists is that, by holding up four fingers in the air, Jake has put himself on the normative hook, taking responsibility for his both having the authority to lay an obligation on the Big Band and his actually having laid an obligation on the Big Band. Were Jake to have no such authority—say, because he is an imposter—or were he to stop conducting at the end of only two bars, then it would be appropriate to correct or admonish Jake for having failed to discharge the obligations (or responsibilities) incurred by his having raised four fingers in the air—once more, all else being equal.

The three cases we have considered highlight two claims fundamental to the normative theory of speech. The first is that an agent's performing an illocutionary act implies that he has the rights, responsibilities, and obligations of being a speaker. The second is that having these normative features plays an important explanatory role. It is in virtue of an agent's having these features that his performing a locutionary act count-generates his performing an illocutionary act. If the normative theory is true, then, illocutionary acts are not count-generated by mere "descriptive" facts about the speaker and her audience, such as what the speaker intends and what the audience expects (although, as I will note in a moment, normative theorists do maintain that these mere descriptive facts often have an important role to play in speech). Rather, the theory tells us that for an agent to perform an illocutionary act by way of performing a locutionary act, he must alter his normative position with respect to his audience, this alteration consisting in the fact that he acquires certain rights, responsibilities, and obligations vis-à-vis his audience, and vice versa. If the normative theory be believed, provided certain arrangements are in effect, it is these normative facts that (at least in part) account for the "hook-up" between an agent's act of uttering a sentence and the speech acts that he thereby performs. In their absence, speech would not occur.

Let me immediately add a qualification to this. While I have presented the normative theory as offering a normative explanation for the count-generation of speech, the view is ontologically non-committal in two important respects. First, when normative theorists claim that normative features are ingredient in the count-generation of speech acts, they do not thereby commit themselves to any claims about that in which these features consist. Strictly speaking, then, their view is compatible with these normative features being determined by anything from social stipulations to the commands of God. Nor do normative theorists commit themselves to any claims about the normative category to which these features belong. The normative theory, then, does not presuppose that these features are moral or should be understood as moral realists believe. As will have already been evident, I believe that the some of the normative features that count-generate speech are moral, but a separate argument is required to defend this further commitment.

I Clarifying the view

In my view, there is much to recommend the normative theory, at least in the basic form in which I have presented it. Before I highlight some of its virtues, however, I want first to fill in some details in my presentation of the position that may help us to understand it better. Let us start with four preliminary points.

In the first place, the Speech Act Argument is couched in terms of the normative standing that a speaker acquires. But, as the cases which I have described will have made evident, the normative dimensions of speech in which I am interested go beyond those that attach to a speaker. Audiences can also acquire normative standings. Suppose that when addressing the Big Band, Jake utters the sentence "I promise I will direct you to play *Mack the Knife* late in our first set," thereby laying an obligation on himself. If what I have said is correct, this implies that his audience has a right against him such that if he fails to intend to do as he says, then (all else being equal) it is appropriate to hold him accountable. As I shall contend later, this is simply the conceptual fallout of principles that link obligations and rights together. For now, however, I want to emphasize that in what follows I shall be interested not simply in the normative standings of speakers. The conceptual net I wish to cast extends beyond them to the normative standings that an audience can acquire. Speech, according to the normative theory, implies that we stand in normative *relations* to one another.

Second, according to the cases I have presented, Jake performs three speech acts: he asserts a proposition, promises to act in a certain way, and commands the Big Band to act in a particular fashion. There are, however, speech acts of types other than these, and one might wonder whether the normative theory applies equally to cases of these other types. Without arguing the point in any detail, I think we can see that it does.

Suppose we follow William Alston and think of speech acts as falling into the following five basic categories:

> Assertives: e.g., alleging, claiming, testifying, etc.
> Directives: e.g., asking, requesting, commanding, etc.
> Commisives: e.g., promising, inviting, offering, etc.
> Expressives: e.g., thanking, expressing contempt, expressing relief, etc.
> Exercitives: e.g., adjourning, pardoning, nominating, etc.[6]

To this point, we have been working with examples from the first three categories. But it is fairly apparent how the account can be extended to the latter two.

Imagine that, upon receiving a new tie as a gift, I (with all apparent seriousness) utter the sentence:

> "What a handsome new tie!"

If this utterance counts as a speech act, it is what Alston refers to as an expressive. According to the normative theory, I have performed the speech act of expressing enthusiasm only if and because I have altered my normative position with respect to my audience. In the case at hand, the alteration consists in my having taken responsibility for the fact that I am genuinely enthusiastic about the tie you have given me. If you rightly detect that my enthusiasm is bluff, for example, you can rightly (if lightheartedly) admonish me for being insincere.

Suppose, somewhat differently, I utter the sentence:

> "I nominate you as our spokesperson."

---

6. Alston (2000), 34. Searle (2010) offers a similar list. I do not claim the list is exhaustive.

If this utterance counts as a speech act, it is what Alston terms an exercitive. According to the normative theory, I have performed the speech act of nominating you only because I have altered my normative position with respect to my audience. What might this alteration consist in? In this case, it includes not only my having taken responsibility for having the authority to nominate, but also my being liable to correction, blame, or reproach if things are not as I present them. If the right to nominate you as our spokesperson belongs not to me but to the entire committee, for example, then you can correct me by reminding me of this fact. At any rate, the point should be clear enough: we can extend the main lines of the normative theory to the whole range of speech acts.

Third, I started our discussion in this chapter by asking the question "In virtue of what does Jake's waving four fingers in the air count as his having directed the Big Band to perform exactly four more bars of music?" The answer that we considered initially says: it is by convention. Jake's locutionary act counts as his having directed the Big Band to act in a particular way in virtue of the fact that certain conventional arrangements are in effect. I said that, in my estimation, this answer is only half right. Since the issue will arise again in the next chapter, let me at least partly explain myself.

Begin by distinguishing *arrangements*, on the one hand, from *conventions*, on the other.[7] For present purposes, we can think of an arrangement for Ψing as an ordered pair of act-types {Φing, Ψing} such that an agent could engage in Ψing by Φing. For example, an arrangement for an agent to assert *that Ella Fitzgerald performed "Mack the Knife"* is an ordered pair consisting of the act-types:

> {Uttering the sentence "Ella Fitzgerald performed *Mack the Knife*," asserting *that Ella Fitzgerald performed "Mack the Knife"*}.

As our discussion of locutionary acts will have made evident, there exists an untold number of possible arrangements for the generation of the single illocutionary act of asserting *that Ella Fitzgerald performed "Mack the Knife."* In principle, one could perform it by raising a single finger in the air or wiggling one's nose. But, if that is

7. I borrow the distinction from Wolterstorff (1980), 198–219, and (1995), 89–91.

right, what brings it about that an arrangement such as that specified by the ordered pair above is in effect for Jake and his audience?

The answer appears to be: it is by convention that an arrangement such as this is in effect. That is, it is because there is something like a social stipulation in place or a received practice that holds for qualified parties that Jake can employ the arrangement:

> {Uttering the sentence "Ella Fitzgerald performed *Mack the Knife*," asserting *that Ella Fitzgerald performed "Mack the Knife"*},

to state *that Ella Fitzgerald performed "Mack the Knife."*[8]

For present purposes, then, let us think of conventions as a type of social stipulation (or received practice) that holds for qualified parties. And let us call those arrangements that are in effect by convention *conventional arrangements*. (Of the many arrangements that exist, only a small percentage will be in effect by convention.) At this point, we have a decent idea of how normative theorists think about the interrelation between conventional arrangements, on the one hand, and normative standings, on the other. Suppose we want to know how an agent can acquire the rights, responsibilities, and obligations of being a speaker, thereby engaging in speech. Normative theorists answer: there must be an arrangement in effect for that agent such that she can employ it to acquire the normative standing of being a speaker. As such, conventional arrangements are vehicles for the acquisition of the rights, responsibilities, and obligations of being a speaker. Now, suppose somewhat differently, with respect to some arrangement for speaking, {Φing, Ψing}, we want to know what accounts for the fact that an agent's Φing count-generates his Ψing. Normative theorists answer: it is an agent's having the rights, responsibilities, and obligations of being a speaker that accounts for the hook-up

---

8. However, it may be worth pointing out that not all arrangements for speaking are in effect by convention. A person, for example, can emphatically gesture in certain ways to onlookers and thereby avow that she is in distress, even though there are no socially generated arrangements in place that tell us that performing gestures of that particular type count as avowing that one is in distress. Or, somewhat differently, she can inform us that there is a bear in the near vicinity by performing actions that resemble those performed by a bear. The first case appeals to what the eighteenth-century philosophers called "natural signs." The second appeals to resemblance or iconic relations. Our understanding of speech should allow for cases such as these. See Wolterstorff (1995), ch. 5.

between these two actions, for the count-generation operative in speech consists in an agent's having these normative features.

Let me expand upon this last point. All of us are familiar with cases in which an agent performs one and the same locutionary action but thereby performs very different types of action. For example, suppose that:

> Jake at time t utters the sentence "Ella Fitzgerald performed *Mack the Knife*," but by doing so merely tests whether the microphone before him is switched on.

Suppose, by contrast, that:

> Jake at time t_1 utters the sentence "Ella Fitzgerald performed *Mack the Knife*," thereby asserting that *Ella Fitzgerald performed "Mack the Knife."*

According to these cases, by performing the very same act-type, Jake at one time simply tests whether a microphone is switched on, but mere seconds later (we can suppose) asserts a proposition. These cases help us to see that the mere fact that an agent performs a given locutionary act that is a component of an arrangement for speaking that is in effect is not sufficient to explain his having performed a speech act.

What accounts for the difference? Normative theorists offer the following reply. In the first place, Jake employs different arrangements for acting that are in effect. In the first case he employs the conventional arrangement:

> {Uttering the sentence "Ella Fitzgerald performed *Mack the Knife*," testing whether a microphone is working}.

While in the second case he employs the conventional arrangement:

> {Uttering the sentence "Ella Fitzgerald performed *Mack the Knife*," asserting *that Ella Fitzgerald performed "Mack the Knife"*}.

And what is it to employ an arrangement of the second sort, an arrangement for speaking? According to normative theorists, it is to take responsibility for things being a certain way. Specifically, it is to take responsibility for things being a certain way by performing a locutionary act that is a component of a conventional arrangement for speaking that is in effect. If this is right, the difference between the two cases we are considering is a normative one. In the first case, Jake does not take responsibility for anything about Fitzgerald. By uttering the sentence "Ella Fitzgerald performed *Mack the Knife*," he does not thereby commit himself to any claim about what Fitzgerald has done and, so, is not open to correction if what he says is not true. Rather, by uttering this sentence he simply expresses the intention to test whether a microphone is working. In the second case, by contrast, Jake utters the same sentence, but takes responsibility for the fact that Fitzgerald performed *Mack the Knife*, laying himself open to appropriate correction if he is wrong or fails to believe what he says. If this is right, having the rights, responsibilities, and obligations of being a speaker is doing the explanatory work that normative theorists claim. If we want to know why the performance of the same locutionary act-type generates a speech act in one case but not in another, the answer is that in one case an agent acquires the rights, responsibilities, and obligations of being a speaker by performing that locutionary act, while in the other case he does not. (This is not, I might add, to claim that illocutionary act-types can be individuated solely by appeal to their normative features.)

Before moving forward, two points about this explanation bear mention. The first is that taking responsibility for something can be done in less than a sincere way. To take responsibility for Fitzgerald's having performed *Mack the Knife*, Jake need not believe that she has actually performed this piece. Rather, in ordinary speech situations, Jake need only *present himself* as being genuinely committed to the fact that Fitzgerald performed *Mack the Knife*—where this is determined by a whole host of difficult-to-describe, contextually variable factors that include not only his uttering a sentence, but also such things as his facial expressions and tone of voice.

The second point is that, as normative theorists see things, taking responsibility for something's being the case is ordinarily an intentional action. Accordingly, normative theorists insist that speech acts such as asserting, commanding, promising, adjourning, and the like are typically not events that happen to us. Rather, they are typically actions that we intentionally perform—although I should stress that, in this case, the qualifier "typically" is important. Taking full account of deviant cases of speech would, I believe, require us to stop short of maintaining that all speech acts are intentionally performed.

To illustrate the point, imagine a case in which a person enters a large room in which an auction is taking place but is ignorant of the rules that govern auctions. After briefly observing the behavior of others, he decides to join the fun and shoots up his hand in the air. Given the norms in play, this person is "on the hook" for having bid on an item even though he did not intend to do so; he has (so it would appear) inadvertently performed a speech act. Cases such as this suggest that certain contexts are governed by conventional arrangements for speaking that are particularly strict. In these contexts, it is assumed that everyone who is engaged in a given social practice is or ought to be aware that performing actions of various kinds is sufficient to have rights, responsibilities, and obligations of various sorts ascribed to them. If this is right, taking responsibility for a state of affairs need not be an intentional action.[9]

I turn now to the fourth and final preliminary matter that I would like to address. Up to this point in our discussion I have talked more or less indiscriminately about the rights, responsibilities, and obligations of being speaker. It will be important for the subsequent discussion, however, to make some distinctions, dividing these normative features into different types.

To get our bearings with regard to this issue, imagine that you have been a mid-level US Postal Service employee for years but have recently been appointed Postmaster General. When you were an ordinary US Postal Service employee, you had various rights. Among these rights, we can suppose, is the right to a paid vacation. But you did not have the right to promise your fellow employees a three-percent pay raise. Nor did you have the right to order them to submit to yearly drug testing. You lacked the authority to do these things. Only when you became Postmaster General did you acquire these rights. And when you did acquire these rights, they had a limited scope. They were rights against only US Postal Service employees in certain conditions. Had you, for example, sincerely uttered the

---

9. See note 4. While I realize that there are other ways of diagnosing the auction case, a piece of evidence in favor of the diagnosis offered above is provided by the nature of mitigating conditions. Suppose, for illustration's sake, the relevant authorities were to discover what had happened in the case described. Would they say that the agent is not accountable, since he had failed to bid? I would think not. I would think that the reply would be something like "Given the unusual conditions, we will not hold you accountable for having successfully bid on the item." I thank John Turri for discussion of this point.

sentence "I promise you at least a three-percent pay raise" to a visiting police officer, your speech act would have been malformed. You would have had no authority to promise any such thing; it is not part of your office or position.

Suppose we call this authority on your part a *standing power*. As an initial approximation, think of a standing power as consisting in an agent's having rights of two sorts: first, a permission-right to introduce normative alterations into the world, and second, a claim-right against others that they not try to prevent that agent from bringing about such alterations.[10] Consider, for example, the standing power to promise something. This power is one that consists in your having a permission-right to lay an obligation of a certain kind on yourself, thereby altering your normative status. Were you to lay such an obligation on yourself, your having this right guarantees that the performance of this act would not itself be a violation of those obligations that attach to you in virtue of your being a participant in the discursive practice of giving and receiving promises, since you are permitted to perform this type of act with respect to a certain range of agents in a certain range of conditions. This power, we have seen, also consists in your having a claim-right against others that they not try to prevent you from laying such an obligation on yourself, as you would be wronged if they were to try to do so (all else being equal).[11]

Every standing power is accompanied by general rights, responsibilities, and obligations. Call these *standing rights, responsibilities, and obligations*. Suppose, to stay with our example, that (in ordinary conditions) you were to address members of the US Postal Service, uttering the sentence "I promise you a three-percent pay raise." Attached to the performance of an action of this kind is the obligation to intend to do as you say. Were you to utter this sentence but fail to conform to this obligation, then you would be rightly open to correction, admonition, blame, or the like. Or suppose, somewhat

10. A claim-right is a right against a person that she do or refrain from doing something. A permission-right, by contrast, is not a right against anyone. It is simply a permission that an agent himself has to do or refrain from doing something. The obligations and rights to which I refer in the text are so-called objective obligations and rights.

11. Are all permission-rights accompanied by claim-rights? No. If we are playing a game of sharks and minnows, for example, I have a permission-right to try to swim to the other side of the pool. But I do not have a claim-right against you that you allow me to do so.

differently, that in ordinary conditions you were to utter the sentence "I am stepping down from my position as Postmaster General." Attached to the performance of actions of this kind is the responsibility to present things as they actually are. If you present things as being a certain way and things are not as you present them, then (in ordinary conditions) your audience has the right to correct, admonish, or blame you. Thus described, standing rights, responsibilities, and obligations are doubly conditional. They do not apply to an agent in virtue of his having actually committed himself to some state of affairs by performing some locutionary act. Rather, they specify that *if* an agent presents the world or himself as being a certain way by performing some locutionary act, then he is liable to correction, admonition, or blame *if* things are not as he presents them.

Finally, suppose that in an ordinary speech context you actually address the members of the US Postal Service, uttering the sentence "I promise you a three-percent pay raise." You have now actually presented yourself as laying an obligation on yourself to provide a three-percent raise to the employees of the US Postal Service. They now have the right to hold you accountable if you fail to intend to do any such thing. Similarly, suppose that in an ordinary speech context you address the members of the US Postal Service, uttering the sentence "I am stepping down from my position as Postmaster General." You have now actually taken responsibility for things being as you present them. If things are not as you say—perhaps because you have no intention of stepping down from your position—then your audience is now entitled to correct, admonish, or blame you. Call those normative features generated by your taking responsibility for a state of affairs *generated rights, responsibilities, and obligations*, since they are generated by the performance of locutionary acts of various sorts.[12]

There is, then, a three-fold distinction between (i) standing powers (ii) standing rights, responsibilities, and obligations, and

---

12. Thus understood, generated rights, responsibilities, and obligations come in two varieties. Some are conditional, specifying that if things are not as an agent presents them, then she is liable to correction, reproach, blame, or the like. Other generated rights, responsibilities, or obligations, by contrast, are not conditional. They are normative features that an agent has because, say, things are not as she presents them. You might, for example, be liable to correction because the world is not as you say it is. Unless I indicate otherwise, when I refer to generated rights, responsibilities, and obligations, I will have those of the conditional variety in mind.

(iii) generated rights, responsibilities, and obligations. Two points about this three-fold distinction merit emphasis.

First, in the example I have used, you have the standing power to promise and command various things to employees of the US Postal Service. You have this standing power only because you have a special normative standing: namely, that of being the Postmaster General. Most others who lack this normative standing also lack the standing power with regard to US Postal employees to promise them pay raises or order them to submit to drug testing. Since this is a standing power that attaches only to qualified parties, call this a *specialized standing power*. Some speech-act types, we have seen, are such that they can be performed only by those with the relevant specialized standing power.

But not all are. In ordinary speech situations, you and I can do such things as assert propositions about the weather and request the time. That is, you and I have the standing power to perform such actions. In ordinary speech circumstances, if I were to utter the sentence "It looks as if it is going to rain," no one could rightly say that my speech act is defective on account of my not having the authority to assert this, as I have the right to perform speech acts of this type. Moreover, by all appearances, I have this right simply in virtue of being a participant in the practice of speech; nothing else is required. For ease of reference, we can call a standing power of this sort a *generic standing power*. Generic standing powers, like their specialized counterparts, are accompanied by standing rights, responsibilities, and obligations.

Second, according to the picture sketched previously, the standing power to perform any speech act type is accompanied by a cluster of correlative standing rights, responsibilities, and obligations. According to a natural way of thinking about ordinary speech situations, it is having both standing powers and these standing rights, responsibilities, and obligations that accounts (at least in part) for an agent's having particular generated rights, responsibilities, or obligations on a given occasion.[13] Suppose, once again, you are the

---

13. Particularlists, such as Dancy (2004), who deny that there are any general obligations, would reject this. While I believe that particularists have important insights to offer regarding the nature and explanatory role of normative principles, I am not persuaded by the arguments they offer for their position. So, for present purposes, I am going to lay the view aside, assuming that there are general normative principles that can account for why actions can have particular normative properties.

Postmaster General and that, in an ordinary speech situation, you address the employees of the US Postal Service, uttering the sentence "I promise you a three-percent pay raise." By performing this action, you have thereby altered your normative status with respect to the employees of the US Postal Service. Among the ways you have done so is that, by uttering this sentence, you have put yourself on the normative hook, laying yourself open to rightful correction if you do not have the authority to pronounce this or if you have no intention of giving them a pay raise. That you have the generated obligation to intend to do what you say is, arguably, determined by the fact that there are standing rights, responsibilities, and obligations in place. In ordinary speech conditions, if you utter the sentence "I promise you a three-percent pay raise," then you are obligated to intend to do what you say because there is the standing obligation that:

> In ordinary speech situations, if an agent presents himself as having made a promise, then he is obligated to intend to do as he says.

It is this standing obligation that, in part, accounts for the fact that you have altered your normative relation in a certain way with regard to your audience. Or to put the matter differently, it is this standing obligation that is "triggered" when an agent presents himself as having made a promise.

II Why the normative view?

To this point I have tried to accomplish two things. In the first place, I have been concerned to present the main lines of the normative theory, underscoring its distinctive features. In the second place, I have also attempted to display its appeal, mostly by highlighting the extent to which speech is a normative phenomenon. Rather than leave this appeal simply at the intuitive level, however, I now want to present several considerations that favor its acceptance, spending some time elaborating upon the fourth and final consideration.

First, as I pointed out in the last chapter, Clarke's Insight does not direct us to a surprising or otherwise hidden feature of speech acts.

Speech acts such as promising and commanding, so to speak, wear their normativity on their sleeve. Any plausible account of promising should take into account the fact that by performing locutionary acts of certain kinds (in ordinary conditions), it appears as if the speaker thereby lays an obligation on himself. Likewise, any plausible account of commanding should account for the fact that by performing locutionary acts of other types (in ordinary conditions), it appears as if the speaker lays an obligation of a certain kind on his audience. The normative theory has the virtue of not only taking these appearances seriously, but also offering an account of the appearances that is fairly straightforward: with respect to speech, things are as they seem. Speech genuinely exhibits a normative dimension.

Second, the normative theory has the virtue of offering a highly unified account of the nature of speech acts. In response to the question "What brings it about that a locutionary act count-generates an illocutionary act?" the normative theorist replies "In part, having the rights, responsibilities, and obligations of being a speaker." In this respect, promises and commands do not stand apart as unusual speech acts, because they exhibit a normative dimension. *All* speech acts exhibit a similar normative dimension. The normative theory offers us a streamlined account of that dimension—one that appeals to the notion of a normative standing. Later I will contend that this is a significant virtue of the view.

Third, by claiming that the notion of a normative standing lies at the heart of speech, the normative theorist has not (in the first instance at least) thereby appealed to something dark and philosophically mysterious. Few doubt that we exhibit normative standings. And we seem to understand fairly well that they consist in having certain rights, responsibilities, and obligations. To return to the example used earlier, the possession of these rights, responsibilities, and obligations distinguishes, at least in part, the standing of being an ordinary US Postal Service employee from that of being the Postmaster General. It is the having of these rights, responsibilities, and obligations to which one would appeal were one to explain the difference between being an ordinary mid-level US Postal Service employee and being the Postmaster General.

Finally, it is difficult to find among speech act theories a developed alternative to the normative theory. Admittedly, those working within speech act theory often distinguish the normative theory from the perlocutionary-intention view, as I did in the last chapter. But it is not immediately apparent that these positions are in genuine conflict. Take, for example, Stephen Barker's statement of the perlocutionary-intention view. According to Barker, for an agent S to assert a proposition p is for S to (i) advertise his intention to represent a state of affairs; and (ii) intend for his audience to engage with this commitment by accepting, confirming, or rejecting it.[14] Barker's position is a version of the perlocutionary-intention view, since it says an agent's asserting consists in her advertising intentions to produce in her audience certain kinds of mental state. But it is not immediately clear that it represents a genuine rival to the normative theory. For, charitably understood, both positions affirm the importance of both the perlocutionary and normative dimensions of speech.

Consider, first, the way in which normative theorists think of the perlocutionary dimensions of speech. While normative theorists maintain that perlocutionary-intention theories fail to specify the proper role of perlocutionary act intentions in ordinary discourse, they do not deny that agents ordinarily express perlocutionary act intentions when speaking. Moreover, normative theorists agree that inasmuch as perlocutionary-intention theorists emphasize the communicative dimensions of speech, they have their eye on a fundamental dimension of the practice of speaking—this dimension arguably being what distinguishes it from other practices that involve the use of words.[15]

Both points deserve elaboration. Let me begin with the first. Imagine a case in which you are a member of a choir that specializes in the performance of Byzantine chant. When you engage in this activity, it is governed by norms that require you to use certain tones

14. See Barker (2004), 8. Barker talks of asserting cognitive states rather than propositions. He also speaks of "situations" rather than states of affairs. I have altered the terminology he uses to present his view so that it meshes more exactly with the terminology that I have been using. Schiffer (1972), Bennett (1976), Bach and Harnish (1979), Avramides (1989), and Grice (1989) also develop versions of the perlocutionary-intention view. Harnish (2005) offers an interesting comparison of the perlocutionary and normative approaches. In metaethics, Gibbard (1990) embraces the fundamentals of the perlocutionary-intention position.

15. For a related point, see Wolterstorff (1980), 211, and Alston (2000), 270–1.

at particular points in a performance but not at others. If, while chanting a sticheron, for example, you were to use the first tone when you are supposed to use the fourth, then you would be rightly subject to correction. The script calls for something else. To put the matter in the terminology that I have used throughout this chapter, by participating in the social practice of Byzantine chant, you acquire the normative standing of being a chanter with its constitutive rights, responsibilities, and obligations. Failure to discharge certain responsibilities renders you liable to correction, reproach, or even blame.

Norms of chanting, I have said, are ones that concern how one ought to use words. Clearly, however, the fact that an agent conforms to these norms when chanting Greek sentences makes no contribution to the illocutionary acts performed when chanting. Whether an agent chants a Greek sentence in the first or the fourth tone makes no difference as to what speech act she has thereby performed. Indeed, this should be especially evident in the case in which a person knows how to pronounce Greek sentences, but has almost no idea (nor is there any expectation that she have any idea) of what they mean. In such a case, the norms of chanting apply even though it is questionable whether she is performing any illocutionary acts at all.

It cannot be, then, that what distinguishes the normative standing of being a speaker from other such standings is that it is one that applies to agents in virtue of their doing things with words. For both the normative standings of being a chanter and being a speaker, I have claimed, are acquired by agents in virtue of their doing things with words. What, then, distinguishes them? The answer that both normative and perlocutionary theorists would offer is this: the standing of being a chanter is not bound up with communicative intent in the way that the standing of being a speaker ordinarily is. The rights, responsibilities, and obligations that apply to an agent when chanting— such as norms that concern which tones to use—are not, in the first instance, ones that concern the communication of information to an audience. At least some of the rights, responsibilities, and obligations that apply to an agent engaging in discourse, however, are. The two practices, chanting and speech, have different aims—the aim of the latter being, at least in a wide range of cases, to communicate information. The character of the rights, responsibilities, and obligations that attach to those who participate in these practices reflects these different aims.

If this is right, normative theorists will sympathize with the perlocutionary-intention theorists' claim that communicative intent is central to speech. Arguably, however, perlocutionary-intention theorists should also be in considerable sympathy with the normative theorists' insistence that normative standings are important to speech. For, charitably understood, while perlocutionary-intention views emphasize the role of perlocutionary act intentions in speech, they do not deny that a person's expressing these intentions is accompanied by his having the normative standing of being a speaker. Indeed, the recognition that agents possess such a standing is, arguably, lying just below the surface of their position.

Consider, in this regard, Barker's account of assertion once again.[16] According to Barker's position, an agent asserts a proposition just in case she advertises the intention to represent the world in a certain way and intends her audience to engage with this commitment. Arguably, however, in ordinary speech situations, advertising oneself as being in a representational state of a certain kind just is to "stick one's neck out" in a certain way, thereby laying oneself open to rightful correction if things are not as one advertises. After all, if advertising one's cognitive commitments implied nothing whatsoever about one's normative status *vis-à-vis* one's audience, it is difficult to see why, according to the perlocutionary-intention view, an agent would be *rightly* subject to correction or reproach were things not as she presents them. The implication I draw is that, although perlocutionary-intention theorists do not themselves emphasize the normative dimensions of speech, there is nothing about their view that should lead us to believe that, by emphasizing these dimensions, normative theorists have misdescribed the nature of speech as perlocutionary-intention theorists understand it.

16. While I have employed Barker's position as a case of the perlocutionary-intention view, I find his own attempt to account for the normative dimensions of speech elusive. Some of what Barker says (vii–viii and 16–17) indicates that he believes that the normative dimension can be explained away. But I do not see, in his presentation at least, how this is supposed to happen.

III Against the perlocutionary-intention view

I have claimed that a consideration favoring the normative theory is that, among the available theories of speech, it is difficult to find a developed alternative that is incompatible with it. But perhaps we have not looked closely enough. For it might be said that there is a way to understand the perlocutionary-intention view according to which it is a clear rival to the normative theory. Is there such a way?

There is indeed. According to one understanding of their view, perlocutionary-intention theorists accept the following two claims:

> An agent performs an illocutionary act by performing some locutionary act only if and because he expresses the relevant perlocutionary act intentions when performing that locutionary act.

> In general, an agent's having the rights, responsibilities, and obligations of being a speaker is not that in virtue of which his performing a locutionary act count-generates his performing an illocutionary act. Generally speaking, these normative features do not generate but are generated by speech.

This position (which I will now refer to as the perlocutionary-intention view) is, in effect, the reverse of the normative theory. Normative theorists acknowledge the presence of perlocutionary intentions in speech; they deny, however, that they play a pivotal role in the count-generation of speech. Perlocutionary-intention theorists, by contrast, acknowledge the presence of normative features in speech, but deny that they play a pivotal role in the count-generation of speech. According to perlocutionary-intention theorists, it is not having the rights, responsibilities, and obligations of being speaker but the expression of perlocutionary intentions that accounts for the hook-up between locutionary and illocutionary acts. These philosophers hold that, generally speaking, normative features do not generate but are generated by speech. Promises generate obligations. Requests generate reasons. Assertions generate rights.[17]

---

17. Does this version of the view approximate the views defended by perlocutionary-intention theorists such as Barker, Bennett, and Schiffer? Well, these philosophers accept the first claim stated above. But it is difficult to say whether they would accept the second, since they say little about the normative dimensions of speech in which normative theorists are interested. Harnish (2005) is an exception. He seems to think that the two views might simply be variants of one another.

Why would a philosopher accept this version of the perlocutionary-intention view? Perhaps drawing a parallel will help us see why. Consider epiphenomenalists about the mind. Those who advocate this position claim that mental states such as beliefs and desires exist. They deny, however, that they explain anything worth explaining, such as an agent's behavior. In general, this is because they hold that, although there are entities such as beliefs, appeal to them is explanatorily unnecessary. According to some epiphenomenalists, we can explain behavior adequately without making essential reference to beliefs. Usually, the claim is that behavior can be explained merely by appeal to neural or brain states (where these are not identical with beliefs). According to others, even if such explanations are not forthcoming, we have strong independent reasons for thinking that beliefs could not be explanatorily efficacious. Sometimes the claim is that if they were, this would imply that there are cases of "downward causation," which is impossible.

A case for the perlocutionary-intention view would presumably rest on similar claims. That is, a parallel case would presumably claim that although normative facts exist, appealing to them to explain speech is unnecessary. In this case, it might be said that we can adequately explain the generation of speech acts without making essential reference to them. Or it might be said that even if such explanations are not on offer, we have strong independent reasons for thinking that normative facts could not be ingredient in what count-generates speech acts.

Let me offer some initial observations about this rationale for accepting the perlocutionary-intention view. First, suppose for argument's sake that this rationale for accepting the perlocutionary-intention view were correct. Even if it were correct, this would not be devastating for the Speech Act Argument. For recall that, as I presented it in the previous chapter, the Speech Act Argument implies this pair of claims: first, that moral facts exist and, second, that these facts explain (at least in part) the count-generation of speech. If the rationale under consideration were correct, the perlocutionary-intention view would imply that the second of these claims is false. Normative and, hence, moral facts, it would turn out, do not explain the count-generation of speech. But this is compatible with the claim that the performance of speech acts implies the existence of moral facts. After all, the perlocutionary-intention view does not deny that normative features *attach* to speech acts. If these features do attach to speech acts, and some of them are moral, then it leaves the first claim identified above intact. This, admittedly, is considerably less than I wish to argue for. Still, it is worth emphasizing that even if the perlocutionary-intention view were true (and the argumentation of Chapters 3–6 were correct), an important component of the Speech Act Argument would not be affected.

Second, I think we have reason to believe that the rationale just offered for the perlocutionary-intention view is in fact incorrect. Specifically, I think we have little reason to believe that normative features are not ingredient in the count-generation of speech. Take an obvious case. Suppose that during a game of Major League Baseball, the home plate umpire yells "Strike!" upon a pitcher's throwing a ball toward home plate. Moreover, suppose that while watching the very same pitch on my television screen, I yell the very same thing. By yelling the word "Strike!" the umpire has accomplished two things: he has declared the pitch a strike and the pitch now counts as a strike. In contrast, by yelling the same, I have only managed to startle my napping dog.

There is an apparent explanation of this. The umpire possesses a standing power—one which includes the right to declare pitches strikes in a game of Major League Baseball. I do not. A standing power of this sort may or may not be causally efficacious. However that may be, I am aware of no reason to think that standing powers could not (partially) account in some non-causal way for the performance of illocutionary acts. To the contrary, it seems to me that the case of the umpire reveals standing powers to be exactly the sort of thing that are ingredient in the count-generation of speech. For, to repeat, they appear to be precisely the sort of thing that accounts for the performance of the speech act in question.

I believe there is reason, then, to be suspicious of what appears to be the most obvious rationale for accepting the perlocutionary-intention view, as there appear to be vivid cases in which normative features figure in the generation of speech. Still, the perlocutionary-intention view is worth a closer look, as it represents the most obvious rival to the normative theory. In what follows, I offer three reasons for preferring the normative theory to it.

The first reason

A moment ago I identified two claims that perlocutionary-intention theorists accept. They are, recall:

> An agent performs an illocutionary act by performing some locutionary act only if and because he expresses the relevant perlocutionary act intentions when performing that locutionary act.

> In general, an agent's having the rights, responsibilities, and obligations of being a speaker is not that in virtue of which his performing a locutionary act count-generates his performing an illocutionary act. Generally speaking, these normative features do not generate but are generated by speech.

I believe both of these claims are false. In this section I provide an argument to reject the first.

Suppose we could identify cases in which an agent performs a speech act, but fails to express (or, indeed, have) the requisite perlocutionary act intentions. If we could do this, then we would have strong reason to reject the claim that an agent's expressing a perlocutionary act intention accounts for the generation of speech. I would like to present several such cases. The first is a case in which, by all appearances, a speaker performs an illocutionary act but assumes there is no audience and, hence, forms no intention for an audience to engage with the content of his illocutionary act. The second is one in which, by all appearances, an agent performs an illocutionary act, assumes there is an audience, but does not intend for his audience to engage with the content of his illocutionary act. The third case is one in which, by all appearances, an agent performs an illocutionary act but intends for there to be no audience to engage with its content.

Begin with the first case. Suppose Jake has become immersed in a Nature mystery cult. According to this movement, Nature is a vast impersonal force that can be manipulated by performing incantations of various sorts. Wishing to increase his ability to manipulate Nature, imagine that Jake takes his cult guidebook into his room.

He opens the guidebook, and follows its instructions, uttering the
following sentences:

> Nature is eternal.
> May its power be manifest!

By uttering these sentences, Jake expresses various beliefs he has
about Nature, for he accepts what the mystery cults say about it. But
by uttering these sentences he expresses no perlocutionary intentions whatsoever. For there is no one whom he intends to engage
with the content of his speech acts: not Nature, not other people,
not himself. (Jake has strange views about Nature; but he does not
believe that an impersonal force, Nature, considers the propositional
content of his linguistic acts.) He is, after the fashion of adherents to
the cult, intending to pronounce various things about the world.
However, Jake's aim in doing so is not to communicate but to manipulate. If this is right, Jake has performed a series of illocutionary
acts; among other things, he has pronounced Nature to be eternal.
But he has not expressed any perlocutionary intentions. For he assumes there is no audience to engage with the content of his illocutionary act.

Consider, now, a second case, due in its essentials to Alston.[18] Imagine a deeply pessimistic prophet. God, we may imagine, has told
this prophet to testify to a certain truth p. Given the prophet's background knowledge of what his audience is like, he has no hope that
they will engage with what he says; he is certain that they will simply
ignore him. So, he forms no intention for his audience to engage
with the content of what he says. Indeed, his view of the religious and
moral character of his audience is so dim that he does not even form
the intention to *try* to get them to engage with the content of what
he says. Nonetheless, he wishes to be obedient to God and trusts
God's veracity. So, out of pure obedience, he states p anyway by
vouching for its truth.

By all appearances, the pessimistic prophet has succeeded in
testifying to some fact. If he has, however, then an agent's expressing
a perlocutionary act intention is not a necessary condition for

---

18. See Alston (2000), ch. 2, for the development of such cases. Searle (1969), 46, also
    alludes to such a case, as does Green (2007), ch. 2.

speaking. Unlike Jake in our first case, the prophet assumes there is an audience that can accept, reject, or consider what he says. But he does not intend for them to do so.[19]

Turn now to the third and most radical case. Imagine that Jake were to keep a private diary. In his diary, he records daily happenings in his life and how he feels about certain things and people. Among other things, Jake states that he is tired of the responsibility of being a bandleader, especially when the members of the Big Band are lazy. He asks himself whether he is cut out for the job. And he expresses contempt for audiences ignorant of jazz. By writing these things in his diary, Jake appears to perform various speech acts, including what we earlier classified as directives, assertives, and expressives. But the diary is so private that he intends that no one should become aware of its contents.

If this is right, Jake has performed illocutionary acts of various sorts but intends that no one engage with what he says. Admittedly, one might wonder if this case presents a genuine counterexample to the perlocutionary-intention view, for one might think that Jake himself is the audience of the speech acts he performs. Accordingly, one might believe that what accounts for Jake's having performed speech acts of various types by writing in his diary is the fact that Jake intends that he himself engage with the content of what he says.[20]

This seems to me mistaken. We can rather easily imagine that Jake's aim in keeping this diary is entirely therapeutic. Given his psychological condition, we can suppose, his therapist has strongly

---

19. Barker (2004), 9, n14, maintains that Alston's objection is effective only against views such as those defended by Grice and Schiffer, which hold that sincere assertors intend their audiences to believe that p. Against views such as his own, which maintain only that sincere assertors intend that their audience engages with the content of their assertion by considering, accepting, or rejecting it, Barker claims Alston's objection fails. I believe that this is not so: if the case of the pessimistic prophet has force against Grice's and Schiffer's views, then it also has force against Barker's more permissive view. Let me add to this an additional point. In his engagement with Alston, Barker maintains that the claim "P is true, but I do not intend that you believe it" is akin to a Moorean Paradox such as "It is raining, but I do not believe it." This also strikes me as incorrect. In standard cases of Moorean paradoxical sentences, accepting the second conjunct of a sentence undercuts the warrant for accepting its first conjunct. The same is not true of a claim such as "P is true, but I do not intend that you believe it." For an agent may have excellent reasons for not forming the relevant perlocutionary intention, which do not undercut his reasons for believing that p is true.

20. Avramides (1989) suggests a view along these lines.

recommended that he regularly record what he is thinking and feeling in a diary. In fact, we can imagine Jake going to rather extraordinary lengths to ensure that the diary remains totally private, writing in an ink that disappears shortly after being used. If this is correct, we have another reason to reject the perlocutionary-intention theorist's claim that a necessary condition of an agent's performing a speech act is that he intend that his audience engage with the content of what he says, for some speech acts are performed with the intention that there be no audience to engage with them.

All three counterexamples suggest that, in a range of cases, the perlocutionary-intention view yields the wrong results, since it is false that an agent's expressing one or another perlocutionary intention is ingredient in the count-generation of speech. Still, the point that these counterexamples establishes has to be stated carefully, since it is easily misunderstood. The point of the counterexamples is not that perlocutionary or communicative intentions are generally absent from speech. Nor is it that speech itself lacks a communicative dimension. The point, rather, is that perlocutionary intentions do not play the explanatory role that perlocutionary-intention theorists believe.

It is worth dwelling on the role of communication in speech for a moment. To do so, return to the case, introduced earlier, in which we specified the difference between the normative standing of being a chanter, on the one hand, and being a speaker, on the other. The difference between these two standings, we said, is a function of the aims of the two practices. The norms that govern the practice of chanting are not (in the first instance at least) concerned with the communication of information, while the norms that govern speaking generally are. According to normative theorists, this comparison helps us to see the role of communication in speech. In short, normative theorists emphasize that a fundamental aim of the *practice* of speaking is to allow its participants to communicate information. But this, normative theorists maintain, does not imply that its participants must form intentions to communicate when competently participating in the practice.

In effect, then, normative theorists exploit a gap between the communicative aim of a practice and the communicative intentions of a speaker. That is, normative theorists maintain that although a fundamental aim of the social practice of speaking is to communicate information,

this does not imply that

an agent performs an illocutionary act only if and because he expresses the relevant perlocutionary act intentions when performing it.

To draw an analogy: when it comes to speech, normative theorists wish to occupy conceptual space akin to that occupied by rule consequentialists in ethical theory. While rule consequentialists agree that the institution of morality aims at maximizing value, they deny that this implies that each morally assessable action is or should be directed at maximizing value. The point of a practice need not be the point of every act performed by someone sincerely and competently participating in it.

If this is right, normative theorists can maintain that perlocutionary act intentions are ordinarily present in speech. They can also agree that a mature and rational agent will assume that a fundamental aim of speech is to communicate information.[21] It is for this reason, normative theorists claim, that communicative intentions are often expressed in speech. Still, as I have stressed, this does not imply that we should also believe that in each case in which an agent performs an illocutionary act, these intentions are operative. The point of a practice and the intentions of those who competently participate in it need not coincide.

The second reason

In the previous section I argued that we should reject the claim that the expression of perlocutionary intentions is that which accounts for the hook-up between locutionary and illocutionary acts. I turn now to the second claim that perlocutionary-intention theorists

---

21. The communication of information is not, however, the only fundamental aim of speaking. This is not simply because of the cases of the mystery cult, pessimistic prophet, and private diary. It is also because the fundamental purpose of exercitives such as adjourning is not to communicate information but to coordinate our activities, such as how to end a meeting. To accomplish this end, one must communicate information. Still, the communication of the information is not the ultimate but the proximate aim of the performance of a speech act of this type.

defend. This claim, recall, says that normative features are not, in general, ingredient in what count-generates speech; rather, they are consequent on the performance of speech acts. Assertions generate responsibilities. Promises generate obligations. Commands generate rights. Normative theorists disagree with this, maintaining that at least some of these normative features are that in virtue of which a locutionary act count-generates an illocutionary act.[22]

Let me advance two arguments for believing that normative theorists get the better of this disagreement. The first argument defends the claim that some generated rights, responsibilities, and obligations are not explanatorily downstream from speech. The second argument defends the related claim that some standing powers and standing rights, responsibilities, and obligations are not explanatorily downstream from speech. If these arguments hit their mark, then we should reject the thesis that normative features could not count-generate speech because, in general, they are explanatorily downstream from it.

It will be helpful to begin with some terminology. Return for a moment to Barker's analysis of asserting. Recall that, according to Barker's position, an agent asserts a proposition p only if two conditions are satisfied: she must both advertise that she believes p and intend for her audience to engage with p by, say, considering p, believing p, rejecting p, or the like. I have stressed that it is the acceptance of the second condition—which concerns the role of perlocutionary intentions—that distinguishes the perlocutionary-intention view from that of its rivals. It is worth emphasizing, however, that the first condition is also fundamental to the perlocutionary-intention view. All else being equal, to succeed in getting one's audience to engage with the content of one's cognitive state one must present oneself as

---

22. Of course, both normative and perlocutionary-intention theorists agree that, in ordinary cases of speech, the acquisition of a normative standing is explanatorily downstream of an agent's saying something. Theorists of both sorts, for example, agree that an agent has an obligation to keep a promise because he said he would. According to normative theorists, the saying in question is merely the performance of a locutionary act. According to perlocutionary-intention theorists, by contrast, the saying is the performance of an illocutionary act. A failure to distinguish locutionary from illocutionary acts can lend a superficial plausibility to the claim that normative features are explanatorily downstream from the performance of illocutionary acts.

being in that state. That is how one's audience can determine what it is that one is attempting to communicate.

Let us call the first condition of Barker's analysis of asserting the *commitment condition*. For present purposes, let us say that an agent satisfies the commitment condition just in case she commits herself to the world being a certain way by employing some arrangement for speaking that is in effect. If the perlocutionary-intention view is true, there is nothing unique in the fact that such a condition attaches to asserting. Every speech act-type whatsoever will have attached to it a similar condition. For, if the perlocutionary-intention view is correct, a necessary condition of the performance of any speech act is that the speaker intends for his audience to engage with the fact that he is in one or another cognitive state. And, all else being equal, the only way to make this intention manifest is by committing himself to being in that state by employing some conventional arrangement for speaking.[23]

I pointed out earlier, however, that to commit oneself to being in a cognitive state such as believing a proposition is to stick one's neck out in a certain way. And to do that is to alter one's normative status with respect to one's audience, leaving oneself open to rightful correction if things are not as one presents them. To use a phrase employed earlier, committing oneself to something is to take responsibility for that thing's being the case, thereby becoming liable to correction or blame if things are not as one presents them. If so, an agent's satisfying the commitment condition implies that he acquires what I shall call the *accountability features*—these being a subspecies of generated rights, responsibilities, and obligations. The accountability features include properties such as *being required to present things as they actually are* and *being open to rightful correction if things are*

---

23. I prefer to describe such a condition as one regarding not advertising but commitment. This is because committing oneself to a state of affairs is plausibly thought to be a component of every illocutionary act, but is not itself plausibly viewed as being an illocutionary act type. Advertising oneself as being a certain way, by contrast, is easily thought of as being an illocutionary act type. That invites the suspicion that Barker's view explains one illocutionary act type (namely, asserting) in terms of another (namely, advertising). That said, when I follow Barker's language more closely by speaking of advertising, this is best understood simply in terms of committing oneself to the world being a certain way by the use of some conventional arrangement for speaking.

not as one presents them. If the perlocutionary-intention view were true, the accountability features would presumably be the sorts of thing that are explanatorily downstream from speech.

The first argument I want to present employs a recipe for generating a certain type of problematic case. According to the recipe, we identify a case in which an agent satisfies the commitment condition by employing some conventional arrangement for speaking but fails to express any perlocutionary act intentions. In such a case, that agent will presumably be liable to correction, thereby exhibiting the accountability features. But, if the perlocutionary-intention view is true, he will not have spoken. If there are cases of this sort, then we will have reason to believe that it is false that generated rights, responsibilities, and obligations are explanatorily downstream from speech, contrary to what the perlocutionary-intention view tells us.[24] Rather, they are generated by satisfying the commitment condition itself.

We can develop this argument by returning to the case of the Nature mystery cult. Recall that, in this case, Jake assumes that Nature is a vast impersonal force that can be manipulated by performing incantations of various sorts. Wishing to increase his ability to manipulate Nature, Jake takes his cult guidebook into his room. He opens the guidebook, uttering the following sentences:

> Nature is eternal.
> May her power be manifest!

If the perlocutionary-intention view is true, Jake has failed to perform any speech acts by uttering these sentences. Let us suppose, for argument's sake, that perlocutionary-intention theorists are right about this. If they are, then by uttering these sentences Jake fails to perform a speech act, because he lacks the requisite perlocutionary intentions. If this were correct, however, then Jake would presumably still be liable to correction if what he says is false or unjustified. To see this, imagine that Jake had failed to notice that, during the episode just described, his spouse was lying in bed. Upon hearing Jake utter these sentences, Jake's spouse would presumably be

---

24. I am assuming that while the perlocutionary-intention view may allow that some normative features are explanatorily upstream from speech, these will not be generated rights, responsibilities, and obligations and, specifically, what I am calling the accountability features.

entitled to correct him if what he said was false or unjustified. She might, for example, point out that we have decisive reason to believe that Nature is not eternal.

We have before us a case of the requisite sort. Jake satisfies the commitment condition by employing some conventional arrangement for speaking. As such, he exemplifies the accountability features. But he fails to express any perlocutionary act intentions. If the perlocutionary-intention view is true, however, then he has not performed any speech acts. From which it follows that the acquisition of the accountability features is not generated by his performing a speech act. This, however, is incompatible with the perlocutionary-intention view as we have presented it. For, recall, we presented the position as being committed to the claim that an agent's having the normative features that attach to speech, such as the accountability features, is explanatorily downstream from the performance of speech acts, not the other way around. To which I should add that the possibility of an agent's laying himself open to rightful correction without successfully performing an illocutionary act is not an implication of the perlocutionary-intention view alone. Any view that recognizes the existence of malformed speech acts of certain kinds is committed to this conclusion. For example, were I to utter the sentence "I now pronounce you husband and wife" during a wedding ceremony in which I, an imposter, presented myself as a clergyman, I would have thereby laid myself open to appropriate correction. But I would not have succeeded in either pronouncing you married or marrying anyone.

I turn now to the second argument for rejecting the claim that (in general) the rights, responsibilities, and obligations that attach to speech are explanatorily downstream from it. This argument directs our attention to the relations that standing powers and standing rights, responsibilities, and obligations bear to speech, maintaining that neither sort of normative feature is (in general) explanatorily downstream from speech.

Begin with standing powers. Earlier I said that speech acts bear the following relation to standing powers. First, when an agent performs a speech act in ordinary conditions, she takes responsibility for having one or another standing power. When an umpire pronounces a batter out, for example, he takes responsibility for having the authority to perform acts of this type. Second, some speech acts are such that an agent can perform them only if and because he in fact has the relevant sort of standing power. In a game of Major League Baseball, a person can declare a batter out only if and because he has the requisite authority. It follows from this that some standing powers are not among the normative features generated by the performance of speech acts. Rather, they are ingredient in what count-generated them.

Consider, as a somewhat different case, standing rights, responsibilities, and obligations. Suppose that, during a game of Major League Baseball, an umpire utters the sentence "You have two strikes against you." This linguistic act is subject to the following general norm or standing responsibility:

> In ordinary speech situations, if an agent presents the world as being a certain way and things are not as he presents them, then he is liable to correction, blame, admonition, or the like.

Like standing powers, this liability is also not explanatorily downstream from an agent's performing the illocutionary act of asserting. Arguably, moreover, it accounts (at least in part) for not only an agent's acquiring the accountability features themselves, but also the phenomenon of taking responsibility itself. For suppose the phrase "taking responsibility for a state of affairs" is factive: an agent cannot take responsibility for a state of affairs and fail to acquire the accountability features.[25] It is natural to wonder how this could be so. Why is it that, necessarily, taking responsibility for a state of affairs implies that an agent is liable if things are not as she presents them? A natural suggestion is that the implication holds because an agent "triggers" various sorts of standing rights, responsibilities, and obligations that attach to her, such as the norm specified above. Under this way of thinking, an agent can take responsibility for a state of affairs and thereby acquire the accountability features only if and because there are standing rights, responsibilities, and obligations that attach to

---

25. Alston (2000), I believe, understands the phrase in this way. Of course, a normative theorist would not deny that one can *try* to take responsibility for something and fail to do so, say, by uttering the sentence "I will take responsibility for that." One could, I suppose, deny that taking responsibility is factive. But then the point stated above can be put in terms of successfully taking responsibility: successfully taking responsibility for a state of affairs, which is necessary for an agent to speak, necessarily implies that an agent is liable if things are not as she presents them.

her, such as the norm mentioned above. Were we to assume that the phenomenon of taking responsibility for a state of affairs is ingredient in the count-generation of speech, it would follow that so also are standing rights, responsibilities, and obligations.[26]

I have presented two lines of argument for rejecting the claim that normative features are (in general) explanatorily downstream from speech. The first argument, admittedly, has fairly modest implications. It does not imply that, in general, normative features are ingredient in the count-generation of speech. It implies only that neither the accountability features, standing powers, nor standing rights, responsibilities, and obligations are explanatorily downstream from speech. While modest in its implications, this argument provides sufficient reason to reject the second claim that constitutes the perlocutionary-intention view, namely, that (in general) normative features are generated by speech. The second argument I have offered, by contrast, has more bite. If correct, it establishes that standing powers and standing rights, responsibilities, and obligations are ingredient in the count-generation of speech. If either of these arguments hits its mark, it undercuts an important motivation for accepting the perlocutionary-intention view, which consists in the claim that, since (in general) normative features are explanatorily downstream from speech, they cannot be ingredient in what count-generates it. Not only would these arguments undercut this motivation; they also generate a challenge to those unsympathetic with the normative theory of speech. The challenge is to identify that which is ingredient in the count-generation of speech. If it is neither perlocutionary intentions nor normative features, we need a new proposal that exhibits the sorts of virtues enjoyed by the normative theory.

The third reason

Advocates of the perlocutionary-intention view, I have said, accept two claims. According to the first, the expression of perlocutionary

26. At least it would, given two further assumptions: first, that these normative features are not mere background conditions of what it is to take responsibility for something but explain it; and, second, that explanation is in this case transitive. It is because they explain what it is to take responsibility for something that these normative features also account for speech.

intentions is ingredient in the count-generation of speech. According to the second, the rights, responsibilities, and obligations of being a speaker are not (generally speaking) ingredient in the count-generation of speech; rather, they are generated by speech. I have offered reasons to reject both these claims. It should be forthrightly admitted that these objections are not devastating to the perlocutionary-intention view. To accommodate them, perlocutionary-intention theorists could weaken their position, allowing for the possibility that speech occurs in some cases in which agents to do not express perlocutionary act intentions. (Or, alternatively, they could understand what it is to express an intention in such a way that one can express an intention without having it.) They might, for example, hold that in deviant cases of speech—such as the case of the pessimistic prophet—various conventions for speaking take over, thereby generating speech acts. When modified in this way, the perlocutionary-intention view would be one that purports to explain only paradigmatic speech acts; deviant cases will have to be taken on a case-by-case basis. Advocates of this position might also remind us that hard cases often make bad law.

This response would, however, come at a price. For, even if the perlocutionary-intention view were modified in this way, normative theorists can pull together what has been argued thus far to assemble a case in their favor. The case appeals to the following methodological consideration: take two rival theories, A and B, each of which purports to explain some phenomenon. Imagine that neither view is appreciably simpler than the other; each has basically the same ontological commitments. Suppose, however, that theory A explains the phenomenon in question in a more unified way than theory B. Where theory B must allow for exceptions, theory A does not. Moreover, where theory B claims that theory A must allow for exceptions, there are none. If this is so, then we should prefer theory A to theory B. I claim that this is the position in which the normative theory finds itself in comparison to its rivals.

For the dialectical situation is this. We are looking for some feature or set of features that binds together locutionary and illocutionary acts. Normative theorists propose that it is an agent's having the rights, responsibilities, and obligations of being a speaker that accomplishes this, at least in part. Perlocutionary-intention theorists propose that it is an agent's expressing perlocutionary intentions that plays the required role. In response, normative theorists point out that the latter proposal yields the wrong results in a certain range of cases; in these cases, agents speak without expressing perlocutionary intentions. They also note that in those same cases, their own view yields the right results. In each case in which an agent speaks—even the deviant ones—she alters her normative position by taking responsibility for a state of affairs. On the whole, then, normative theorists maintain that they have offered a unified account of what is ingredient in the count-generation of speech. Normative theorists further contend that the main consideration for believing that normative features are not ingredient in the count-generation of speech fails. For it is false that, generally speaking, an agent's having the rights, responsibilities, and obligations of being a speaker are consequent upon an agent's performing some illocutionary act. In fact, we can point to cases in which the opposite is true, such as those cases in which an agent performs a speech act in virtue of possessing one or another standing power, such as when an umpire declares a batter out. On the whole, normative theorists maintain, their view is superior; given its theoretical virtues, it ought to be preferred to the perlocutionary-intention theory.

It would, nevertheless, be too quick to declare the normative theory the position of choice, as there is an option that we have not yet considered.[27] To see this, bring to mind the normative theory once again. As I presented it, the core of the view is the claim that an agent performs an illocutionary act in virtue of altering his normative position with regard to his audience, acquiring rights,

---

27. There is another view that I am omitting from full consideration. According to this view, it is the expression of not perlocutionary but illocutionary act intentions—roughly, intentions to perform one or another illocutionary act—that is ingredient in what count-generates speech. I have registered sympathy for the view that such intentions are important to speech, as they are (in a wide range of cases) the means by which an agent takes responsibility for a state of affairs. But I doubt that they are essential to speech. The auction case illustrates why. This case, recall, suggests that an agent can speak by unintentionally presenting himself as being committed to something, as when an agent bids on an item at an auction by raising his hand. If this is right, some cases of speech are like getting a speeding ticket: behavior of certain kinds can get one on the normative hook, even when it is the result of being ignorant of various arrangements that are in effect. In light of such considerations, I believe that the most attractive version of the normative theory is one that is not intention-based, as it has the sort of generality we are looking for.

responsibilities, and obligations of various kinds. It might be said, however, that we should distinguish two aspects of this alteration. On the one hand, there is the phenomenon of an agent's *taking responsibility* for a state of affairs. On the other, there is *having certain rights, responsibilities, and obligations*. The first phenomenon, it might be observed, is not identical with the second. The first is an action, while the second is not. Furthermore, while there is a sense in which the first phenomenon is normative, it is only derivatively so. Taking responsibility for something is normative only inasmuch as it implies that an agent has one or another normative property. But—so it might be claimed—it is not itself a normative property or a state of affairs that consists in an agent's having such a property.

Suppose, then, we distinguish an agent's taking responsibility for a state of affairs from an agent's having the normative features that result from performing such an action. An agent's taking responsibility for a state of affairs is an element common to all the cases of speech we have considered—even the deviant ones. In the cases of both the diary and the auction, for example, by employing conventional arrangements for speaking, the agent commits himself to things being a certain way—taking responsibility for them. In the former case, the presenting is intentional. In the latter case, it is not. It looks, then, as if there is a rival view with which the normative theory must reckon. This rival view says that the phenomenon of taking responsibility for a state of affairs is non-normative; it implies the existence of normative facts but is not itself one. It is this phenomenon of taking responsibility for a state of affairs, according to the rival position, that is ingredient in what count-generates speech and not any normative feature that results from it. The normative features are determined by an agent's taking responsibility for a state of affairs, but they do not account, even in part, for speech.

This may be the best option available to opponents of the normative theory. For like the normative theory, it offers an apparently unified account of that in virtue of which the performance of a locutionary act count-generates the performance of an illocutionary act. And it does so by appeal to entities that nearly all parties agree exist and can enter into count-generation explanations, namely, an agent's taking responsibility for something. That said, I do not think the view accomplishes what it aims to, for the following reason.

According to the rival view under consideration:

(i) S's employing a conventional arrangement for speaking;

(ii) S's taking responsibility for p; and

(iii) S's being liable to correction, reproach, or blame if p is not the case,

represent a series of distinct but nested states of affairs. By performing the action specified by (i), an agent performs that action specified by (ii). By performing the action specified by (ii), he brings about the state of affairs specified by (iii).

Part of this seems correct. We should agree that

(i) S's employing a conventional arrangement for speaking

is not only an act-type distinct from but also generates

(ii) S's taking responsibility for p.

But it is not so obvious that

(ii) S's taking responsibility for p

in any sense generates

(iii) S's being liable to correction, reproach, or blame if p is not the case.

Why not?

In the first place, as indicated earlier, I take the natural interpretation of expressions such as "taking responsibility for p" and "leaving oneself liable to correction" to be factive. Under this interpretation, which is accepted by normative theorists, one cannot take responsibility for p and fail to be responsible for p if p is not the case. Nor can one leave oneself liable to correction if p is not the case and not be liable to correction if p is not the case. Under this understanding, the relationship between the event specified by (ii) and the state of affairs specified by (iii) is very different from paradigmatic generation relations, such as that which obtains between (i) and (ii). For the event specified by (ii) cannot occur without (iii) obtaining. Which brings me to my second observation: there is a very intimate relationship between an agent's being responsible for p and his being liable to correction, reproach, or blame if p is not the case. By all appearances, to be responsible for p just *is* to be liable to correction, reproach, or blame if p is not the case.

I can now state why I think we ought to reject the proposal under consideration. The reason is that the action specified by (ii) no more generates that specified by (iii) than my taking a walk generates my being on a walk. Rather, it is a trivial conceptual implication of my taking a walk that, from the time at which I take a walk, the state of affairs of my being on a walk obtains. Similarly, it is a trivial conceptual implication of an agent's taking responsibility for p that, from the time at which he takes responsibility for p, the state of affairs of his being liable to correction, reproach, or blame if p is not the case obtains.

The point I wish to press, however, is not simply that there is no interesting sense in which the event specified by (ii) generates the state of affairs specified by (iii). Rather, it is also that since (iii) is a trivial implication of (ii), we should deny that (ii) is a non-normative event. Now, admittedly, I have no general criterion to offer for what counts as a normative state of affairs or event. I submit, however, that if a paradigmatic normative state of affairs, such as that specified by (iii), is a trivial implication of an event, such as that specified by (ii), then it would be cutting things too finely if our view were to imply that the latter is not also a normative state of affairs. After all, any adequate specification of what it takes for someone to take responsibility for a state of affairs would make essential reference to normative features, such as being liable to correction, reproach, or blame.

In other cases, it is worth noting, fulfilling this condition is sufficient for us to denominate a state of affairs as normative. Consider, for example, the received understanding of rights. According to the received view:

(iv) S's acquiring (or having) a right against S* that S* refrain from performing some action A

trivially implies

(v) S*'s being liable to correction, admonition, blame, or the like, if he performs A.

Everyone agrees, however, that acquiring or having a right is a normative phenomenon. The reason seems to be that any adequate specification of what it takes for someone to have a right would make reference to normative features, such as an agent's being liable to blame if she acts or fails to act in certain ways. If this is correct, though, then we should also say that the state of affairs specified by (ii) is a normative state of affairs. For, if what I have said is correct, any adequate specification of what it takes for someone to take responsibility for a state of affairs would make reference to normative features, such as his being liable to correction, reproach, or blame.

Where, then, does this leave us? With two ways of running the normative theory, I believe. Common to both versions is the conviction that an agent's taking responsibility for a state of affairs is a normative phenomenon. They agree, moreover, that at least some of the rights, responsibilities, and obligations that attach to speakers—such as what I have called standing powers and the accountability features—are not explanatorily downstream from speech. They differ, however, in this important respect: the first version of the view maintains that an agent's taking responsibility for a state of affairs is ingredient in what count-generates speech, but an agent's having the accountability features is not. According to this view, while an agent's taking responsibility for a state of affairs conceptually implies the existence of generated rights, responsibilities, and obligations, these normative features nevertheless play no explanatory role in the generation of speech. The second version of the view, by contrast, is more inclusive. It tells us that both an agent's taking responsibility for a state of affairs and the rights, responsibilities, and obligations that are thereby conceptually implied are that in virtue of which a locutionary act counts as an illocutionary act.

For my purposes, it is not crucial which version of the normative theory we accept, as either version could be employed to develop the Speech Act Argument. For suppose that standing powers and standing rights, responsibilities, and obligations play an important explanatory role in the performance of speech acts such as directives, commisives, and exercitives, since one cannot take responsibility for a state of affairs without them. Then that will be enough to vindicate the claim that rights, responsibilities, and obligations of a certain range play a crucial role in the generation of speech. They are that which account for how an agent can take responsibility for a state of affairs. In fact, if what I suggested earlier is true, these normative features *constitute* what it is to take responsibility for a state of affairs.

That said, it will be evident that my sympathies lie with the second version of the normative theory. My reasons are straightforward. I see no non-arbitrary reason to affirm that

(ii) S's taking responsibility for p

is ingredient in what count-generates an agent's performing a speech act, while

(iii) S's being liable to correction, reproach, or blame if p is not the case

is not. Given that (iii) is a trivial implication of (ii), it is very difficult to see why the state of affairs specified by (ii) is ingredient in the count-generation of speech but that specified by (iii) is not. In my judgment, claiming that there is this asymmetry would be like insisting that Jake's taking a walk at some time accounts for why he has traveled from A to B but his being on a walk at that time does not.

At any rate, it might be helpful for our purposes to have a summary statement of the normative theory of speech. I propose the following:

> An agent's performing some locutionary act Φing count-generates her performing some illocutionary Ψing in virtue of her having the rights, responsibilities, and obligations of being a speaker. These normative features include the standing power to perform actions of certain kinds that are constitutive of Ψing, such as her having the right to lay obligations on herself and others. They also include the standing rights, responsibilities, and obligations that accompany this standing power, such as her having the obligation to present things as being a certain way only if they are that way. An agent's taking responsibility for things being as she presents them conceptually implies that she has generated rights, responsibilities, and obligations of certain sorts, such as being liable if things are not as she presents them. Depending on one's favored version of the view, these are also ingredient in the count-generation of speech.

As I have just stated, I hold that generated rights, responsibilities, and obligations are ingredient in the count-generation of speech.

IV An objection to the normative theory

At the close of the previous chapter, I formulated what I called the Speech Act Argument for moral realism. Recall that according to the argument's second premise:

(2) Illocutionary acts are count-generated by locutionary acts. But locutionary acts are not sufficient for the count-generation to occur; there must be something else that explains why it occurs.

This raises the question of what it is that explains the count-generation in question. In this chapter, I have defended the answer provided by the argument's third premise, namely:

(3) It is an agent's having the rights, responsibilities, and obligations of being a speaker that explains (at least in part) why the count-generation of illocutionary acts occurs.

The argument I have offered for this last claim comes in two main stages. In the first stage I highlighted various virtues of the normative theory of speech. I pointed out, for example, that speech appears to be suffused with normativity. Rights, responsibilities, and obligations of various sorts appear to attach to the performance of illocutionary acts such as assertions, promises, and commands. The normative theory has the virtue of not having to explain away these appearances but taking them at face value. I also noted that it is difficult to identify a genuine rival to the normative theory. At first blush, perlocutionary-intention views, for example, do not deny that when performing speech acts, agents take responsibility for states of affairs of various sorts. If this is so, however, it is difficult to see that the two views are fundamentally opposed.

In the second stage I identified a version of the perlocutionary-intention view that is genuinely incompatible with the normative theory. This rival position, I claimed, is committed to two central claims. First, locutionary acts count as illocutionary acts in virtue of the speaker expressing perlocutionary intentions. Second, the normative features that accompany the performance of speech acts are (generally speaking) explanatorily downstream from the performance of speech acts. They do not account for speech.

I presented three reasons to reject this position. First, through a series of counterexamples, I argued that we can perform speech acts without expressing perlocutionary intentions. In these cases, the perlocutionary-intention view yields the wrong results. If so, expressing these intentions is not among the necessary conditions for speaking. Second, I claimed that there is good reason to believe that there are rights, responsibilities, and obligations that are not explanatorily downstream from the performance of illocutionary acts. Some, such as what I called the *accountability features*, attach to agents simply in virtue of their committing themselves to states of affairs of various sorts, such as the world's being a certain way, by way of the employment of arrangements for speaking. If this is true, I argued, the primary consideration for holding that normative features are not ingredient in the generation of speech is off the table. Third, I argued that even when we modify the perlocutionary-intention view to handle some of these objections, the normative theory still offers a more unified account of speech. When discussing this last point, we identified a potential ambiguity in the normative theory that might lead one to believe that normative features are not that in virtue of which we speak. I claimed that, upon closer inspection, this apparent ambiguity does not jeopardize the normative theory.

In what remains, I would like to consider an objection to the normative theory that I believe deserves attention. This objection raises the concern that normative theorists exaggerate the extent to which speech is a normative phenomenon. For—the objection runs—it appears as if creatures such as non-human animals, which lack normative standings altogether, can speak. That is, it appears as if animals such as dogs, gorillas, and dolphins can communicate to us that they are hungry or that they are content without thereby acquiring rights, responsibilities, or obligations of any sort.

Put more crisply, the objection runs thus:

1* If the normative theory is true, then, necessarily, an agent performs a speech act Φ only if she has a Φ-correlate normative standing.

2* It is, however, possible for non-human animals to speak without having such a standing.

3* So, the normative theory is false.

While I believe this objection fails, it will be instructive for our purposes to explore why. As a first step toward fashioning a reply, let me introduce a three-fold distinction between speech acts, proto-speech acts, and communicative acts, respectively.

Speech acts are as I described them earlier. They are illocutionary acts such as asserting, affirming, asking, adjourning, baptizing, confessing, declaring, expressing a wish, promising, requesting, and so on. If the normative theory is true, they are acts generated (at least in part) by an agent's having the rights, responsibilities, and obligations of being a speaker.

Proto-speech acts, as I shall think of them, are "honorific" speech acts. They are purposive acts such that, when they are performed by some agent (and not malformed), one can properly ascribe to that agent the status of having performed a speech act (or something close thereto) in virtue of the fact that that agent is being treated as a participant in the social practice of speaking. Perhaps very small children perform proto-speech acts. Given their level of cognitive development, very small children—say, those under two years old—cannot acquire the rights, responsibilities, and obligations of being a speaker. Still, when we induct them into the social practice of speaking, we treat their utterances as if they count as speech acts. Baby Jane utters "Juice," thereby doing something like requesting a cup of juice. We treat this utterance as a request and, hence, a reason for us to give her a cup of juice even though we know that it is likely that Baby Jane will promptly throw the cup on the floor when it is handed to her. We have treated her linguistic act as an honorific speech act. When she has sufficiently matured and gotten the hang of how to participate in the practice of speaking, she becomes a full-fledged participant in this practice and, hence, a speaker. (In that case, she will have some explaining to do if the juice ends up on the floor again.)[28]

---

28. Another approach would be to hold that small children do in fact speak. According to this approach, children can put themselves on the normative hook by employing arrangements for speaking. But they cannot recognize this. That is why, it might be suggested, we make so many allowances for them, not admonishing or correcting them in the way we do ordinary adults. For present purposes, it does not matter whether one accepts this view or the position that small children perform mere proto-speech acts.

Finally, *communicative acts*, as I shall think of them, are simply acts by which some individual communicates information to another individual, but are not proto-speech acts or speech acts. Growling, wincing, winking, rolling one's eyes, or baring one's teeth are all examples of communicative acts. As these cases make evident, these acts can be more or less intentional in character.

With these distinctions in hand, let me offer a diagnosis of the objection under consideration. The objector is using the term "speak" in a fairly loose sense to refer either to what I have called "communicative acts" or "proto-speech acts." Now there is nothing particularly objectionable about using the term "speak" in this way; it seems to me that ordinary language licenses such a use. But if the term is being used in this way, normative theorists have no objection to the argument's second premise. They agree that non-human animals can perform an impressive array of communicative acts whereby they communicate information to one another and to us. Moreover, we have learned that members of some species, such as the gorilla and the dolphin, can also perform a wide range of proto-speech acts in which they, among other things, "proto-request" things of us by using sign language.[29] The ability to understand our speech and to perform proto-speech acts indicates not only that these creatures share prelinguistic interpretive capacities with human beings (in some cases, due to our shared evolutionary history), but also that they form beliefs and intentions of certain kinds (or at least something similar thereto), revising them when they make mistakes or to pursue goals of different kinds.[30] The normative theory, then, is not motivated by the concern to highlight the differences between non-human animals and human beings, while downplaying the commonalities. The broadly interpretive and conceptual capacities that non-human animals of certain kinds and human beings share are both extensive and significant.

While normative theorists can (and, I think, should) agree with all this, they will, nonetheless, deny that the argument's conclusion

29. Koko the gorilla, apparently, requested of her caretakers that they give her a kitten to care for. See *National Geographic,* Vol. 167 (January 1985).
30. If Alasdair MacIntyre is correct, non-human animals form and revise beliefs and intentions, but they are of a fairly indeterminate sort. See MacIntyre (1999), chs. 1–5, and Searle (2010), ch. 4.

follows. For normative theorists maintain that an agent's having the rights, responsibilities, and obligations of being a speaker is necessary for the performance of not communicative or proto-speech acts, but of full-blown illocutionary acts. Although there are dissenters, the thesis that non-human animals do not perform illocutionary acts is not terribly controversial. Indeed, it is telling that the philosophical debate about the cognitive capacities of animals has not focused on whether animals can speak; that they cannot has more or less been taken for granted.[31] The fulcrum of the debate has been whether they could have beliefs and intentions without being language users—that is, without being the types of creature that employ a natural language with a particular vocabulary, syntax, and semantics that might enable them to perform speech acts in a social practice. Although let me add that, in principle, there is no reason that normative theorists must deny that non-human animals speak. The issue of whether they can speak, if it is settled at all, is one that would have to be decided (at least in part) by empirical investigation. Given more investigation, perhaps we will learn that dolphins can do such things as promise and command.

In any event, the claim that, to the best of our knowledge, non-human animals do not speak will invite two questions. First, haven't normative theorists evaded the force of the objection under consideration by simply stipulating what they mean by "speech"? And, second, if normative theorists are correct, what feature is it that human beings possess, but non-human beings do not, that accounts for the fact that humans, but not animals, are speakers?

I shall have to be brief in reply to these questions. The answer to the first question is: true, normative theorists use the term "speech" in a fairly circumscribed sense. But that is not due to mere stipulation. Nor is it an artifact of the normative theory itself. Rather, it is because communicative acts, proto-speech acts, and illocutionary acts are different types of act. One way to get at their difference, which does not simply presuppose the truth of the normative theory, is this: illocutionary acts are, in the paradigm case, intentional acts. Special cases aside, an agent performs an illocutionary act of a given type by way of performing some locutionary act only if he intends to

---

31. Millikan (2005), 158, is perhaps a dissenter.

perform that illocutionary act. (Of course, the intention need not be explicit to the speaker.) Proto-illocutionary acts and communicative acts, however, are not like this. In the paradigmatic case, to communicate to me that you are hungry, you need not intend to assert *that you are hungry*. And, thus, you need not deploy the concept 'being an assertion.' To be sure, normative theorists offer a particular account of the role of intentions in speech, while perlocutionary-intention theorists offer another. But advocates of both approaches agree that there are differences between speech acts, on the one hand, and communicative and proto-speech acts, on the other, which should be explained. It is worth adding that everyone agrees that a creature such as Koko the gorilla can communicate to us that she is hungry. She can even "say" "Koko want banana." But, apparently, she does not distinguish this from related phrases such as "Banana Koko want" and "Banana want Koko." These sentences are treated as equivalent. Our best evidence suggests, then, that while creatures such as gorillas can use names such as "Koko," they cannot understand the syntactical arrangements of language that determine meaning. If one accepts the plausible claim that to be a speaker an agent must be able to be guided by (or sensitive to) such arrangements, it follows that while Koko performs proto-speech acts, she does not speak.[32]

As for the second question, normative theorists can, in principle, offer different answers to it. Perhaps Robert Brandom is right to claim that the primary difference between sapient beings such as humans and other creatures is that sapient beings deploy concepts—where deploying a concept is (in part) actualizing an ability to put forth something that can serve as and stand in need of reasons, to authorize its use as a premise for further inferences, and to undertake responsibility for it in a social practice.[33] Or perhaps it will lie in some other related feature of our broadly rational nature. But it does seem that, at the very least, the difference in question will lie in the fact that we have capacities for choosing between many different ways of communicating information or coordinating actions.

32. See Searle (n.d.). For complications, see <http://ngm.nationalgeographic.com/2008/03/animal-minds/virginia-morell-text/7>.
33. See Brandom (2000), 11, 33.

For, as I have emphasized, human beings have at their disposal untold numbers of arrangements for the communication of information or the coordination of action. Some of these arrangements are in effect by convention. And, of the arrangements in effect for qualified parties, humans typically have a choice to employ any number of them to communicate information to an audience or co-ordinate actions. If Jake wishes to communicate to the Big Band that he wants them to continue to perform a piece they are presently per-forming, he can, among other things, shout "Keep going!" or circle his index finger in the air by his head. Not only this, of the arrange-ments in effect that can be deployed, an agent can deploy their com-ponents in multiple, often non-standard, and even deceptive ways. By shouting "Keep going!" Jake can exhort, command, condemn, entreat, express a wish, illustrate a point of grammar, participate in a game of make-believe, exercise his vocal chords, practice pronoun-cing a sentence, test a microphone, and so on.

To effectively communicate information and to coordinatinate ac-tivities, then, we need to not only choose to implement different ar-rangements that are in effect, but also commit ourselves to certain of their uses, laying ourselves open to appropriate correction in the process. Were we not to so commit ourselves, it is difficult to see how (in conditions like those we occupy) we could effectively employ the various systems of communication that are available to us. It is, then, at least in part, our status as creatures that can choose between, in-tend to use, and commit ourselves to the use of a wide and sophisti-cated assortment of arrangements to communicate information and coordinate activities that renders us speakers. Illocutionary acts are, as it were, the fruit of there being animals that can do such things as these.

3

The Moral Dimensions
of Speech

My purpose in the previous chapter was to argue that speech is a thoroughly normative phenomenon. Only if agents have the rights, responsibilities, and obligations of being a speaker, I claimed, do their locutionary acts count as illocutionary acts. What, however, should we say concerning the nature of these normative features? Are some of them best viewed as *moral* rights, responsibilities, or obligations?

Some philosophers believe not. Consider what Robert M. Adams says in the course of defending a divine command theory of moral obligation. Adams maintains that moral obligation is determined by God's commands. But the discursive practice of commanding itself, Adams contends, is constituted by not moral but premoral obligations:

> That we have such premoral conceptions of commanding and obligation seems to be evident from such facts as the following. I can use the concept of commanding, obeying, and disobeying to describe goings-on in social systems that I regard as morally questionable or worse. It would not normally occur to me to put shudder quotes around 'command' in such a context. We can imagine a morally undeveloped society in which people speak of the chief, for example, as issuing commands, and themselves as having obligations arising from the chief's commands, without ever raising the question about the moral validity of these commands and obligations. Even if we asked them whether they had a "real" obligation to obey the chief's commands, and whether it would "really" be wrong to disobey them, we may suppose, they would hardly know what to make of our questions; they would not see them as a subject for intelligent discussion. In this case they would not have a genuinely *moral* conception of obligation; yet they would have concepts of

command and obligation that serve them effectively in describing their social system and living within it, and that we too could use as anthropologists in describing their system.[1]

Suppose that the approach to commanding that Adams advocates could be extended to other discursive practices, such as asserting and promising. The result would be a normative but non-moral account of speech.

I am going to argue that this view is mistaken: some of the rights, responsibilities, and obligations ingredient in the count-generation of speech are moral. The overarching argument I shall present is one to the best explanation, consisting in two parts. The aim of the argument's first part is to establish that we have strong reason to believe that some of the rights, responsibilities, and obligations that constitute the normative standing of being a speaker are moral. This part of the argument, however, has little chance of succeeding if we have sufficient independent reasons for thinking there are no moral rights, responsibilities, or obligations. The purpose of the argument's second part is to contend that these reasons do not exist. The argument's first part will be my concern in this chapter; its second part will be my topic in the next three chapters.

The issue of whether speech exhibits moral dimensions is not one to which philosophers have devoted much attention. This is true even of those who advocate the normative theory of speech. Almost none of these philosophers consider the matter at any length. And to the extent that they do consider the issue, almost none of them defends the claim that moral features are ingredient in the count-generation of speech; they either deny the claim or remain silent about it.[2] The thesis I am going to defend in this chapter, then, is not one that has been widely embraced, even by defenders of the normative theory. For better or worse, it goes beyond what most advocates of the view have affirmed.

1. Adams (1999), 243.
2. Brandom, for example, shows no sympathy with the idea that moral norms count-generate speech. Alston and Searle appear opposed to it. Mitchell Green is non-committal. Only Wolterstorff defends it—although he seems drawn to the strong claim, which I reject, that all the rights, responsibilities, and obligations that constitute speech are moral. See Searle (1969), 188; Wolterstorff (1995), ch. 5; Alston (2000), 61–2 n8; Brandom (2000); Green (2007), 71 n17.

I Six assumptions

Let me begin by introducing a series of assumptions that will guide the subsequent discussion.

First, I will assume that we should be pluralists about the normative domain. According to pluralism, there are various types of rights, responsibilities, and obligations, including epistemic, legal, prudential, and practice-based rights, responsibilities, and obligations—the latter being such that they attach to particular roles that one plays in a social practice, such as being a teacher or a government employee. Accordingly, I will not presume that if an agent has an obligation or right to some good, she thereby has a moral obligation or right to that good. Nor will I take it for granted that if an agent has a moral obligation or right, then it should be understood in a realist way.

Second, I will assume that our rights, responsibilities, and obligations can be overdetermined. If our ordinary practices of classification are to be trusted, for example, the performance of one and the same action can violate both a legal and a moral obligation. If, say, I drive my car at high speed through an intersection filled with pedestrians, then (all else being equal) I have thereby violated both a legal and a moral requirement.

Third, I will assume that while the lines demarcating the different normative domains are vague, this often does not prevent us from seeing what falls within the moral domain. Given that we have focal cases with which to work, we can often determine which of the various rights, responsibilities, and requirements that an agent may have are moral.

Fourth, I will assume that not only are the boundaries demarcating the different normative domains vague, but that these domains are also entangled, overlapping, and interpenetrating one another in a variety of interesting ways.

Let me elaborate. Suppose we think of a normative domain as a system of interrelated normative concepts including 'being a right,' 'being a responsibility,' 'being an obligation,' and so forth. To say that two normative domains A and B are entangled is to claim that an accurate and perspicuous account of a range of concepts belonging to A would involve essential recourse to the concepts belonging to B;

indeed, in some cases, entanglement implies that concepts belonging to one domain constitute those belonging to the other.

Take the prudential domain as an illustration. Suppose an agent were to fail to conform to a norm of practical rationality such as the so-called means/ends rule, which (at a first approximation) tells us that, if an agent desires to Φ, and believes that by Ψing, she will Φ, then she ought to Ψ. Most philosophers would agree that such a failure is one of practical rationality, at least when satisfying the desire in question by acting in that way is not manifestly incompatible with her own well-being. Still, there are different *ways* of failing to conform to the means/end rule. An agent, for example, might fail to conform to it because she has failed to pay sufficient attention to her desire to achieve some end or neglected its significance to her well-being.

We have ways of describing failures of practical rationality that are descriptively rich. Rather than simply lump them together by using thin evaluative terms such as "irrational," we say that they are cases of being intemperate, being badly negligent about forming a coherent life-plan, being shortsighted about one's future well-being, being willingly obtuse to practical advice, being self-destructive, and the like. How best to categorize these defects? The prudential dimensions are evident enough. Being intemperate and being unreceptive to practical advice have a tendency to undercut one's ability to pursue one's own good. As any parent knows, for children to form a conception of their own good, they must pay attention to the advice they are given. But such defects also appear to have moral dimensions. A defect such as being badly negligent about forming a coherent life-plan, for example, counts as a moral demerit in virtue of its being a failure to appreciate and care for one's own good, which is something that deserves an agent's own appreciation and care. It is a failure of self-respect or what Bishop Butler called "reasonable self-love."[3]

To take a somewhat different case, consider the epistemic domain. Suppose an agent were not to draw an inference supported by the best evidence or were to pursue a half-baked plan of inquiry. When

---

3. Adams (2006), ch. 7, which draws upon Butler, offers a helpful discussion of this issue.

evaluating behaviors such as this, philosophers are also prone to employ thin terms of assessment such as "irrational." But, in cases such as these, we also have more descriptively rich terminology at our disposal. We describe such cases as ones in which an agent is careless with the evidence, insufficiently open-minded with respect to the views of others, unduly partial, overly rigid in her convictions, and so forth.

Broadly conceived, these are all failures of epistemic rationality. But in these cases, too, it proves fairly difficult to offer a more precise categorization of them according to which they fall neatly into a single normative category. Normative failures such as exhibiting undue partiality seem (in a wide range of circumstances) to have both epistemic and moral dimensions. The epistemic dimensions are apparent. Exhibiting undue partiality towards one's own positions is an epistemic defect, presumably because it tends to hinder an agent from representing reality aright. We often, after all, need to revise our views in the light of what others say. But it is also a moral defect, because the agent who exhibits it tends to overestimate the accuracy and worth of his own powers and convictions, while underestimating those of others. In fact, in this case, an agent's having the tendency to fail to represent reality aright for these reasons *consists* in his overestimating his own powers and convictions while underestimating those of others. It is because an agent badly overestimates his own powers and underestimates those of others that he tends not to represent reality aright. Accurately characterizing this failing involves making essential reference to both its epistemic and moral dimensions.

The phenomenon of normative entanglement is, I believe, significant. For if it is true that the moral domain is intimately intertwined with normative domains such as the aesthetic, prudential, and epistemic domains, it should not be surprising if it were also enmeshed with other normative domains such as the discursive practices of giving and receiving commands and giving and receiving promises. That is, provided that we deploy moral concepts, it would be unsurprising that accurately characterizing the normative dimensions of discursive practices such as these were to involve recourse to them. Likewise, provided that we are not already assuming that the moral domain is empty, it would be unsurprising if some of its members

were also members of domains such as the discursive practices
of giving and receiving commands. If they were, it would be only
one more instance of a more general pattern of normative
entanglement.

The fifth assumption I shall make is that, were there moral obligations and rights, then there is a reliable strategy for determining
whether someone has a moral obligation to act in a certain way or a
moral right to some good. The strategy is to take a case in which an
agent fails to conform to an obligation or to honor a right and to ask
whether, in failing to conform to that obligation or to honor that
right, that agent thereby suffers from a moral demerit or disexcel-
lence, such as having wronged another. How does one determine
that? Presumably, by applying well-entrenched, socially established,
and refined methods of moral evaluation to cases in which an agent
fails to conform to an obligation or to honor a right.

It is, after all, difficult to see where else one could reasonably turn,
at least initially. To draw an analogy: imagine you were to hear a
piece of classical music, but are unsure whether it is a fugue, rondo,
strophe, sonata, or the like. Where else would you turn for illumin-
ation on the matter but to well-entrenched, socially established, and
conceptually refined methods of music evaluation? Of course, it may
be that social practices such as these incorporate concepts that fail to
stand for anything in reality. Perhaps there are no such things as
moral obligations or sonatas despite there being concepts thereof.
(There is the possibility that the concepts expressed by the phrases
"being a moral obligation" and "being a sonata" are incoherent.
While one has to remain alive to such a possibility, I know of no good
reason to believe that these concepts are incoherent.[4]) And perhaps
our understanding of these concepts needs to be modified in certain
ways given our best empirical knowledge of the world. Indeed, it
might be that there are cases in which we conclude that making
sense of a given practice requires employing entirely new methods
of investigation and evaluation. Still, if what I have said thus far is

---

4. Although see Loeb (2008), which presents the beginnings of a case for what he calls
"moral incoherentism." If I understand it, Loeb's case proceeds on the assumption
that if a concept is incoherent, then it fails to stand for anything. Although I will not
argue the point here, this assumption seems to me false.

correct, appealing to well-entrenched and refined practices of evaluation and the concepts they incorporate is where we should begin.

The final assumption I will make is that there is a range of rights,
responsibilities, and obligations—the likes of which I will specify in
a moment—such that if they appear to fall under moral concepts,
then this is a *pro tanto* reason for holding that they are moral rights,
responsibilities, and obligations. I make this assumption not because
I suppose that, in the normative domains and elsewhere, things are
pretty much as they seem to be, unless there is substantial evidence
to the contrary. Nor is it because I assume that we should interpret
positions in such a way that they are likely to come out true. Rather,
the approach I am taking is broadly Reidian.

Call a practice in which we deploy concepts of a certain range to
form judgments a *doxastic practice*. Examples of such practices would
be the perceptual practice in which we deploy concepts such as
'being a tree' to form judgments about our environment and the
introspective practice in which we deploy concepts such as 'feeling
dizzy' to form judgments about how we are feeling. Imagine that a
particular doxastic practice is socially well-established over time,
deeply entrenched (or, in the limit case, practically inescapable), endowed with sophisticated methods of evaluating judgments made
in that domain, including appeals to its own array of experts and
criteria for reliability. Imagine, furthermore, that many of its central
claims are not subject to systemic disagreement among competent
participants. Let us call a practice that satisfies these criteria a doxastic practice in *good working order*. The Reidian view says that we have
pro tanto reason to take the outputs of a doxastic practice in good
working order to be reliable—the outputs being understood to include judgments that consist in the application of concepts constitutive of the practice.

It is, after all, unclear what the viable alternatives would be. One
alternative would be to hold that none of our doxastic practices is in
good working order and, hence, reliable. Call this position the *skeptical hypothesis*. It is not easy to see why we should believe this position. For, presumably, any consideration that someone might offer
in its favor would itself be the deliverance of (or grasped via the employment of) a doxastic practice—such as memory and reasoning—
that we have no reason to trust. Another option would be to hold

that only some doxastic practices in good working order are reliable. Call this option *partiality*. Accepting partiality, though, would be nearly as unattractive as accepting the skeptical hypothesis, as partiality is a view that recommends that we not treat like cases alike, thereby enjoining us to pick and choose. We should reject this position. Our best strategy, according to the Reidian view, is to be inclusive. We have *pro tanto* reason to take the deliverances of any doxastic practice in good working order to be reliable.[5]

Call that social practice that consists in deploying moral concepts to form moral judgments the *moral doxastic practice*. The moral doxastic practice, I assume, appears to be in good working order. For the moral practice is socially well-established over time; moral thinking is not a recent development in the history of humankind. Moreover, it is deeply entrenched—so deeply, in fact, that, for all practical purposes, it is inescapable; try as we might, most of us cannot avoid forming moral judgments. Furthermore, we also have fairly sophisticated methods of evaluating moral judgments, which include determining whether they were formed in hospitable conditions, bringing them into reflective equilibrium, engaging in experiments in living, consulting the opinions of those who exhibit moral excellences, and so forth. Finally, as I shall note in Chapter 7, there is a significant range of moral judgments—apparent truisms or "fixed points" such as *that it is wrong to engage in recreational slaughter of fellow persons*—that are not the subject of disagreement among competent moral agents and appear to be constitutive of moral thinking. If all this is correct, were we to discover that a certain range of rights, responsibilities, and obligations fall under paradigmatic moral concepts, the Reidian approach would imply that we have a *pro tanto* reason to hold that they are moral.

---

5. This is, I realize, merely to dip a toe into deep methodological waters. I develop the Reidian view in more detail in Cuneo (2011a), (2011b), and (2011c), offering more detailed explorations of these issues. Reid's own articulation of his methodology is scattered throughout Reid (1997), (2002), and (2010). The most thorough contemporary development of the Reidian position of which I am aware is Alston (1991), ch. 4. It is from Alston that I borrow the term "doxastic practice." It might be worth adding that the Reidian view is consistent with holding that doxastic practices can be reliable to different degrees. So, while the perceptual and moral practice might both be in good working order, we might also have reason to hold that the former is more reliable than the latter.

I can now present the argument that I wish to develop in this section. Assume that the argument from the previous chapter is correct: the rights, responsibilities, and requirements of being a speaker are ingredient in the count-generation of speech acts. Presumably, though, there are no such things as generic rights, responsibilities, and obligations. Just as there are only shades of redness, so also there are only kinds of rights, responsibilities, and obligations. If so, our task is to identify the kinds of rights, responsibilities, and obligations that are ingredient in the count-generation of speech.

With that in mind, suppose we were to reflect on various cases in which speech takes place, trying to ascertain the character of the normative features in play. More specifically, suppose we were to consider those cases introduced in the last chapter in which Jake asserts something to his audience, promises something to the Big Band, and directs the Big Band to act in a certain way. If we were to do so, there is excellent reason to believe, I claim, that some of the rights, responsibilities, and requirements that are ingredient in the count-generation of these speech acts fall under moral concepts. For if we attempt to offer an illuminating and sufficiently nuanced characterization of these normative features, we will find ourselves appealing to moral concepts to describe them. And the best explanation of this, so the argument runs, is that there are moral rights, responsibilities, and requirements that fall under these concepts. I shall contend, then, that an examination of these cases gives us strong *pro tanto* reason to believe that moral rights, responsibilities, and obligations are among the rights, responsibilities, and obligations that constitute the normative standing of being a speaker.

II The case for moral dimensions

During the Big Band's performance, Jake asserts to his audience that Ella Fitzgerald performed *Mack the Knife*. According to the normative theory, by uttering the sentence

"Ella Fitzgerald performed *Mack the Knife*,"

Jake has thereby altered his normative position with respect to his audience, taking responsibility for its being the case that things are as he presents them. Now suppose that what Jake says is true. However, let us also suppose that Jake has no idea whether what he says is true. When he uttered this sentence, Jake had no evidence for believing that Fitzgerald performed *Mack the Knife*. He claimed as much simply because he was intent on impressing his audience—a group of poorly informed foreign students studying for a class in music history. In having behaved this way, I assume, Jake suffers from a normative demerit of some kind, for he is now rightly open to reproach. Is the demerit in question best thought of as a moral one? It would appear so. After all, by all appearances, Jake has wronged his audience. He has behaved in an unusually condescending way, assuming that because his audience is a group of foreigners it does not really matter what he tells them or what views they hold. On the assumptions that Jake is required not to act in this way and that our characterization of his conduct is correct, he has a moral obligation (or a moral reason) to not behave in the way he did.

We can look at the same situation from the angle of rights. By making claims simply to impress his audience, Jake fails to accord his audience due respect, thereby leaving himself open to reproach. If this is true, it is plausible to assume that his audience has a right to hold him accountable for what he says. Is the entitlement in this case best thought of as a moral right? On the assumptions that, in this context, acting in an unusually condescending fashion implies that Jake has wronged his audience, then the answer is Yes; by uttering this sentence about Fitzgerald, Jake has laid himself open to rightful reproach or admonition—this being an implication of the fact that *not being treated in a condescending fashion* is, in ordinary conditions, a good to which we have rights.

Let us now turn to our second case. Before the show, Jake promises the Big Band that he will lead them in a rendition of *Mack the Knife* late in the first set. If the normative theory of speech is true, Jake has altered his normative position with respect to the Big Band, for by uttering the sentence

"I promise I will direct you to play *Mack the Knife* late in our first set,"

he has thereby put himself on the normative hook, committing himself to intend to lead the Big Band in a performance of this piece late in the first set.[6] Suppose, however, that immediately prior to having uttered this sentence Jake thinks to himself:

> I dislike performing *Mack the Knife*. But I know the Big Band enjoys performing it. I also know, however, that the Big Band will perform better in the first set if I tell them that we will play *Mack the Knife*; it will boost their enthusiasm. So, I shall promise them that we will perform it late in our first set. But I shall close our first set with *Birdland* instead, making up an excuse and promising to play *Mack the Knife* the next time we perform.

According to this description, Jake at once promises the Big Band that he will lead them in a performance of *Mack the Knife*, but has no intention to do anything of the sort. Clearly, Jake's failure to intend to do what he promised implies that he suffers from a normative demerit of some kind, for he is, we think, open to reproach for having behaved as he did. Is the demerit in question best thought of as a moral one? Presumably, yes. Jake, by all appearances, has wronged the Big Band. He has manipulated them for entirely selfish reasons, choosing to satisfy his own preferences rather than intend to keep his word. If so, then we have good reason to believe that Jake has failed to satisfy a moral responsibility that he acquires by way of having committed himself to having the intention to lead the Big Band in a performance of *Mack the Knife*.

Consider the same situation from the angle of the Big Band. Jake, we have said, is open to reproach for having failed to intend to act as he promised. If this is true, then presumably the Big Band is entitled to express its disapproval of Jake's behavior, for Jake has (among other things) treated them in a highly manipulative manner. Is the entitlement or right in question best thought of as a moral one? On the assumption that manipulating others for entirely selfish reasons implies, in this context, that Jake suffers from a moral demerit, then the answer is Yes; the Big Band has a moral right not to be treated in this way—this being an implication of the fact that *not being manipulated for purely selfish reasons* is, in ordinary conditions, a good to which we have rights.

---

6. In what follows, I say that Jake takes responsibility for having a given intention. I might equally well have spoken of his having taken responsibility to perform a given action. For present purposes, I think nothing hangs on the issue; we could put the matter either way.

Let us turn to the third and final case in which Jake, by raising four fingers in the air, directs the Big Band:

> To play exactly four more bars of the piece they are presently performing.

As the normative theory glosses things, Jake has once again altered his normative position with respect to the Big Band, for by raising his four fingers in the air he has vouched for the fact that he has the authority to lay on them an obligation to play exactly four more bars of *Mack the Knife*. Suppose, however, that the members of the Big Band tend to be petty, inordinately resenting the constructive criticism that Jake offers them. Wishing to express their resentment, suppose that the Big Band refuses to stop playing when Jake commands them to, paying absolutely no heed to his directive. In this case, the Big Band's failure to act as directed implies that they suffer from a normative demerit of some sort, for they are liable to censure for having acted in this way.

In this case, is the demerit in question also best thought of as being a moral one? By all appearances, yes. After all, in this case, things are as Jake advertises: Jake has the authority to direct the Big Band and they know it. The Big Band, however, has chosen to disregard Jake's directive because they resent him. In doing so, however, they have (by all appearances) wronged Jake, for their behavior is deeply insulting. In fact, the Big Band appears to have violated two obligations: the standing obligation to obey such directives as Jake may issue that fall within the office of his being their bandleader and the generated obligation to stop playing *Mack the Knife* when exactly four more bars of music have passed. Their violations, admittedly, may not be heavily freighted with normative significance; not all moral violations are. In some cases, apologies are sufficient for reparation; in others, they are not. Still, if our characterization of their behavior is accurate, then the Big Band has failed to satisfy a moral obligation (or honor a moral reason).

Once again, we can approach the same situation from the angle of rights. The Big Band, we have claimed, is open to reproach for having disregarded Jake's directive, refusing to acknowledge his authority because they are nursing resentment. On the plausible assumption that, special cases notwithstanding, for every obligation there is a correlative right, Jake is entitled to better behavior from the Big Band, for things are as he presents them. If so, Jake has at least two rights against them: a standing right that they obey those directives that he issues that fall within his office as band director and the generated right that they stop performing *Mack the Knife* at the end of exactly four more bars of music. Are these rights best thought of as being moral?

Suppose that by disregarding Jake's directive the Big Band has behaved in a deeply insulting fashion. On the assumption that, in this context, this implies that they have wronged him, then the answer to our question is Yes. For Jake has a moral right not to be treated in the manner in which the Big Band has treated him—this being an implication of the fact that *not being treated in a deeply insulting way* is, in the ordinary case, a good to which we have rights. If this is correct, then the Big Band's refusal to acknowledge Jake's authority by continuing to perform *Mack the Knife* violates a generated moral right. By violating this right, however, they have also thereby violated the standing right to obey such directives that Jake may issue that fall within his office as band director. For the violation of this right is no less an expression of disrespect than the violation of the generated right that they stop performing *Mack the Knife*. And this, if what I have said is correct, is reason to believe that the standing obligation they have violated is also a moral obligation.

The three cases I have described share a common structure. Each assumes that in order to speak, an agent must take responsibility for things being as he presents them. The cases then specify what the normative implications are, in certain types of circumstances, when things are either not as a speaker presents them or his audience fails to acknowledge that things are as he presents them. The rights, responsibilities, and obligations on which I have had my eye, then, are not loosely connected to speech. Rather, they are those rights, responsibilities, and obligations that attach to agents in virtue of their doing what it takes to speak. As such, they are excellent candidates for being among those normative features ingredient in the count-generation of speech.

Rather than simply dropping the case for there being moral dimensions of speech, let me now double back for a moment, revisiting the passage I quoted earlier from Adams in which he claims that it is

clear that we have a premoral conception of speech acts such as commands. This should help to address several possible concerns about
what I have said.

In this passage, Adams presents two types of case. The first concerns a morally undeveloped society. In this case, we are to imagine
a society in which people speak of the chief as issuing commands—
and themselves as having obligations that accompany the chief's
commands—without ever raising the question about the moral val-
idity of these commands and obligations. These people, says Adams,
would not have a genuinely moral conception of obligation. And yet
they would have concepts of commanding and obligation that serve
them effectively in living within their social system.

The second type of case, to which Adams only alludes, concerns
goings-on in a social system that is "morally questionable or worse."
As an example of such a case, imagine a Norwegian during the time
of the Quisling regime. Suppose this person were ordered by an official of this regime to publish a virulently anti-Semitic tract. On the
face of things, this official has successfully commanded this person
to act in a certain way, which implies that he lays an obligation on
him. But presumably the obligation in question is not a moral one; it
is not (or does not generate) a moral reason for the person to obey.
If anything, the obligation is practice-based—one generated by actions constitutive of the discursive practice of giving and receiving
commands.[7]

What shall we make of Adams' cases? At least this, I think: they
are consistent with what I have argued for. Earlier, when I claimed
that the normative standing of being a speaker is constituted by
rights, responsibilities, and obligations, I did not *identify* these with
moral rights, responsibilities, and obligations. Rather, my claim was
merely that some of these rights, responsibilities, and obligations
are best thought of as being moral. This, however, is compatible
with Adams' proposal that some of the rights, responsibilities, and
obligations that constitute the discursive practice of giving and

---

7. This example is taken from Wolterstorff (1995), 94. Wolterstorff attributes the
   example to Adams, although Adams himself does not introduce it in Adams (1999).
   I am assuming that Adams holds that a premoral society would have a premoral
   conception of not only commands but also promises.

receiving commands are also premoral in character. We do not have
to choose between one option or the other.

That said, some of what Adams says indicates that he thinks it possible to describe, in an accurate and perspicuous way, the linguistic
activity presented in these cases without making recourse to moral
notions at all. Of this I am dubious. For imagine a case in which the
chief commands a young male member of the tribe to keep the night
watch. When receiving the chief's command, let us suppose that this
man responds by insulting the chief, his purpose being thereby to
"show up" the chief. Or, to choose a different case, suppose the chief
were to promise one of his subjects, a widow, that he will give to her
an extra week of provisions so that she can feed her family. And suppose that while issuing the promise, the chief—viewing the promise
as simply a way to keep the woman from bothering him any time
soon—were not to intend to do as he promised.

Let us agree that in both cases obligations are generated. By uttering the sentence "Keep the night watch!" the chief thereby generates an obligation for the young man to keep the night watch.
Likewise, by uttering the sentence "I promise you an extra week of
provisions," the chief has thereby laid an obligation on himself to
give his subject an extra week of provisions. What is difficult to see is
how—if we take the appearances at all seriously—it could be the case
that, in both instances, moral obligation is absent. To focus on the
second case, it is difficult to see how it could be the case that (i) the
chief at once lays an obligation on himself, (ii) fails to intend to act
in the manner he promises for the reasons just given, but (iii) it is
not accurate to ascribe to him a moral demerit such as *being unfaithful* or *having wronged his fellow society-member*. Or to get at the
matter from another angle, there seems to be no reason why it would
be inaccurate to say that the woman to whom the provisions are
promised is such that she would be wronged were the chief not to
intend to provide the promised provisions. Aside from a commitment to a sweeping form of moral skepticism, which Adams himself
rejects, there does not seem to be anything about the situations thus
described that would make ascriptions of these types false or inapt.
Certainly the fact that the chief or his fellow society-members fail to
see any moral dimensions to commanding or promising does not
imply that they are absent or that a perspicuous description of these

speech acts would not appeal to moral concepts. (Once again, I do not assume that the normative properties that these notions describe should be understood in a realist fashion.)

There is, I believe, a still stronger claim that can be made. Call to mind the standing obligation, when promising, to intend to act as one promised. In ordinary speech situations, when an agent fails to have this intention, it appears as if she has failed to conform to a moral obligation. The full nature of the matter, however, is this: it is not simply that things appear this way. Rather, it is also that we do not have available a sufficiently nuanced and illuminating pre- or non-moral vocabulary to describe such an obligation. (It is no accident that, when moral intuitionists such as W. D. Ross drew up a list of basic *prima facie* moral obligations, the obligation to keep one's promises appeared on the list.) So, it is not as if there are plausible but competing ways to describe such an obligation, some of which make recourse to moral concepts, while others do not. Any reasonably nuanced and articulate description of such an obligation would tell us that the obligation in question is moral—specifically, one of fidelity.

Recall, however, that Adams also alludes to a different sort of case—one in which (according to the elaboration I offered) a Quisling official commands a person to publish an anti-Semitic document. In contrast to the case of the widow, it looks as if this case is one in which commanding takes place but moral obligation is absent. Accordingly, it appears as if this case requires different handling.[8]

Normative theorists, I believe, should say the following with regard to this type of case. First, it is consistent with their view to hold both that the Quisling official succeeds in commanding something, and that in doing so his audience acquires no moral obligation to publish the anti-Semitic material. Once again, this is because the normative theory is not committed to the position that all the normative features constitutive of speech are moral.[9] In this case, the obligation

8. Searle (1969), 188, devotes a paragraph to why he believes the obligation to keep a promise is not moral. What he says appeals to a variant of the Quisling-style case.
9. Indeed, it may be worth noting that the normative theory is not even committed to the thesis that laying an obligation on one's audience is constitutive of commanding. It may be that to command an agent must, by performing some locutionary act, simply *present* himself as having the authority to lay an obligation on his audience.

that accompanies the command may be a non-moral one. Indeed, given the fact that one would not exhibit a moral demerit by ignoring it, we have good evidence that it is not in fact a moral obligation.

Second, normative theorists might maintain that, in the case described, the Quisling official does in fact generate a moral obligation by performing the locutionary act in question. But, normative theorists might remind us that all such obligations are merely *pro tanto* in character. Since the official lacks the moral authority to command the publication of the tract, he generates no actual obligation that is binding on his audience. Under this interpretation, the Quisling case does not present us with an example of speech in which practice-based obligations are present but moral ones are not.

Third, it is open to normative theorists to claim that the official's speech act is sufficiently malformed that he fails to lay any sort of obligation on his audience. According to this response, certain normative conditions attach to commanding—among these, that the commander has the authority or standing power to command what he does. But no one, this response maintains, has the standing power to command the performance of actions that are morally wrong. To be sure, the Quisling official may use the words "Publish this tract!" And he may be able to exercise force against someone who does not conform to his wishes. Still, none of this implies that he lays any sort of obligation on his audience by uttering this sentence. For, to say it again, he lacks the authority to issue the command. If so, the official in the case either fails to perform a command altogether or performs a badly malformed command. Under this interpretation, the Quisling case does not present us with an example of a (well-formed) speech act in which practice-based obligations are present but moral ones are not.

III The case continued

The view I have defended thus far is compatible with normative pluralism. It tells us that the normative standing of being a speaker is constituted by rights, responsibilities, and obligations. In principle, these normative features could be of different sorts. I have argued for the relatively modest claim that at least some of them are best viewed as being moral in character, as they fall under moral concepts. But

I have resisted any inclination simply to identify the totality of these normative features with moral ones, noting that pluralism of this type is unremarkable. For we are, I argued earlier, already familiar with cases in which different normative domains, such as the prudential and epistemic domains, overlap and interpenetrate one another. The fact, then, that there is also overlap between the discursive practice of giving and receiving commands, on the one hand, and moral rights, responsibilities, and obligations, on the other, is not surprising. In this section, I want to move the argument forward another step by contending that the moral dimensions of speech are considerably more extensive than I have indicated so far.

The best way to do so is to consider cases once again. Take a case in which you assert a proposition. According to the normative theory of speech, you have done this in virtue of taking responsibility for things being as you present them. This, I have said, implies that you are liable to correction, admonition, reproach, or blame if either the world is not as you say it is or you do not believe that the world is as you say it is. Of course, speech acts are not performed in the void; they are always performed in certain circumstances. Suppose, then, we specify a range of circumstances in which you could assert a proposition p. Among these circumstances are those in which:

> You know that p.
> You believe that p is false.
> You fail to believe that p, although p happens to be true.
> You reasonably believe that p, although p is false.

We can now specify a series of conditional generated rights that attach to you or your audience upon your asserting that p:

> You have the right against your audience to its taking you at your word if you know that p.
>
> Your audience has a right to admonish you for being dishonest if you believe that p is false.
>
> Your audience has a right to reproach you for exhibiting disrespect toward them if you fail to believe that p, although p happens to be true.
>
> Your audience has a right to correct you if you reasonably believe that p, although p is false.

With a little more thought, we could identify still more rights of this sort. For present purposes, however, the important thing to see is that, when an agent asserts, he introduces a whole panoply of conditional rights into a speech situation. Importantly, some of these conditional rights appear to be moral. The rights in the first three cases, for example, are to goods such as *not being treated with under-respect* and *not being deliberately deceived*. Still, probably not all of the conditional rights mentioned are best described as being moral. Perhaps, for example, the right to correct someone who has inadvertently uttered a falsehood belongs simply to the discursive practice of asserting—this practice being like, say, the game of baseball inasmuch as its participants have rights, responsibilities, and obligations simply in virtue of their being participants in that practice.

Agents, I have been claiming, alter their normative position with respect to their audience when they assert. By all appearances, the alteration is not merely a normative but also a moral one. For all cases of asserting are such that a speaker introduces into a speech situation a range of conditional moral rights, including those mentioned above. And some cases of asserting, we have seen, are also such that, by performing some locutionary act, speakers and their audience have actual (that is, non-conditional) moral rights. Say you utter the sentence "Ella Fitzgerald performed *Mack the Knife*" in ordinary conditions. In doing so, you have thereby introduced a series of moral conditional rights into that speech situation, including those mentioned above. If, like Jake, you were to fail to believe what you present yourself as believing, then your audience would also have an actual moral right to reproach you for having treated them in the way that you have.

As a somewhat different example, consider a case in which you promise. According to the normative theory of speech, you promise to act in a certain way (at least in part) in virtue of your taking responsibility for having an intention to act as you say you will. This, in turn, implies that you are liable to correction, admonition, reproach, or blame if things are not as you present them. Consider, now, a range of circumstances in which you might take responsibility for intending to Φ at some future time t. Among such circumstances are those in which:

> You intend to Φ and truly and reasonably believe that you can Φ.
>
> You decide (at some time prior to t) not to Φ simply because it is inconvenient, although you truly and reasonably believe that you can Φ.

You do not intend to Φ, although you truly and reasonably believe that you can Φ.

You intend to Φ, although you falsely but reasonably believe you can Φ.

We can, once again, specify a series of conditional rights that attach to you or your audience when you promise to Φ:

You have a right against your audience that they not blame you for failing to intend to Φ if you intend to Φ and truly and reasonably believe that you can Φ.

Your audience has a right to hold you accountable for being unfaithful if you decide (at some time prior to t) not to Φ simply because it is inconvenient, although you truly and reasonably believe that you can Φ.

Your audience has a right to reproach you for being dishonest if you do not intend to Φ, although you truly and reasonably believe that you can Φ.

Your audience has a right to correct you if you intend to Φ, although you falsely but reasonably believe you can Φ.

In this case, too, we could identify still other rights that attach to promisers and their audiences. The crucial point to appreciate, however, is that when an agent promises, he introduces a range of conditional rights into a given speech situation. Like the assertion case, many of these conditional rights appear to be moral, as they are rights to goods such as *not being treated with under-respect* and *not being deliberately deceived.* Of course, some of the conditional rights enjoyed by you or your audience in such a case may be non-moral. It may be, for example, that the right to inform someone that it is impossible to act as she has promised is a mere practice-based right belonging simply to the discursive practice of promising.[10]

As with asserting, agents alter their normative position with respect to their audience when they promise. And like asserting, the normative alteration that occurs is, in part, a moral one. For all cases of promising are such that a speaker introduces into a speech situation

---

10. Although, it is probably worth adding, even in this case there are moral dimensions of the situation that come into play. Suppose an agent's promise were reasonably and competently made, but the agent, through no fault of her own, cannot act as she has promised. (Perhaps, for example, she has fallen ill.) If so, then it would appear that she has a moral right not to be blamed for her failure, for to blame her would be, among other things, unfair. Through no fault of her own, the world has not co-operated with her intentions.

a range of conditional moral rights, including those mentioned above. And some cases of promising, as we saw earlier, are also such that speakers and their audience have actual (that is, non-conditional) moral rights. Imagine—to stay with our earlier example—that, in ordinary conditions, you were to utter the sentence "I promise to lead you in a performance of *Mack the Knife* late in the first set." In doing so, you would have thereby introduced a series of moral conditional rights into that speech situation, including those mentioned above. If you, like Jake, were not to intend to do what you present yourself as intending to do, then your audience would also have an actual moral right to hold you accountable for having treated them in the way that you have.

Here and elsewhere, I have spoken of the right to hold a speaker accountable if things are not as she presents them. While there is probably no harm in speaking thus, we can now see that it is also potentially misleading. For when an agent speaks, her audience does not simply acquire this general conditional right. Rather, it acquires a very large conjunction of specific conditional rights, such as those mentioned above. One way to think of the relationship between the general conditional right and these more specific conditional rights is this: the right to hold a speaker accountable if things are not as she presents them is a right that necessarily manifests itself in the form of these more specific rights, much in the way that the property *being red* is a color that necessarily manifests itself in colors such as *being scarlet*. In the case of speech, the character of the manifestation is determined by various contextual features, such as the speaker's own beliefs. However that may be, we now have greater insight into the nature of the normative alteration that occurs when agents speak. If what I have said is accurate, an agent's "putting himself on the hook" consists in his altering his normative status with regard to his audience. That, in turn, consists in his introducing a panoply of generated conditional rights into a speech situation. These are, in large measure, conditional moral rights. If so, morality is not incidental to speech. Rather, moral features are constitutive of the normative alteration that occurs when agents speak.

My aim in this section has been to present the normative theory in more detail, indicating the extent to which morality is implicated in speech. But, in a way, I have only scratched the surface, since I have said almost nothing about the role of moral obligations and responsibilities, focusing almost exclusively on the role of rights. Let me now, however, address what may be a lingering concern. I have claimed that, in an ordinary speech situation, an agent's altering his normative status with regard to his audience by taking responsibility for a state of affairs introduces rights, responsibilities, and obligations into the picture. I have also claimed that many of these rights, responsibilities, and obligations are moral. It might be objected, however, that the argument I have offered falls short of establishing the claim that these moral features are ingredient in the count-generation of speech.

For consider the following claim, which I will call the *Coincidence Thesis*. According to this thesis, in every speech situation there are practice-based rights, responsibilities, and obligations that are ingredient in the count-generation of speech. In some cases, such as those to which I have drawn attention, there are moral rights, responsibilities, and obligations that coincide with these practice-based normative features. This, however, is compatible with the further claim that these moral rights, responsibilities, and obligations are not ingredient in the count-generation of speech. After all, given what has been argued, it may be that only practice-based normative features account for speech—the moral rights, responsibilities, and obligations that coincide with them being simply "along for the ride." It follows that, even if agents acquire moral rights, responsibilities, and obligations in ordinary speech situations, we need additional reason to believe that they, like their practice-based counterparts, are ingredient in the count-generation of speech.

I fail to see why. There is, after all, no incompatibility between the Coincidence Thesis and the argument that I have developed in this chapter. To illustrate the point, consider an ordinary speech situation in which you perform a promise. According to the normative theory, you are liable to reproach if things are not as you present them. In being liable, your audience will have both conditional practice-based and conditional moral rights against you, as the Coincidence Thesis avers. Moreover, if things are not as you present them—say, because you have no intention of doing what you say you will—then your audience will have both actual (that is, non-conditional) practice-based and moral rights against you, as the Coincidence Thesis says. Normative theorists can agree with this, adding that rights of both sorts account for speech. The alternative would be to claim that normative features of both sorts are present but only those of one sort explain anything. Unless, however, there were special reasons to believe that normative features of only one sort were suited to do the necessary explanatory work, this would be to exercise arbitrary partiality. But I am not aware of any reason to believe that practice-based but not moral features are especially suited to be that in virtue of which locutionary acts count-generate illocutionary acts. If so, our approach to explanation should be inclusive.[11]

It might help to reflect for another moment on the type of worry that the objection from the Coincidence Thesis raises. For the worry is just a more specific version of a more general concern about the argument developed over the previous two chapters, which is that it establishes only that normative (and indeed moral) facts *attach* to speech acts but do not *explain* them. At various points in Chapter 2, I touched upon this concern. We are now, however, in a good position to pull together the different things that I have said about it. Let me, then, offer a summary of the line of argument I have presented.

As formulated earlier, the Speech Act Argument hinges on the assumption that:

(2) Illocutionary acts are count-generated by locutionary acts. But locutionary acts are not sufficient for the count-generation to occur; there must be something else that explains why it occurs.

The proposal that I have defended is that normative facts and, indeed, moral facts account (at least in part) for the count-generation of speech.

I have argued that this answer, which is offered by normative theorists, has the following to recommend it. In the first place, normative features look like the sort of thing that could be and are

---

11. One might suggest that since practice-based normative features are present in all cases of speech, but moral ones are present in only some cases of speech, entities of the former but not the latter sort are ingredient in the count-generation of speech. This proposal strikes me as dubious for various reasons—one reason being that it assumes that there is no case of speech such that the practice-based normative features ingredient in its count-generation are identical with moral ones. In Section V I offer an argument for thinking that this assumption is false.

ingredient in the count-generation of speech. There is no apparent reason to believe that they are ill-suited for the job. Concerns about causal overdetermination or downward causation are simply not relevant, as the explanation in question is not causal. Nor, as far as I can see, are there analogs to these worries that would cause problems for the normative theory. For there to be a concern about over-determination, for example, we would need reason to believe that there is some feature (or set of features) that is ingredient in the count-generation of speech such that it renders normative features explanatorily redundant. We have, however, located no such feature (or set of features). To the contrary, there appear to be vivid cases in which normative features explain (at least in part) the performance of speech acts such as pronouncing someone guilty. Only agents with the relevant authority can do that.

Normative features, then, appear to be viable candidates for being among those features ingredient in the count-generation of speech. Does a view that appeals to such features better explain the performance of speech acts than the major alternatives? To this question, I have offered an affirmative answer, in large measure because the normative theory offers a highly unified account of speech. One alternative would be to appeal to conventional arrangements—ones which specify that the performance of actions of one kind count as the performance of actions of another kind. But the appeal to arrangements such as these, I suggested in Chapter 2, would shed little light on the phenomenon to be explained. Why, after all, is it that employing conventional arrangements of this type allows us to speak? To be told that an act Φ counts as an act Ψ because certain conventional arrangements hold, which specify that actions of that first type count as actions of that second type, does not help. We want to know what the counting as *consists in*. Normative theorists do better, for they tell us what the relation consists in.[12] A second alternative is to appeal to perlocutionary intentions. But expressing (or even having) perlocutionary intentions, I argued, is neither necessary nor sufficient for speech. A last alternative would be to appeal to the phenomenon of taking responsibility for a state of affairs, where this is understood

---

12. Recall that this response is not intended to rule out the possibility that the normative features in question are themselves in effect by convention.

to be a non-normative event. However, this option, I claim, fares no better than the others. For one thing, I suggested that the very phenomenon of taking responsibility depends on agents being subject to standing rights, responsibilities, and obligations. For another, there does not seem to be any reason why the phenomenon of taking responsibility for a state of affairs and not the generated rights, responsibilities, and obligations that it conceptually implies account for speech. Denominating one but not the other as ingredient in the count-generation of speech seems to have no basis.

If the lines of argument just offered are correct, we have good reason to believe that normative features are ingredient in the count-generation of speech. What, however, can we say about the character of these normative features? One thing we can say is that they are practice-based, as they have their home in discursive practices such as giving and receiving commands. But we can, I have argued, say more than this, for some of these features also fall under moral concepts. And unless we have powerful reasons to the contrary, I have said, we should conclude that some of these features are moral. Granted, one could raise the concern that these moral features merely attach to but do not explain speech. But there is no good reason, so far as I can tell, to believe that among the normative features that count-generate speech, only non-moral ones do the relevant explanatory work.

IV Convention and practice

My project in this chapter has been to explore the nature of the normative alteration that occurs when agents speak, arguing that it has moral dimensions. In this section I wish to supplement this argument. Doing so will not only provide additional reasons for accepting the claim that some of the normative features that constitute speech are moral. It will also take a step toward addressing a residual worry, which I have not faced head on, namely, that the form of moral realism that I defend is extremely weak, since it is compatible with moral considerations being no more robust than those that constitute social practices such as Byzantine chant, baseball, or etiquette. According to the argument I am now going to present, we should reject the claim that the rights, responsibilities, and obligations that constitute speech are merely conventional. On the further assumption that, were moral rights, responsibilities, and obligations to exist, they would also not be merely conventional, we have additional reason to believe that the normative features that constitute our practices or speech are moral: they fit the same explanatory profile.

To present the argument, it will be helpful to back up for a moment. When engaging with Adams' view, I conceded that it is plausible to hold that the rights, responsibilities, and obligations that constitute speech are practice-based normative features. They attach to agents simply in virtue of their being participants in practices of speech, such as the discursive practice of giving and receiving promises. But in following Adams on this matter, it should be noted, I did not identify practice-based normative features with what I shall call *mere conventional norms*. In fact, there seems to me good reason to distinguish practice-based from merely conventional normative features.

To see why, note that some practices in which we engage are deeply contingent in the sense that we can easily imagine worlds very similar to ours but in which these practices do not arise. For example, we can easily imagine a world fairly similar to ours but in which we never developed the game of baseball or Byzantine chant. Call a social practice that is contingent in this way a *deeply conventional practice.*

Let us now note that social practices themselves are by and large norm-governed. As such, they are composed of activity types that one can perform well or badly, correctly or mistakenly. The game of baseball, for example, is such that one can execute a bunt poorly; the practice of Byzantine chant is such that its participants can sing a wrong note. Of special interest for our purposes is the recognition that some of the norms that actually govern these practices have the following essential feature: they are arbitrary. These norms are such that, while they in fact govern social practices of a certain range C, there are other norms that could be in effect for participants in C and which would basically serve the same purpose as the norms that are actually in effect. Call norms of this variety *deeply conventional.*[13]

---

13. Here I echo Marmor (2009). Let me make two points regarding conventions. First, while I have borrowed from Marmor's helpful discussion, some differences between our ways of thinking about convention are worth noting. Most importantly, Marmor thinks of conventions as themselves being norms. I, in contrast, have claimed that

I can now explain what a mere conventional norm is. A *mere conventional norm* is a deeply conventional norm that is part of a deeply conventional practice. The norms of baseball provide a vivid example of mere conventional norms. The game of baseball, we noted earlier, is a deeply conventional practice. Although it is difficult to imagine a world similar to ours in which we did not devise and engage in games, it is easy to imagine a world fairly similar to ours in which we never devised and played the game of baseball. (It would, in this respect, be a world vastly impoverished in comparison to ours!) Moreover, many of the norms of baseball are deeply conventional. For example, the present rules of baseball dictate that if a batter has three strikes called against him (and the catcher catches the third strike), then he is out. But we can easily imagine that a different rule had been implemented—one according to which a batter is out if he has only two strikes called against him, whose implementation would basically serve the same purpose as the present rule. Indeed, we can even imagine the present rules of baseball being altered to a two-strike format if there were sufficient reason to do so—in order, say, to shorten games, making them more exciting.

Mere conventional norms, then, are deeply conventional norms that are part of a deeply conventional practice. It should now be apparent why I have not identified them with practice-based ones: practice-based normative features need not be deeply conventional or part of a deeply conventional practice. Admittedly, to this point, I have not offered anything like an account of what practice-based normative features are, settling instead for simply pointing to examples, such as the rules of Byzantine chant, baseball, and etiquette, and the rights, responsibilities, and obligations that attach to the par-

conventions are not themselves norms but are akin to social stipulations. I prefer this latter way of thinking of convention because of its flexibility. It allows us to distinguish conventional arrangements for acting, such as those that specify that acting in one way counts as acting in another way, from conventional norms, which are directives. Second, there are delicate issues regarding how to individuate social practices about which I wish to remain neutral. Consider, for example, a social practice SP that is governed by a set of norms N. Imagine that there is another set of norms N* such that the participants in SP could implement N* and that N* would serve the same basic purpose as N. Were N* implemented, would SP cease to exist, being supplanted by a new social practice? Or is SP such that it could survive the implementation of these new norms? I do not know the answer to these questions. Hence, I shall not commit myself one way or the other regarding them.

ticipants in these practices. Still, even if we have only paradigmatic examples of such normative features before us, that is enough to see that not all of them are merely conventional.

To appreciate the point, reflect on speech for a moment. By everyone's lights, our practices of speech are contingent; it is easy to imagine worlds in which they never arise, such as worlds in which there are no rational agents. Still, our discursive practices are not deeply conventional. For among the needs that lie deepest in human life are those to communicate reliably with one another and to have available ways of solving what David Lewis refers to as coordination problems, such as how to end a meeting or render a verdict.[14] Indeed, given the depth and scope of these needs, it is very difficult to imagine a world at all like ours in which there were no speech.

What about the norms that inform our practices of speech? It is clear that some are arbitrary. We could easily imagine, for example, arrangements for promising different from ours and yet serving the same purpose. Such arrangements might dictate that promises are to be performed only by uttering sentences that have the grammatical form of interrogatives. That said, it is equally evident that many of the norms that inform speech are not arbitrary. It is not, for example, an arbitrary feature of promising that one promises by presenting oneself as intending to lay an obligation on oneself. Nor is it an arbitrary feature of promising that, all else being equal, one is rightfully open to blame or admonition if one fails to intend to do what one presents oneself as intending to do. Nor, finally, is it an arbitrary feature of promising that, in ordinary conditions, it is inappropriate to praise someone for having both promised to act in a certain way and not formed the intention to act in that way. In short, the types of rights, responsibilities, and requirements that attach to the performance of promises are, in Searle's terminology, constitutive of promising; they define the character of the speech act in question.[15] There are not other ways in which an agent can alter

14. See Lewis (1972). Lewis thinks of conventions as arrangements to solve coordination problems. As will have been evident, the notion of convention with which I have been working is broader than this. See also Marmor (2009), ch. 1, for a treatment of Lewis' view.

15. Searle (1969), 33. As noted earlier, however, Searle holds that these normative features are not moral but merely "institutional." One could, in principle, offer

his normative status with respect to his audience such that by altering his status in just those ways he would have thereby performed the act of promising.

My immediate purpose in distinguishing merely conventional norms from practice-based normative features has been to contend that, while the normative features that constitute speech are practice-based, they are not merely conventional. But, I have indicated, my more general aim is to provide further reason to believe that some of the normative features that constitute speech are moral. Let me now provide that reason by turning our attention from speech to morality.

Most of us in our everyday lives form and evaluate moral judgments, hold others morally responsible, pursue strategies for character improvement, and so forth. To use the terminology employed earlier, we engage in the moral doxastic practice. The moral doxastic practice, however, appears not to exhibit the contingency characteristic of deeply conventional practices such as baseball and chess. It is difficult to imagine a recognizably human form of life in which we do not perform activities such as forming and evaluating moral judgments, holding others responsible, and the like. The explanation for this lies close at hand. Like our discursive practices, the activities that constitute the moral practice are rooted in needs that are themselves deeply entrenched in human social life. Our lived situation is such that we need, among other things, to protect the vulnerable from harm, engage in shared projects, and determine how to allocate scarce resources. The role of forming moral judgments and holding others responsible is crucial to engaging in these enterprises successfully, for (among other things) we often need to place limits of very specific kinds on the ways in which it is permissible to treat each other.

About this much, most philosophers agree. It is more controversial, however, to claim that our moral practices are also constituted by moral norms, such as norms that specify under what conditions it

---

various explanations as to why these normative features are constitutive of promising. One could say, for example, that the aims of our practices of speech include communicating information and successfully coordinating activities of various sorts. Only if speakers take responsibility for states of affairs, it might be claimed, could the practice achieve its aims.

is permissible to hold others accountable for their actions. At this point, however, we need not come down one way or the other on the question of whether there are such norms. Sufficient for the purpose at hand is to affirm the following conditional claim: if there were moral norms that constitute our moral practices, then a wide range of them would not be deeply conventional. For if such norms exist, then many are such that there are not norms other than those presently in effect that would basically serve the same purposes as those in effect. For example, it is not an arbitrary feature of our practices of justice that it is morally permissible to protect the innocent from violent aggression and to hold those who have engaged in such behavior accountable (or otherwise deter them from engaging in such behavior in the future). For one major aim of these practices is to protect the innocent from harm.[16]

This last point about the connections between justice and accountability deserves more attention than I can give it here. But it is worth pointing out that, according to thinkers such as Stephen Darwall, a distinctive mark of moral obligations is that there is a conceptual tie between them and having the authority to express attitudes such as blame, resentment, and indignation toward those who flout them. In Darwall's vernacular, moral obligations are conceptually linked to "second-person accountability," which is (in part) the authority to make accountability-seeking demands of one another. If what I have contended is correct, the rights, responsibilities, and obligations that constitute the normative standing of being a speaker also exhibit this feature; they are linked with the so-called reactive attitudes in the way Darwall contends moral obligations are. Indeed, second-person accountability, if the normative theory of speech is correct, lies at the very heart of speech; it is, in part, what accounts for the hook-up between locutionary and illocutionary acts.[17]

---

16. This, of course, is compatible with highly idiosyncratic views about who counts as an innocent.

17. See Darwall (2006). Those familiar with Darwall's book will recognize that there is a fair amount of congruence between the sorts of things Darwall says about the connections between the moral domain and speech and what I claim here. Specifically, in Darwall's discussion, one finds an emphasis on the connection between having what I have called a standing power to perform speech acts of various sorts and moral obligation. That said, there may also be points of disagreement. In some places, for example, Darwall indicates that moral obligations depend on the possi-

Call those rights, responsibilities, and obligations that are non-arbitrary features of deeply rooted social practices *deeply non-conventional*. If the line of argument just offered is on the mark, then we should hold that if there are normative features that inform our practices of speech and morality, then some are deeply non-conventional. They are, moreover, deeply non-conventional in virtue of the roles they play in human social life, which includes protecting each other from harms of certain kinds, such as being given false information when being told the truth matters a great deal.

This coincidence, if I am right, is telling. For to this point, I have framed the discussion by *contrasting* practice-based rights, responsibilities, and obligations with moral ones. If the line of argument developed in this section is on the mark, however, the contrast needs to be softened. For if there are normative features that belong to each category, then they have this in common: they are deeply non-conventional.

Let me summarize the argument I have just offered. Consider the rights, responsibilities, and obligations that are ingredient in the count-generation of speech. These rights, responsibilities, and obligations exhibit the following three features: they are deeply non-conventional, rooted in deep needs such as being told the truth when being given false information would be very harmful, and conceptually linked with reactive attitudes such as blame, resentment, and indignation. Now consider moral rights, responsibilities, and obligations. Were these features to exist, then they would have these same qualities: they would be deeply non-conventional, rooted in needs deeply embedded in human social life, such as protecting one another from harm of certain kinds, and conceptually linked with reactive attitudes such as blame, resentment, and indignation. This coincidence is striking. An elegant explanation of it is that some of the rights, responsibilities, and obligations of being a speaker are moral; they fit the same profile.

We have, then, a second argument for believing that some of the rights, responsibilities, and obligations ingredient in the count-generation of speech are moral. It is, however, important neither to

---

bility of issuing orders or requests (8). If what I have argued is correct, this cannot be true.

overstate nor understate the strength of the conclusion for which I have argued. While the argument I have offered rules out the view that moral features are deeply conventional, this is a fairly modest conclusion, as it does not imply that moral features ought to be understood as realists believe. In Chapter 6, I will offer an argument for this more substantial conclusion. Still, if the argument hits its mark, it yields the conclusion that we have good reason to believe that if moral features exist, then they do interesting explanatory work, as they are ingredient in the count-generation of speech. This, I believe, is also a substantial conclusion.

VI Conclusion

This completes the first stage of the argument that I wish to offer for the thesis that some of the rights, responsibilities, and obligations that constitute the normative standing of being a speaker are moral. I mentioned at the outset of our discussion, however, that the argument has another stage that requires development.

This is for two reasons. In the first place, the argument I have offered appeals to assumptions about the way concepts work that some philosophers dispute. In particular, it assumes that when we deploy moral concepts, these concepts function in such a way as to describe or stand for moral features of various kinds. This, however, is somewhat controversial. Philosophers who belong to the expressivist tradition deny it.

In the second place, we may have strong independent reasons to believe that, while there are normative features of various kinds, there could be no moral features—the appearances that such features are ingredient in the count-generation of speech being systematically misleading. If so, any initial reason to believe that some of the rights, responsibilities, and obligations of being a speaker are moral would be defeated. Philosophers who identify themselves as error theorists take this approach.

I address these important topics in the next two chapters, beginning with the second concern.

4

Against the Mixed View

Part I

Whe Jake Stephens promised the Big Band that he would lead them in a performance of *Mack the Knife* but had no intention of doing so, he suffered from a normative demerit. What sort of demerit? In the previous chapter, I argued that his failing is best thought of as being moral. For, I claimed, it is difficult to see how we could accurately and perspicuously describe Jake's failing without maintaining that he has wronged the Big Band by manipulating them for entirely selfish ends. If we use the phrase "to break a promise" somewhat loosely to stand for the phenomenon of failing, when promising, to intend to do as one says, the argument from cases offered in the last chapter implies:

The Normative Claim: It is morally wrong to break one's promise simply because one feels like it.[1]

Most philosophers would grant that the Normative Claim appears to be true. Some would go further, claiming that it appears also to be a conceptual truth in the sense that we have strong *pro tanto* reason to

---

1. Let me add two points. First, I understand the phrase "breaks one's promise simply because one feels like it" broadly, so that it covers cases in which an agent either (i) wants not to keep his promise or (ii) simply does not care about keeping his promise. Second, I have stated the Normative Claim in such a way that it does not have any qualifications attached to it. It might be, however, that it (and similar claims) should be understood to be qualified by an implicit *ceteris paribus* rider, since there might be highly unusual circumstances in which breaking promises (in the sense specified above) is morally permissible. Under this interpretation, the Normative Claim would express a *ceteris paribus* norm, which is apparently necessarily true. This understanding of the Normative Claim is compatible with the overarching argument I wish to make.

believe that were anyone sincerely to deny it, that person would suffer from a conceptual deficiency, such as having a confused grasp of its constituent concepts or failing to see or acknowledge their manifest implications.[2]

We are, nonetheless, all familiar with claims that appear to be true—even on extended reflection—but turn out to be false. Might the Normative Claim be such a claim—the moral equivalent of an optical illusion? In the previous chapter, I suggested that there are two ways to defend the view that, in this and similar cases, the appearances mislead. One way to defend this claim, which error theorists advocate, is to maintain that we have powerful independent reason to believe that there are no moral facts. If this were correct, the Normative Claim might appear true—even to those who reject it—but we would have sufficient independent reason to believe that it is not, since there are no moral facts. A second way to defend the view that the appearances mislead, which expressivists embrace, would be to contest the assumption that moral concepts function descriptively. According to this strategy, there might be a deflated sense in which we can *say* that the Normative Claim is true (and that it is true that particular cases of promise-breaking are wrong). Still, if this approach were correct, the concepts constitutive of the Normative Claim (and moral judgments more generally) would not play the role of representing moral reality, such as the property of *being wrong*. The truth of this position would undercut the assumption, central to the argument from cases, that when we categorize various normative failings as being moral, we are describing them, as opposed to doing something else, such as simply expressing disapproval of them.

My project in this chapter is to argue that neither of these strategies succeeds. The main argument I present begins by calling to mind the most prominent arguments for holding that moral facts do not exist. These arguments, I suggest, fall into two types. On the one

---

2. Cuneo and Shafer-Landau (2014) develop this position, although it is anticipated in Jackson and Pettit (1996); Foot (2002), chs. 7 and 8; and Reid (2010). In the previous chapter, I made the additional observation that when you or I judge that promise-breaking is wrong, our judgment not only appears true but is also the output of a doxastic practice in good working order, namely, the moral doxastic practice. That, I said, is reason to believe that our judgment is reliably formed.

hand, there are those that, if sound, would provide reason to reject apparent truisms such as the Normative Claim. But these arguments, I contend, would also provide equally good reason to reject the existence of practice-based norms, such as those that attach to bandleaders and baseball players. This is problematic, I claim, because antirealists are naturally understood to embrace a position that I call the *mixed view*.[3] Friends of the mixed view maintain that there are various practice-based rights, responsibilities, and obligations, such as those that attach to bandleaders and baseball players. Among these rights, responsibilities, and obligations, they also claim, are those that belong to the discursive practices of giving and receiving promises, giving and receiving requests, performing and responding to assertions, and so forth. However, it is said, these are not moral rights, responsibilities, or obligations, as we have sufficient independent reason to believe that moral facts do not exist. Hence the "mixed" character of the view: there are normative facts aplenty but no moral ones.[4]

On the other hand, there are those arguments against realism that, if sound, would provide reason to reject propositions such as the Normative Claim but would provide no independent reason to reject practice-based norms. Proponents of these arguments, I maintain, are subject to a charge of arbitrariness, since it is difficult to see why they accept certain intuitively plausible claims about the moral realm

3. According to the way that I define moral realism in Chapter 1, constructivism is a version of antirealism. I will not, however, have my eye on this family of views in this chapter, focusing instead on versions of antirealism which either deny that moral facts exist or that moral thought purports to represent them. I engage with constructivist views in Chapter 6. It is also worth noting that some moral antirealists might not reject the Normative Claim, maintaining instead that it is trivially true, since we cannot promise. In the next chapter, I shall consider this view at more length. It might also be worth emphasizing that nothing hangs on using promising as the focal example of a speech act whose performance has moral implications. For if the argument of the previous chapter is correct, we can formulate claims similar to the Normative Claim that pertain not to promising but to asserting and commanding. At any rate, in this chapter, I will assume that antirealists generally do not wish to deny that we perform speech acts such as promising, asserting, and commanding.

4. In the previous chapter, I argued that we should relax the contrast between moral features, on the one hand, and practice-based ones, on the other, claiming that some of the rights, responsibilities, and obligations that constitute speech belong to both categories. In this chapter, I will not help myself to this argument, assuming only that some of the practice-based normative features that constitute speech appear to be moral.

while rejecting others, such as the Normative Claim. In principle, this charge of arbitrariness could be discharged. I contend, however, that it is not. Since neither rejecting the existence of practice-based norms nor methodological arbitrariness is acceptable, the mixed view should be rejected.

Or so I shall argue. My argument for this conclusion will, admittedly, be incomplete. Of the various arguments ordinarily offered for the non-existence of moral facts (or moral antirealism more generally), I am going to consider only four. Two prominent arguments, I will contend, fall prey to the first half of the dilemma. Two others of equal significance, I will argue, are subject to the second half of the dilemma. Since important parts of this dilemma hinge on the assumption that concept descriptivism—roughly, the view that moral concepts purport to represent moral properties—is true, I will defend this assumption in the next chapter.

An advantage of this "fast-track" approach is that, if it hits its mark, it yields an interesting conclusion with considerable economy. A disadvantage is that the conclusion it yields is merely provisional. For, if sound, it establishes only that a healthy representative sample of the most prominent reasons marshaled in favor of moral antirealism is unacceptable. It might be that right over the horizon new and better arguments await. Still, if the strategy works it will yield the conclusion that, at this point in the debate, the most prominent reasons for believing that the normative dimensions of speech are not as they seem are themselves not compelling. And that is sufficient for my purposes.

I The first horn of the dilemma: practice-based norms must go

The Knowledge Argument

The first argument I would like to consider attempts to exploit a tension that, according to some, realists have difficulty alleviating. The tension is that, on the one hand, realists are committed to there being a realm of moral facts that are objective in the sense that they are not merely conventional. In this regard, they look rather different from

the norms of baseball or etiquette. On the other hand, these philosophers are committed to the claim that morality is practical in the
sense that moral facts of certain kinds would help to guide action. By
noting that an act is morally forbidden, for example, an agent can
determine some of the reasons he has not to perform it. If this is correct, however, then it is plausible to believe that at least some moral
facts would be within our ken. It would be strange to say, for example,
that such facts exist but cannot guide our actions, since they are cognitively inaccessible.

These assumptions place a burden on realists to explain how we
acquire moral knowledge. Advocates of the mixed view maintain
that this burden cannot be satisfactorily discharged, as realists face:

The Knowledge Argument

(1.1) If moral facts exist, then there must be a satisfactory account
of how we reliably grasp them. This account would tell us how
facts that consist in agents having moral rights, responsibilities, and obligations reliably produce the corresponding
states of moral knowledge.

(1.2) There is no satisfactory account of how we reliably grasp moral
facts. That is, to the best of our knowledge there is no account
that tells us how facts that consist in agents having moral
rights, responsibilities, and obligations reliably produce the
corresponding states of moral knowledge.

(1.3) So, moral facts do not exist.

For present purposes, I am not interested in whether realists can
reasonably reject either premise of this argument. Nor am I particularly interested in why advocates of the mixed view accept premise
(1.2). Suffice it to say that some seem to believe that were moral
rights, responsibilities, and obligations to exist, then they could not
enter into causal relations, which would render them cognitively inaccessible. Others seem to believe that we must identify some mechanism by which we acquire moral knowledge, which we have not
done. Others might take yet a different approach, claiming that,
unlike the norms of baseball and etiquette, there is (if realism is
true) no plausible story to tell about the emergence of moral norms,
which might provide the beginning of an account of how we might

reliably grasp them. At any rate, the underlying worry should be clear enough: realism leaves us entirely in the dark as to how we might know moral reality.

The Knowledge Argument raises difficult issues about the nature of moral knowledge that realists must address. These issues are serious enough that I shall return to them in Chapter 7. For now, let me indicate why I believe that the Knowledge Argument cannot be considered an adequate rationale for accepting the mixed view.

The primary problem is this: advocates of the mixed view are committed to there being practice-based rights, responsibilities, and obligations. As I have said, among these normative features are those that constitute the discursive practices of making and receiving promises, giving and receiving commands, and performing and responding to assertions. For example, there is the standing right, which attaches to the audiences of those who assert, that:

> In ordinary speech situations, if things are not as a speaker presents them, then her audience has the right to hold her accountable.

Earlier I emphasized that rights such as these appear to be constitutive of the practice of asserting. In ordinary speech situations, there is no way for an agent to take responsibility for a state of affairs and not be open to rightful correction if things are not as she presents them. I also claimed that we have good reason to believe that, in some of their manifestations, rights such as these are moral. Among other things, they are not merely conventional; they do not exhibit the degree of arbitrariness that characterizes so many other practice-based norms, such as those that govern Byzantine chant and baseball. They are, moreover, rooted in deep social needs, such as the need to receive accurate information about one's environment, especially when being given false information would be very harmful. Furthermore, the violation of such rights appears to bear the types of conceptual connections to the reactive attitudes of resentment, blame, and indignation that moral features would, were they to exist. Indeed, I claimed, in some cases, we have available no other illuminating way to think of the normative features that constitute our practices of speech except as being moral.

The objection I wish to advance against the Knowledge Argument, however, is not that we have powerful reason to suppose that practice-based normative features such as that just mentioned are moral. It is rather that these features *appear* to be moral, even after extended reflection. After all, even if the argument from cases were to fail, it would still be true that:

> Some of the normative features that constitute our practices of speech are, for all intents and purposes, indistinguishable from moral properties. In fact, if we did not know better, we would be fooled into thinking that they just are ordinary moral properties.

Suppose, though, we were to combine this claim with the second premise of the Knowledge Argument, which tells us that:

> There is no satisfactory account of how we reliably grasp moral facts. That is, to the best of our knowledge there is no account that tells us how facts that consist in agents having moral rights, responsibilities, and obligations reliably produce the corresponding states of moral knowledge.

This would generate a problem for defenders of the mixed view. Given that we have no illuminating way to distinguish (a significant range of) those normative features ingredient in the generation of speech from moral ones, then what holds for the former should also hold for the latter (and *vice versa*). According to the Knowledge Argument, however, we have no satisfactory story to tell about how we could reliably grasp moral facts. But if so, then the same holds for (a certain range of) those normative features that are ingredient in the generation of speech, such as the norm concerning assertion mentioned above. For these features, no more than moral ones, do not appear to enter into the causal flow of nature. We seem not to have identified any mechanism that explains our knowledge of them. And we cannot point to some social stipulation—unlike the norms of baseball or etiquette—that accounts for their coming into existence. The conclusion to draw, I believe, is that the Knowledge Argument overreaches, since when combined with the claim that speech exhibits normative dimensions such as those identified in the previous chapter, it would imply that we do not speak.

The charge that the Knowledge Argument is overly strong could, in principle, be discharged. The key would be to locate some way in which practice-based normative features are different from moral ones, such that grasping the former would be importantly different from grasping the latter. I am prepared to concede that reflection might reveal differences between features of both kinds. But I fail to see that any such difference would imply that grasping the former would be importantly different from grasping the latter. That is, I see no principled reason to believe that we have an informative story to tell of how we reliably grasp those normative features that, say, constitute the discursive practices of giving and receiving promises that would not also apply to moral ones. In fact, if there were such a story, then realists have a ready reply to the Knowledge Argument, borrowed from quasi-realists such as Simon Blackburn: show us how you account for knowledge of those normative features that constitute the discursive practice of giving and receiving promises, and we shall show you how we gain moral knowledge.

If this is right, we ought not to accept the mixed view on the strength of the Knowledge Argument. Provided that we are committed to the existence of practice-based rights, responsibilities, and obligations that behave very similarly to moral ones, were they to exist, we ought not to accept the mixed view on the basis of an argument which (with relatively minor changes) implies that there are no practice-based normative features such as those that constitute our practices of speech.

The Explanation Argument

Let us turn now to a second argument that is vulnerable to the same type of complaint. In its most basic form, this argument tells us that we ought not to accept the existence of moral facts because, were they to exist, they would fail to explain anything worth explaining. Those familiar with this argument know that philosophers sympathetic with it have not ordinarily offered a crisp and non-contentious account of that which is worth explaining (or, for that matter, what it is for one thing to best explain another). Crispin Wright's work is an exception to this tendency, however. Wright claims that were we to have reason to believe that moral facts exist, these facts would have to explain the existence of a sufficiently wide array of types of non-moral fact, especially those that do not consist in our holding moral beliefs.[5]

Let us say that if facts of a given type explain a sufficiently wide range of non-moral fact, then they play a *privileged explanatory role*. According to Wright, an ordinary descriptive fact such as *that the oven is hot* plays such a role. For, among other things, it explains the existence of a wide array of types of non-moral fact, including the facts *that I feel that the oven is hot, that I have burned my hand,* and *that the pot of water is boiling.* It is the failure of putative moral facts to play a privileged explanatory role, contend those sympathetic with Wright, which speaks against their existence. For, strictly speaking, were moral facts to exist, they would not do much of anything. Were they to explain anything, it would only be in virtue of the fact that we represent them in certain ways.

Taking Wright's suggestion into consideration, we can formulate:

The Explanation Argument

(2.1) We have reason to believe that moral facts exist only if such facts play a privileged explanatory role.

(2.2) Moral facts do not play a privileged explanatory role: they do not explain the existence of a sufficiently wide array of non-moral facts—at least not independently of their being represented by the contents of our propositional attitudes.

(2.3) So, we do not have reason to believe that there are moral facts.

---

5. Wright (1992), ch. 5. Joyce (2013) articulates and endorses the suspicion that drives the argument, using Wright's work: "If moral judgements can be fully explained without reference to moral facts, then this casts immediate doubt on whether moral facts are needed to explain *anything*... [F]or what possible instance would we recognize of a moral fact playing a role in explaining phenomenon X, where this act of recognition did not involve the use of moral judgement? Moral facts appear to have what Crispin Wright calls "narrow cosmological role...their causal impact always involves someone's having made a judgment concerning their presence" (10).

I need to add a point of clarification regarding Wright's own views, however. Wright intends his argument to establish only that "robust" moral facts do not exist—where a fact's being robust is a matter of its being such that it can be "seriously represented" by the content of our attitudes and is not merely a "shadow" of our propositional attitudes (181–2, 200). Wright does not, then, intend for his argument to imply that moral facts do not exist in some thinner, deflationary sense and, so, I will not attribute the Explanatory Argument to Wright himself. For present purposes, however, I shall put some of Wright's claims to a broader use, presenting them as purporting to establish the non-existence of moral facts. In the next chapter, I offer my reasons for resisting a version of the argument that attempts to establish that moral facts exist in only a deflationary sense.

For present purposes I propose to ignore the issue of what needs to be added to this argument if it is to yield an antirealist conclusion. I also propose to bracket the issue of whether realists should reject one or another of its premises. Instead, I suggest that we focus on the issue of whether advocates of the mixed view should embrace the Explanation Argument. It seems to me that they should not.

To see why, consider a practice other than speech—in this case, our legal practices. On the face of things, our legal practices appear to be constituted by legal norms of various sorts. One such norm states that:

> If during a court hearing a plaintiff expresses egregious disrespect for the judge, the court has the permission-right to hold him in contempt of court.

Were such norms to exist, then we could legitimately say that they explain various happenings in the world. Imagine, for example, that you are a plaintiff who has, during court proceedings, engaged in an angry outburst directed toward the judge. As a result, you not only believe that you will be held in contempt of court, but also fear that you will face a hefty fine because of your behavior. Arguably, legal norms such as that mentioned above account (at least in part) for your being in these cognitive states.

Explanations such as these appeal to legal norms to account for happenings in the world. But the explanations are elliptical. It is only because legal norms such as that mentioned above enter into the contents of our attitudes that they explain our behavior. It is, for example, only because the judge believes that there are legal norms that prohibit disrespectful behavior of certain kinds that she pronounces you in contempt of court. And it is only because you believe that you are in contempt of court that you fear that you will face a hefty fine. Were these things not believed, then you neither would fear being held in contempt of court, nor would you be so held. If this is right, however, then legal norms do not explain non-legal happenings in the world independently of their being represented by the contents of our propositional attitudes. In this regard they appear to be exactly like moral norms—at least as they are described by proponents of the Explanation Argument.

This is not a happy result for advocates of the mixed view, as these philosophers are committed to the existence of practice-based norms of various kinds, such as legal ones. Is there a way, then, to understand the Explanation Argument so that, in the eyes of its proponents, it yields just the right results, ruling out the existence of moral norms but allowing for the existence of practice-based ones? Well, it might be thought that in this case there is an additional point that deserves attention. For if the argument in Chapter 2 is correct, there is at least one type of explanation in which practice-based normative features might enter: count-generation explanations. It is in virtue of the fact that there are rights, responsibilities, and obligations that constitute the discursive practices of promising and commanding, for example, that locutionary acts of certain kinds count as illocutionary acts of various sorts. And relevant for present purposes is the further fact that these normative features account for the generation of speech acts independently of their being represented by our propositional attitudes. Given that the proper conditions are in place, when an agent acquires the rights, responsibilities, and obligations of being a speaker, that is sufficient for her locutionary act's counting as, say, a promise. And this, it might be thought, is enough to establish that practice-based normative features of a certain range play a sufficiently wide explanatory role, which would insulate them from skeptical worries.

I suspect that this is correct. Were practice-based normative features to count-generate speech acts, then that would be exactly the sort of thing that could be employed by advocates of the mixed view to establish that the Explanation Argument does not prove too much. But the fact that normative features count-generate speech could hardly be used to argue for the mixed view. For advocates of the mixed view would also have to establish that none of the practice-based normative features that count-generate speech are moral. Mere appeal to the Explanation Argument, however, could not settle this issue. If this last claim is true, then the Explanation Argument fares no better than the Knowledge Argument; it does not provide any reason to accept the mixed view.

Let me sum up: advocates of the mixed view, I have claimed, maintain that while there are practice-based normative features of various kinds, such as those that inform our practices of speech, there are no moral facts. Proponents of this position, I have claimed, face a dilemma: either their arguments are too powerful, as they call into question precisely the sorts of normative entities they believe to exist, or they suffer from an arbitrariness problem. I have argued that the Knowledge Argument and the Explanation Argument succumb to the first horn of the dilemma. Let us now turn to the dilemma's second horn, which will require a more extensive discussion.

II The second horn of the dilemma: arbitrariness

The Categoricity Argument

In *The Myth of Morality*, Richard Joyce defends a version of the mixed view, claiming that there are normative features of various kinds, such as the norms of etiquette and practical rationality, but no moral facts. Joyce rests his primary case for this position on one argument, which we can call:

The Categoricity Argument

(3.1) Necessarily, if there are moral facts, then there are categorical reasons.

(3.2) There are no categorical reasons.

(3.3) So, there are no moral facts.[6]

To appreciate this argument, it will be helpful to say something about the broadly Kantian way of thinking of reasons that lies behind it. According to this way of thinking, reasons come in two broad types. On the one hand are categorical reasons, which Joyce at one point refers to as the "real reasons."[7] For present purposes, we can understand categorical reasons to be those that favor behavior on the part of an agent regardless of whether engaging in that behavior

---

6. See Joyce (2001), 42; see also Mackie (1977), ch. 1. I offer a condensed version of Joyce's argument. Joyce offers a more elaborate version of it in Joyce (2011).

7. Joyce (2001), 51. In his later work, *The Evolution of Morality*, Joyce voices reservations about using the conceptuality of categorical reasons, preferring to talk of "moral clout" and "practical oomph." For the sake of expediency, I will formulate the primary argument he offers against moral realism in terms of categorical reasons; nothing of importance, I believe, will be distorted.

serves any of her desires. Categorical reasons, as it is sometimes put, apply to agents simply in virtue of their being rational agents; in this sense, they are inescapable. On the other hand are hypothetical or Humean reasons, which, as we may understand them, are those that favor behavior on the part of an agent only because engaging in that behavior serves one or another of her desires. On the assumption that rational agents can have rather different desires, it follows that Humean reasons apply selectively to rational agents. Were all reasons Humean, an agent would have no reason to conform to some norm if doing so were to fail to serve her desires. It may be worth adding that moral realists themselves differ over whether there are categorical moral reasons. Some believe there are; others believe there are not. The version of moral realism that I am interested in defending here, it will be recalled, is neutral on this issue.

Joyce has much to say in favor of the argument's second premise. For present purposes I propose to pass over these arguments in order to focus on why we should accept the argument's first premise. We should accept this premise, Joyce claims, because it is a deeply entrenched feature of ordinary moral experience. If we are to make any sense of such practices as holding others accountable for their behavior, Joyce argues, we must assume that ordinary morality is committed to there being categorical moral reasons. Indeed, nothing, Joyce says, could count as a moral system that denied the existence of such reasons. In this sense, the argument's first premise expresses a conceptual truth.[8]

The Categoricity Argument is an example of the second type of argument I specified at the outset of this chapter. If sound, it would

---

8. When spelled out more fully, Joyce's thought is this: our practice of holding wrongdoers morally accountable appears to presuppose that wrongdoers have moral reasons not to act as they do. If there were such reasons, however, then they would have to be categorical; otherwise wrongdoers could get off the hook by sincerely denying that they care about morality or the welfare of those they harmed. But the lack of such desires is precisely the type of consideration that those of us who engage in practices of holding others accountable find morally irrelevant. To the extent, then, that our practices of holding others morally accountable actually reveal our moral commitments, we have strong reason to believe that we are committed to the existence of categorical moral reasons (and that these reasons carry considerable weight). Indeed, our commitment to there being such reasons is so deeply entrenched in our moral practices, Joyce adds, that any "system of values that leaves out categorical imperatives" would lack the authority that we expect of morality, and simply "not count as a 'morality' at all" (2001), 177.

provide reason to reject propositions such as the Normative Claim, but not the existence of practice-based norms, such as those of etiquette and Byzantine chant. According to Joyce, this is because putative moral facts, such as that expressed by the Normative Claim, would have to provide categorical reasons to act, but paradigmatic practice-based obligations, such as those of etiquette or Byzantine chant, would not.

With this in mind, let us now note the following feature of the Categoricity Argument: defenders of the argument take the appearances of ordinary moral thought and practice very seriously. The reason we should accept the argument's first premise, says Joyce, is because it appears to make the best sense of how we conduct ourselves in the moral domain, such as when we hold wrongdoers morally accountable. Yet it is a striking fact that these philosophers do not take the appearances of other dimensions of ordinary moral thought and practice with the same degree of seriousness, as they reject propositions such as the Normative Claim—this in spite of the fact that ordinary moral thought and practice also seem to commit us to them. Indeed, as I have already indicated, it is plausible to assume that the Normative Claim itself is a conceptual truth in the same sense that the first premise of the Categoricity Argument is supposed to be: it is a non-negotiable feature of ordinary moral practice, a fixed point. All else being equal, any normative system that failed to incorporate it would simply not count as a moral system.

Herein lies the tension I want to exploit. For suppose we agree, for argument's sake, that there are no categorical reasons. Why, at the outset of theorizing, would we take this to be a reason for rejecting the Normative Claim rather than the first premise of the Categoricity Argument? After all, on the assumption that moral concepts function descriptively, both the first premise of this argument and the Normative Claim appear to be non-negotiable features of anything that could count as moral thought and practice. Accordingly, it is difficult to see why the advocate of the mixed view should embrace:

> **Argument A**: It is conceptually necessary that, if there are moral facts, then there are categorical reasons. But there are no categorical reasons. So, there are no moral facts. However, if there are no moral

facts, then an agent cannot exhibit a moral demerit. Suppose, now, that in an ordinary speech situation, an agent fails to intend to honor her promise to act in a certain way simply because she does not feel like it. It follows that the Normative Claim is false: for in ordinary speech situations, an agent fails to intend to honor her promise to act in a certain way simply because she does not feel like it and yet she does not thereby exhibit a moral demerit, such as having acted wrongly,

rather than accept:

> **Argument B**: It is conceptually necessary that, in ordinary speech situations, if an agent fails to intend to honor her promise to act in a certain way simply because she does not feel like it, then she thereby exhibits a moral demerit, such as having acted wrongly. Suppose that, in an ordinary speech situation, an agent fails to intend to honor her promise to act in that way simply because she does not feel like it. It follows that she exhibits a moral demerit, such as having acted wrongly. But if she exhibits a moral demerit, then moral facts exist. Since she does exhibit such a demerit, moral facts exist. There are, however, no categorical reasons. So, the first premise of the Categoricity Argument is false: there are moral facts, but there are no categorical reasons.

This, at any rate, is the challenge I wish to pose to proponents of the Categoricity Argument. Since it owes a debt to the style of argument that G. E. Moore pressed against skeptics regarding the external world, I will call it the *Moorean-style Objection*.[9]

Can the Moorean-style Objection be met? In principle, yes. An adequate reply would be one in which proponents of the Categoricity Argument identify reasons why we should embrace Argument A rather than Argument B. To my knowledge, however, advocates of the Categoricity Argument have not identified these reasons. I am going to contend that there are none.

---

9. See Moore (1953). McPherson (2009) notes that, interestingly, Moore never employed this type of strategy when defending his own metaethical views. McPherson goes on to suggest that there might be a reason for this, as the Moorean strategy is less plausible when applied in metaethics. It is worth emphasizing, though, that the Moorean strategy that McPherson considers is more ambitious than the one I employ here. The strategy I employ counsels not that we reject Argument A in favor of Argument B, but only that we have no more reason to accept Argument A than Argument B.

To make headway on this issue, let me note that ethical theories, as Joyce himself argues, are themselves assessable along two main dimensions. In the first place, one can ask of a given theory, whether it commits us to types of entities that we would rather not accept if we could get away with it because they would be highly mysterious or clutter our ontology. In the second place, one can ask of a theory whether it does an adequate job of preserving deeply embedded features of ordinary thought and practice. Ideally, a good moral theory would aim to satisfy both these desiderata, although, as Joyce notes, they often tend to pull against one another.[10]

Let us consider the first criterion of assessment. Does accepting the second argument just offered—what I have termed Argument B—violate this criterion? It seems not. Were advocates of the mixed view to claim that all moral reasons are Humean, then they would not have thereby admitted the existence of a type of entity that they would rather not accept if they could get away with it. Advocates of the mixed view such as Joyce, after all, do not blanch in the face of Humean reasons; they have no reservations about admitting that reasons of this type exist. Nor, for that matter, would advocates of this view have introduced new and unwanted complications into their position by admitting that there are such reasons. For if the mixed view were correct, then moral reasons would simply be a species of Humean reasons. If that is right, however, accepting Argument B introduces no type of entity that is new and objectionable into the picture. At most, it implies that there are more types of Humean reasons than we first thought. And it is difficult to see why that should induce us to embrace Argument A rather than Argument B.[11]

---

10. Joyce (2007), 5–6.
11. Olson (2011b) is an error theorist who rejects the existence of hypothetical reasons as they are usually understood. According to Olson, "error theorists should deny that hypothetical reasons are properly understood in terms of the counting-in-favor-of relation." Rather, according to error theory, "claims about hypothetical reasons are true only if they reduce to empirical claims about agents' desires and (actual or believed) efficient means of bringing about the satisfaction of those desires" (78). Would a view such as this escape the Moorean-style Objection? Not obviously. Olson goes to considerable lengths to argue that we should accept premise (3.1) of the Categoricity Argument, because it best fits with deeply entrenched features of ordinary moral practice. Yet he rejects the Normative Claim, which is also deeply embedded in ordinary moral thinking. Olson never says, however, why we should reject one deeply entrenched feature of ordinary thinking rather than the other. Granted, it is true that rejecting both the Normative Claim and the existence of hypothetical

Turn now to the second criterion of assessment, which concerns whether a theory does a good job in preserving deeply entrenched features of ordinary moral thought and discourse. Does accepting Argument B violate this criterion? The issue in this case is more delicate. If we concede Joyce's contention that our moral practices commit us to the existence of categorical moral reasons, then moral realists who believe that all moral reasons are Humean will have to grant that ordinary moral thought and practice are in error.

But it is important to describe the error accurately. In various places, Joyce writes as if the claim that all moral reasons are Humean implies that moral thought could not play its characteristic roles, such as "silencing" competing prudential considerations. For example, toward the end of his book *The Evolution of Morality*, Joyce writes:

> So the question we need to ask is whether moral discourse could carry on playing whatever role it does play if the connection between its prescriptions and the reasons people have to comply were merely a reliable contingent one. If not, then we have grounds for doubting that such a framework counts as a "moral" system at all.[12]

Joyce continues, arguing that if this view were true, moral thinking could not play its fundamental roles:

> Moral thinking has a function...and deliberations in terms simply of what we want and need will not suffice. The moralization of our

reasons (as they are usually understood) allows error theorists to not admit the existence of a type of entity that they would rather not accept if they could help it. However, it does not follow from this that we should accept premise (3.1) but reject the Normative Claim. The error theorist still owes us an argument why we should hold that rejecting the Normative Claim and the existence of hypothetical reasons (as they are usually understood) is on the whole preferable to accepting the Normative Claim and the existence of hypothetical reasons (as they are usually understood). To which it should be added that Olson's proposal strikes me as dialectically puzzling. Olson takes Stephen Finlay's relativist view of reasons to task (73–7), since it comports poorly with phenomena deeply entrenched in ordinary moral practice, such as the fact that we appear to disagree about moral claims in asserted contexts. But a view of hypothetical reasons according to which they are merely empirical predictions can hardly be said to fit better with our deeply entrenched practices of evaluating others' behavior than a relativist account of reasons. The fact that you fail to act in accordance with an empirical prediction does not illuminate why, in a large range of cases, we would say that you are practically irrational for failing to take the necessary means to satisfy one or another of your deeply entrenched desires.

12. Joyce (2006), 202.

practical lives contributes to the satisfaction of our long-term interests and makes for more effective collective negotiation by supplying license for punishment, justification for likes and dislikes, and bonding individuals in a shared framework of decision-making. It is, I submit, precisely the purported authority and inescapability of moral prescriptions that enable them to perform these functions. Thus, a value system lacking practical clout could not so effectively play the social roles to which we put morality, and thus we could not use it as we use morality…[13]

When Joyce refers to the authority and "practical clout" of moral considerations, he primarily has in mind what we might call their *silencing function*.[14] An example might best illustrate how Joyce is thinking.

Suppose that Jake is faced with the choice as to whether to lie to the Big Band. He knows that doing so would be wrong. But he also knows that lying will probably save him from the experience—highly undesirable in his mind—of having to listen to *Mack the Knife* on this particular day. If Jake genuinely understands that lying on this occasion is wrong, however, then this should have the effect of putting out of mind rationalizations that might tempt him to lie. It should shrink the space of deliberative possibilities so that he does not engage in any sort of cost-benefit calculation. Of course, Jake may go ahead and lie anyway. But the price will be an awareness that he deserves to be the object of disapprobation.

Now return to the passages just quoted. In these passages, Joyce seems to move from the realists' claim that:

All moral reasons are Humean,

to the further claim that:

If all moral reasons are Humean, then moral thought could not perform a silencing function—one in which it trumps competing considerations such as prudential ones.

But such an inference would be erroneous. Moral thought might tend to play a silencing function even if all moral reasons were Humean. For it might be that moral thought tends to misdescribe

13. Joyce (2006), 208.
14. See Joyce (2006), sect. 4.2.

the nature of moral reasons, taking them to be categorical when they are really Humean.

Let me explain more fully what I have in mind. Realists believe that there are moral facts such as those reported by the Normative Claim. They also believe that there are moral reasons, although some hold that they are Humean.[15] Although realists of this variety believe that all moral reasons are Humean, they also believe that many of us—and perhaps most of us—have moral reasons to conform to the requirements of morality. Insofar as they accept that Joyce has accurately described ordinary moral thought and practice, however, they concede that moral thought and practice tend to incorporate a mistake. The mistake consists in taking the moral reasons that many of us have to be categorical when they are really Humean.

It is in this respect that some realists (at least if they agree with Joyce's description of ordinary moral thought and practice) believe that ordinary moral thought and practice tend to incorporate an error. To soften the blow of this consequence of their views, these realists might say various things about why it might be useful for us to misdescribe the nature of moral reasons. On this occasion I will not explore this issue.[16] The important point to see is that by admitting that moral reasons are Humean, realists of this sort need not also claim that moral thought and discourse fail to play the types of function that Joyce believes they must to count as components of a moral system. For, once again, Humean realists can hold that ordinary moral thought typically assumes moral reasons are not Humean but categorical.

To this point, I have explored the implications of accepting Argument B—my aim being to identify the theoretical costs of doing so, which include accepting a localized error. Let us now look at the alternative, which is to accept Argument A. Philosophers who accept Argument A, recall, believe that not only is the Normative Claim false, but also that there are no moral truths whatsoever. These philosophers are error theorists about morality. They hold that while our

---

15. By "moral reasons" I mean simply moral considerations that—perhaps in conjunction with other things, such as an agent's own commitments—genuinely favor behaving in certain ways.

16. For more on this, see Cuneo (2012), 123.

moral judgments purport to represent moral reality, they fail to do so, as there is no such reality to represent.

In Chapter 6, I shall engage with the error theory at more length. For now, it is worth asking whether the error theory satisfies the two criteria of theory evaluation with which we have been working. The answer is that, since the error theory does not appear to introduce any new and problematic entities into our moral theories, it fares no worse than realism with respect to the first criterion. Things are different, however, when it comes to the second criterion. In this case, the error theory fares considerably worse than realism of the Humean variety. For unlike realism of this type, the error theory does not simply countenance a fairly localized error about the way we tend to think of the nature of moral reasons. Rather, it claims that there simply are no moral facts; apparent truisms such as the Normative Claim fail to express truths. In addition, the error theory implies that there are no moral reasons of any sort. Given the assumption that moral thought and discourse purport to represent such facts and reasons, then we are, according to the error theory, in massive and systematic error. The error theory earns its name. If it were true, it is difficult to see how we could be more mistaken about moral matters.

All philosophical views come at a cost. The task of the theorist is usually to determine which costs are, on the whole, less onerous than others. Arriving at such a determination can be a difficult procedure; often it is not apparent how we should weigh certain costs against others. But assessing the costs of the case at hand, it seems to me, is fairly straightforward: the theoretical cost of accepting Humean realism is considerably less than that of embracing the error theory. For both theories, we have seen, do fairly well with regard to the first criterion of theory assessment: neither is appreciably more simple than the other. However, error theory, I have maintained, fares very poorly with respect to the second criterion, as it implies that our moral thinking is in massive error. If so, it is better to accept a view according to which there are moral reasons that we tend to misdescribe rather than one according to which there are no such reasons at all.

Let me summarize: suppose we assume that ordinary moral thought and practice are committed to there being things that have moral features of various kinds. If so, advocates of the mixed view that propound the Categoricity Argument are liable to a charge of arbitrariness. The problem, recall, is that while error theorists take the appearances very seriously by accepting claims such as:

Necessarily, if there are moral facts, then there are categorical reasons,

they take equally plausible claims such as:

It is wrong to break one's promise simply because one feels like it,

to be illusory. But it is not easy to see why we should argue from this first claim to the rejection of the latter, rather than the reverse. In principle, error theorists, we have seen, could reply to this charge, claiming that we should reject Argument B rather than Argument A, since doing so is preferable according to the two criteria for theory evaluation identified earlier. But if what I have argued is correct, this is not so. In fact, the evidence points in the opposite direction: we should accept Argument B rather than Argument A. If so, we ought not to reject realism on the strength of the Categoricity Argument.[17]

At this point, however, I can imagine advocates of the mixed view becoming impatient. They will protest as follows: suppose it is true that realism of the Humean variety is in certain important respects less problematic than the error theory since the nature of the error it countenances is considerably less severe than that admitted by the error theory. This, we can admit, is a point in favor of realism. Still, it might be said, it does not follow that we should accept realism according to the two criteria of theory selection that we have employed. For inasmuch as the type of realism under consideration rejects the

---

17. One might worry that the strategy I have used to respond to the Categoricity Argument is not available to realists who believe that moral reasons are categorical. This is a problem, it might be said, because I have claimed to defend a version of realism that is officially neutral regarding the issue of whether moral reasons are categorical or Humean. Let me say two things in response: first, the strategy I have employed is designed to be maximally concessive in the following respect. It aims to establish that, even if we concede a very controversial assumption—namely, that there are no categorical reasons—to advocates of the mixed view, the Categoricity Argument does not go through. The view I defend is, however, compatible with rejecting this controversial assumption. In fact—and this is the second point—realists who believe that moral reasons are categorical can still maintain that the error theorist's methodology is arbitrarily partial. They might say that since there is no more reason to reject premise (3.1) of the Categoricity Argument than the Normative Claim, we should reject the argument's second premise.

existence of categorical moral reasons, it fails to offer an account of a moral system at all. But the criteria for theory evaluation that we have employed are (among other things) ones for assessing *metaethical* theories—theories that describe moral systems. If so, Humean realism might be better than error theory in some respects, but it is not a better metaethical theory, for it simply fails to describe a moral system.

The cogency of this objection hangs on what exactly philosophers such as Joyce have in mind by a moral system. In one of the more memorable passages in *The Myth of Morality*, Joyce says this:

> It is not necessary for me to claim that absolutely every piece of recognizably moral language implies the validity of categorical imperatives, only that a sufficient portion of them do, such that if we were to eliminate categorical imperatives and all that imply them from the discourse, whatever remained would no longer be recognizable as—could not play the role of—a *moral* discourse. Any system of values that leaves out categorical imperatives will lack the authority that we expect of morality, and any set of prescriptions failing to underwrite this authority simply does not count as a "morality" at all. Moral discourse, in other words, is a house of cards, and the card at center bottom has "categorical imperative" written on it.[18]

This passage is interesting, because Joyce tends to slide between talking about what is necessary for a discourse or system of concepts to count as moral, on the one hand, and what it is for a system of values or set of prescriptions to count as moral, on the other.

Let us suppose that when Joyce speaks of a system of morality being a system of values and prescriptions, he means that it is a system of putative rights, responsibilities, and obligations. If so, then Joyce's claim is that if a system of putative rights, responsibilities, and obligations were not to include categorical reasons, then it could not count as a moral system. In principle, this might be correct. But we need an argument to believe it. Joyce's argument, recall, is that moral discourse could not play a silencing function if the system it purports to describe were not to include categorical moral reasons. I have argued that this is not so. For all we reasonably believe, our moral thinking could carry on pretty much as it always has even if our system of rights, responsibilities, and obligations included

---

18. Joyce (2001), 176–7.

no categorical reasons. Of course, ordinary thought about this system would be erroneous in certain respects. But it might be both difficult and undesirable to avoid the error.

Suppose, by contrast, that Joyce means by a system of morality a system of moral concepts. If so, Joyce's contention is that a system of concepts could not count as moral if it did not include the concept of a categorical moral reason, which is such that it has (or is taken to have) genuine application. Now, however, we need to distinguish. On the one hand, the system of concepts in question might be that which is employed by most ordinary people in their everyday moral deliberation. Call this the *ordinary moral system*. On the other, it might be that system that is employed by Humean realists when describing the nature of moral reasons. Call this the *Humean moral system*.

If by "moral system" we mean the ordinary moral system, then we should not reject realism of the Humean variety on the grounds that it offers a distorted picture of our ordinary moral concepts. For realists of this sort are not offering an account of such a system at all. Rather, they are offering us an account of the nature of *reasons*. And, so, it cannot be said that, if their view were true, our ordinary folk concepts would cease to play a silencing role. To say it again, Humean realism has no implications whatsoever regarding which concepts ordinary agents employ when engaging in moral deliberation.

However, if it is the Humean moral system that is at issue—the system of concepts that Humean realists use when describing the nature of moral reasons—then there is, admittedly, a point to press against the Humean realists. For when describing the nature of reasons, Humeans employ the concept not of categorical but of Humean reasons. By doing so, it might be charged, these philosophers fail to capture enough of ordinary moral thought since, were their account of reasons explicitly accepted, moral thought would then fail to play a silencing role.

Let us focus for a moment on this last counterfactual claim: were Humean realism accepted, then moral thought would fail to play a silencing role. Is its truth enough to vindicate the accusation that realists who hold that all reasons are Humean have failed to provide an account of a moral system at all? I doubt it. While I have no full-blown argument to establish this, the following two considerations, I believe, should give us pause.

First, consider a case analogous to the one Joyce offers. Many have thought—Plato, Hobbes, Locke, and Kant come to mind—that moral obligations must be tied to a system of rewards and punishments, typically meted out by a divine being. The idea, presumably, is that something could count as a moral system only if conformance to the rights, responsibilities, and obligations that constitute it were ultimately in one's best interest and lack of conformance were not. (This, incidentally, is not the same idea as silencing, which Joyce invokes. According to the system-of-rewards picture, moral considerations override all others. But they do so only because conforming to them is ultimately in one's own self-interest. If this view were true, proper moral deliberation could involve cost-benefit calculations, which reveal that acting virtuously is in one's ultimate interest. But this is precisely the sort of reasoning that silencing is supposed to rule out.) It is a plausible conjecture that, by making these claims, some of these philosophers were not introducing novel elements to the ordinary moral thought of their time, but accurately describing important elements of it. If so, one could imagine someone arguing that any view that rejected the system of rewards position would fail to capture enough of ordinary moral thought since, were it accepted, moral thought would then fail to represent moral obligations as overriding in the sense that conforming to them ultimately redounds to one's own well-being.

In fact, however, many today reject the system of rewards position. But we would not say of such people that, when they describe their view, they are describing something other than a moral system. For our moral practices appear to be supple enough to allow for differences of opinion as to whether moral considerations are tied to a system of rewards. If that is right, though, then the question to ask of positions such as Joyce's is why we should think that morality could survive the rejection of the system of rewards view but not the rejection of categorical moral reasons. As best I can tell, we do not have a good answer to this question. That moral considerations must play a silencing function and that anything worth calling virtue must ultimately contribute to one's own well-being are both convictions deeply entrenched in ordinary moral thought. It is, I believe, unclear why morality could survive the rejection of one conviction but not the other. Let me emphasize that, by drawing attention to this parallel, I do not mean to suggest that just about anything could count as a moral system. There are limits to what could count as a moral system and, hence, the changes it could absorb, although it may be difficult to say in the abstract what these changes would be. Rather, the point is that we should distinguish between a description of a moral system M according to which M has various serious theoretical blemishes, since it fails to capture deeply embedded features of ordinary morality, and one that fails to describe a moral system at all. I am prepared to say that Humean realism falls into the first category. But I see little reason to believe it falls into the latter, at least when the view is cast in a charitable light.

Second, recall that the charge that we are considering is that Humean realists have failed to capture enough of ordinary moral thought since, were their view accepted, then moral thought would fail to play a silencing role. But one could reasonably worry that if this counterfactual were true, it would imply that too many positions that we would ordinarily call metaethical views are not metaethical views at all, since they would fail to describe a system of moral concepts.[19] Consider expressivism, for example. Expressivists believe that moral thought does not even involve attributing moral properties to things, let alone thinking that there are requirements that yield categorical moral reasons.[20] If expressivism were accepted by the folk, then they would not think of moral considerations as generating categorical reasons that silence cost-benefit calculations. It follows that, according to the line of argument Joyce has offered, expressivism should be dismissed on the ground that it fails to offer us an account of a system of moral concepts.

Or consider moral fictionalism—a view that Joyce himself has defended.[21] Fictionalists such as Joyce propose that we should reform ordinary moral thought and discourse in such a way that those who participate in them engage in a type of pretence wherein they

---

19. Or at least it would imply this on the further assumption that these theories do not inadvertently commit themselves to the reality of categorical reasons.
20. This is not quite accurate, as I point out in Chapter 5, but it is true of prominent versions of expressivism.
21. See Joyce (2001), chs. 7–8. Actually, Joyce claims that the fictionalist position he defends is a version of expressivism. If so, then the considerations adduced earlier regarding expressivism apply to it.

pretend there are categorical moral reasons. But pretending to believe and genuinely believing there are categorical moral reasons, as
Joyce emphasizes, are different; they are different stances one can
take toward moral propositions. Now imagine a scenario under
which fictionalism were accepted. Under this scenario, we would not
believe but merely pretend to believe there are categorical moral
reasons. Would pretending to believe there are moral reasons play
the silencing function that Joyce believes is a non-negotiable dimension of genuinely moral thought?

   In some cases it probably would. But, then again, in other cases
it probably would not. For it is important to remember that, according to fictionalists such as Joyce, those who engage in the
moral pretense know that they are doing so; they are not having
the wool pulled over their eyes by an elite few who propagate something like Plato's noble lie. So, consider a variant of an example
introduced earlier in this chapter: Jake is tempted to lie to the Big
Band simply to save himself from an unpleasant experience. No
one will find out if Jake lies. Nor will doing so alter his long-term
commitment to the fiction of morality. In this scenario it is difficult
to see why the thought that the fiction of morality requires Jake not
to lie would rule out his engaging in a cost-benefit analysis. To the
contrary, I imagine that a moral thought of this sort would, for the
clear-eyed fictionalist who is minimally committed to the moral fiction, simply be an invitation to engage in exactly the sort of cost-
benefit analysis that Joyce believes is ruled out by genuine moral
thought and discourse. Why is that? Well, the offense in question
would not in any sense be a failure of rationality. Moreover, the
clear-eyed fictionalist knows exactly why he often engages in moral
pretense: it is for broadly instrumental reasons. He does so because
he wishes to bolster self-control and increase social cohesion.[22] But,
by hypothesis, Jake's lying in this case would threaten neither of
these goods.

   Earlier we saw that, in Joyce's view, parallel considerations were
enough to rule out realism of the Humean variety. Something could
not be a genuinely moral thought if it invited an agent who is minimally committed to morality to engage in a cost-benefit analysis

---

22. Compare the discussion of Joyce (2001), 7.1.

about whether to conform to putative moral demands. If this is right, however, then it would appear that moral fictionalism should also be dismissed on the ground that it fails to offer us an account of a system of moral concepts, since the normative concepts that we deploy in the fictive mood need not play a genuinely silencing function.

Let me pull together the strands of the preceding argument. I have argued that there are three ways to understand the claim that, were Humean realism true, it would not describe a moral system. Under the first interpretation, a moral system is a system of putative, rights, responsibilities, and obligations. I have claimed that if these putative rights, responsibilities, and obligations were as Humean realists say, this would give us no reason to believe that ordinary moral thought would fail to play a silencing function. Under the second interpretation, a moral system is a system of concepts, albeit it is that employed by ordinary people when engaging in ordinary moral thought and discourse—what I called the "ordinary moral system." I have contended that, if Humean realism were true, Joyce's argument provides no reason to believe that these concepts would fail to play a silencing function. For Humean realists need not claim that ordinary people think of moral reasons as being Humean. Under the third interpretation, a moral system is a system of concepts that ordinary people would use were they to accept some metaethical view, such as Humean realism. This is what I called the "Humean system." When addressing this third interpretation I have made two replies: first, we have reason to believe that our moral practices are supple enough to incorporate significant changes in moral thinking—even one according to which we come to think of moral reasons as being Humean. Second, if it is true that moral thought must play a silencing function, then Joyce's argument would imply that a rather wide range of what we ordinarily call metaethical theories fail to describe a system of moral concepts. This is because were these views accepted, moral thought need not play a silencing function.

For a robust moral realist who believes in the reality of categorical moral reasons, this last claim would be too good to be true. A single line of argument would suffice to dispose of Humean realism, expressivism, moral fictionalism, moral subjectivism, and other views, since they all fail to describe a system of moral concepts. But—and this is the point I wish to press—it should not be *that* easy to dismiss these rival views. If I am right about this, the charge against the Categoricity Argument stands. We ought not to accept the mixed view on the basis of this argument.

The Motivation Argument

In the previous section we considered an argument for the mixed view that appeals to the non-existence of categorical reasons. I claimed that proponents of this argument are liable to a charge of arbitrariness. Let us now consider another argument that is subject to a similar concern.

Recent defenses of expressivism, such as those developed by Blackburn and Allan Gibbard, rely heavily on a single line of argument, which claims that moral judgments are intrinsically motivating.[23] Blackburn, for example, writes that "expressivism in ethics has to be correct." This is because "we have no conception of a 'truth condition' or fact of which mere apprehension by itself determines practical issues. For any fact, there is a question of what to do about it."[24] Gibbard says something similar. Like Blackburn, Gibbard maintains that expressivism regarding ought judgments "*must* be right."[25] The problem with realism, Gibbard continues, is that it "downplays choice" by "treating acting" as "an afterthought." Prominent versions of realism "leave us conceptually in the lurch, with no refined concepts for thinking" our "way to decision."[26] Expressivism, by contrast, furnishes an account of moral judgments according to which they are tailor-made to move us to action. In Gibbard's case, this is because

---

23. I use the term "moral judgment" to stand for those mental states expressed by the sincere utterance of a predicative moral sentence. See Gibbard (1990) and (2003), ch. 1, Blackburn (1998), ch. 3, Timmons (1999), and Horgan and Timmons (2000) and (2006) for defenses of expressivism. Gibbard, as I indicate later, defends the intrinsically motivating character of judgments that concern the "all things considered ought." I should also add that, in what follows, I offer a particular interpretation of expressivism—one that I believe fits well with much of what expressivists say. In the next chapter, I note different ways in which the view can be developed.
24. Blackburn (1998), 70.
25. Gibbard (2003), 7.
26. Gibbard (2003), 10–11; cf. also 13.

some just *are* decisions to act; as such, they are intrinsically motivating "by definition."[27] If these philosophers are right, moral judgment must consist in something other than the mere apprehension of a moral fact or the acceptance of a moral proposition.

When deployed as a premise against moral realism, advocates of the mixed view defend:

The Motivation Argument

(4.1) Moral judgments are intrinsically motivating: it is conceptually necessary that if an agent judges that she morally ought to act in a certain way, then she is motivated to some degree to act in that way.

(4.2) If moral judgments express moral beliefs, then moral judgments are not intrinsically motivating.

(4.3) So, moral judgments do not express moral beliefs.

(4.4) If moral judgments do not express moral beliefs, then there are no moral facts.

(4.5) So, there are no moral facts.

The thought behind the argument's last premise is this: it would be bizarre if moral facts were to exist and yet for moral thought and discourse not to express beliefs, which purport to represent these facts. For suppose moral facts were to exist. We saw in our discussion of the Knowledge Argument that, were such facts to exist, then they would guide action; this is what we mean when we say that these facts are practical. But if these facts were to guide action, then at least some of them would be within our ken, for only then could they guide our actions. If moral facts were within our ken, however, then presumably moral judgments would successfully represent some of them. What would stand in the way?

Look at the matter from the opposite angle. Suppose that moral judgments were not to express moral beliefs, as the antecedent of

---

27. Gibbard (2003), 17 and 219. In characterizing Gibbard's view thus, I am taking some liberties with it. Strictly speaking, Gibbard (2003) offers an argument "that it is possible to have concepts that work as expressivists say our normative concepts work" (7). Still, Gibbard admits that "in the back of his mind…is the hypothesis that important parts of actual language work this way" (8). I assume that ordinary moral language is included in the "important parts" of which Gibbard speaks.

(4.4) states. Then positing moral facts would appear to be entirely superfluous; they would explain nothing regarding the nature of moral judgment or action, as there would be no apparent sense in which moral judgments tracked these facts. But if so, then we have a powerful reason not to accept any theory that implies that they exist. Either way you look at things, we have good reason to accept (4.4), the last premise of the Motivation Argument.

Thus understood, the Motivation Argument is an example of the second type of argument identified at the outset of this chapter. If cogent, it would provide grounds to reject the Normative Claim. But it would not raise doubts about the existence of practice-based norms, such as those that constitute the practices of Byzantine chant and baseball, for presumably judgments concerning these norms are not intrinsically motivating.

For present purposes I propose to ignore reasons to reject one or another premise of The Motivational Argument. Instead, let us focus on why someone might accept the argument's first premise. This premise is not supposed to be a case of abstract metaphysics, the fruit of high-level theorizing. Rather, it is supposed to be something that emerges from reflection on the nature of ordinary moral thought and practice. To claim something like "Yes, I sincerely believe that I ought not to murder, but I am not against it" appears paradoxical. How could one sincerely believe that one ought not to murder and not be against it? As R. M. Hare put the matter some time ago, it looks as if a person who says such a thing were using the term "ought" in a non-standard way, employing it with "inverted commas."[28]

In this sense, advocates of the Motivation Argument defer to the appearances of well-formed ordinary moral thought and discourse. But it is a striking fact that with respect to other apparent truths in the neighborhood, there is no such deference. For consider the Normative Claim once again. Like the first premise of the Motivation Argument, it has an excellent claim to being a truth to which sincere participants in ordinary moral practice are committed. Indeed, if what we said earlier is correct, it looks as if any reasonably comprehensive moral system would have to include

28. See Hare (1952), 172.

it. And yet to accept the mixed view, I have emphasized, is to reject the Normative Claim.

We now have an apparent tension on our hands. For suppose we concede, for argument's sake, that if moral judgments were to express moral beliefs, then these judgments would not be intrinsically motivating. Why should we take this to be a reason to reject the Normative Claim rather than the first premise of the Motivation Argument? After all, both the first premise of this argument and the Normative Claim appear to be truths deeply embedded in (or presupposed by) ordinary moral and thought and practice. Accordingly, it is difficult to see why the advocate of the mixed view should accept:

> **Argument A**: It is conceptually necessary that moral judgments are intrinsically motivating. If this is right, however, then moral judgments do not express moral beliefs. And if this is so, then there are no moral facts. Suppose, now, that in an ordinary speech situation, an agent fails to intend to honor her promise to act in a certain way simply because she does not feel like it. It follows that the Normative Claim is false: for in ordinary speech situations, an agent who fails to intend to honor her promise to act in a certain way simply because she does not feel like it does not thereby exhibit a moral demerit, such as having acted wrongly,

rather than embrace:

> **Argument B**: If an agent fails to intend to honor her promise to act in a certain way simply because she does not feel like it, then she thereby exhibits a moral demerit, such as having acted wrongly. Suppose that, in an ordinary speech situation, an agent fails to intend to honor her promise to act in that way simply because she does not feel like it. It follows that she exhibits a moral demerit, such as having acted wrongly. But if so, then moral facts exist. Suppose, however, it is true that if moral judgments do not express moral beliefs, then there are no moral facts. If moral facts exist, then moral judgments express moral beliefs. Given the truth of premise (4.2), it follows that the first premise of the Motivation Argument must be false: it is possible for an agent to judge that she morally ought to act in some way, but not be motivated to do so.

So, once again, we have the broadly Moorean charge that advocates of the Motivation Argument exercise an arbitrary preference for accepting some apparently well-entrenched truths and not others. Can the charge be met in this case?

It might appear so. As a first move, friends of the Motivation Argument might simply concede that primitive versions of expressivism, which deny that there is any interesting sense in which the Normative Claim is true, are vulnerable to the charge of arbitrariness. But they will also insist that more sophisticated versions of the view are not. The reason is that sophisticated expressivists can distinguish two interpretations of the Normative Claim, maintaining that the Moorean-style Objection goes through against only one such interpretation.

Under the first interpretation—call it *the robust reading*—the Normative Claim reports a robust fact, something that can form the representational content of our moral judgments. Under the second interpretation—call it *the deflated reading*—the Normative Claim does not report any such fact. Accordingly, to accept the Normative Claim is not to predicate of gratuitous promise-breaking the property of being wrong. Rather, it is simply to express a first-order ethical judgment that condemns gratuitous promise-breaking. To judge that gratuitous promise-breaking is wrong, defenders of the deflated interpretation propose, is to do something like express one's commitment to condemning gratuitous promising-breaking no matter what the circumstances in which it may take place (and perhaps to enjoin others to do so as well).[29]

With this distinction in hand, let us return to the Moorean-style Objection. The Moorean-style Objection, say defenders of the Motivation Argument, assumes the truth of the first interpretation we have just identified—the robust reading—according to which moral concepts function descriptively. But in this context, it might be said, the robust interpretation is not something that can simply be assumed, for it incorporates an account of the way in which moral concepts function, which is precisely what defenders of the Motivation Argument reject. To make the Moorean-style Objection

29. See Bennett (1993) Blackburn (1993), 153; and also Gibbard (2003), 7. Blackburn claims that expressivism is compatible with there being moral properties, albeit in a deflated sense. I address this position in Chapter 6. Let me also note that, when characterizing their view, expressivists tend to offer accounts not of what it is for a moral claim to be true but what it is for someone to judge, accept, or *say* that a claim is true. Although I believe this tendency obscures the important issues that divide expressivists from realists, in my characterization of their view I have not marked this distinction.

stick, realists would need to furnish an additional argument that theirs is the better interpretation of the Normative Claim, which they do not.

This response seems to me correct as far as it goes. Advocates of the Moorean-style argument cannot simply assume that the robust reading is correct. Still, I doubt that this response goes far enough, since it threatens to relocate the problem to which the Moorean-style Objection draws our attention. To see this, it is helpful to have firmly in mind the strategy that defenders of the Motivation Argument employ. When faced with the Moorean-style Objection, defenders of the Motivation Argument propose that we take the argument's first premise at face value; the claim that moral judgments are intrinsically motivating says exactly what it appears to say. They then suggest that the Normative Claim is different, for it admits of two interpretations—one which assumes that moral concepts are descriptive, the other of which does not. Under the first interpretation—the robust reading— the Normative Claim should be rejected, for it is incompatible with the claim that moral judgments are intrinsically motivating. Under the second—the deflated reading—it is not. Defenders of this strategy then propose to accept both the claim that moral judgments are intrinsically motivating and the Normative Claim, albeit the latter under the deflated reading.

It will be convenient to have a way of referring to this last combination of claims, which conjoins the claim that moral judgments are intrinsically motivating with the Normative Claim under the deflated reading. Let us call it the *expressivist pairing*. Those who advocate the expressivist pairing, such as Blackburn, often advertise it as the natural position to accept.[30] In a moment I will indicate why this strikes me as dubious. In the meanwhile, the point I wish to press is that employing this strategy is risky, for realists can mimic it to achieve their own ends. It is a gambit that can be played by two.

To see the point, consider a realist who says that there is a default reading of the Normative Claim, which is its face-value sense. According to the face-value interpretation, the Normative Claim says exactly what it seems to say: gratuitous promise-breaking has the property of being necessarily wrong. To accept the Normative

---

30. Blackburn (1998), ch. 3, and (2005), ch. 5.

Claim, accordingly, is not simply to issue a first-order moral judgment in which one condemns promise-breaking. Rather, it is to attribute *being wrong* to gratuitous promise-breaking. In this regard, realists maintain, accepting the Normative Claim is exactly like making other ordinary normative judgments. Consider, for example, judgments such as *you are required to file an affidavit within 24 hours* or *one ought to avoid playing a diminished scale against a major seventh chord*. Virtually no one maintains that to judge that one is required to file an affidavit within 24 hours is merely to endorse the action of filing an affidavit within 24 hours. For, among other things, one could be deeply averse to performing this action. If so, realists maintain, we have strong reason to accept the face-value reading of the Normative Claim. The reason is that, on the face of things, what goes for the semantics of other normative judgments should also go for ethical ones. In the next chapter, I will develop this point in more detail. For now, it is enough to see that if the deflated reading were correct, then this sort of parity would not hold.[31]

Realists, then, maintain that we should accept the Normative Claim under its face-value interpretation. They then propose to disambiguate the claim that moral judgments are intrinsically motivating. This claim, realists maintain, admits of two readings.

Under the first—call it *the descriptive reading*—it says what proponents of the Motivation Argument claim: it is impossible that an agent judge that she morally ought to act in a certain way and not be motivated to act in that way. However, under the second reading—call it *the normative reading*—the claim that moral judgments are intrinsically motivating is implicitly normative. Under this interpretation, the first premise of the Motivation Argument says something like:

> Moral judgments are intrinsically motivating: it is conceptually necessary that if an agent judges that she morally ought to act in a certain way, then she is motivated to some degree to act in that way, provided that her judgment is well-formed.

In principle, realists can understand the "well-formedness" of moral judgments in different ways. One such way is to take inspiration from

---

31. Chrisman (2011) presses a similar point in a different context.

Gibbard, supposing that operative within ordinary agents are two types of system.[32] On the one hand is the representational system, which is roughly a cluster of capacities whose aim is to represent the world in certain ways—the outputs of which include judgments. On the other is the motivational system, which is roughly a constellation of propensities to be moved to act in certain ways, which include instincts, desires, and emotions of various sorts. These two systems do not operate independently of one another. Rather, they work together when outputs from the representational system, such as the belief that an action would be fatal to one's loved ones, yield appropriate affective states, such as fear or aversion. A well-formed judgment, we can say, is the output of these two systems working together as they should.

Moral judgments, according to this way of seeing things, can also be well-formed. They are well-formed when beliefs such as that an action is required yield motivational states of the appropriate sort, such as a desire or intention to perform that action. If this is right, were a judgment that an action is required fail to yield such an affective state, then it would be malformed; it would be like a belief that an action would be fatal to one's loved ones but nonetheless fails to yield any desire to prevent it.

For present purposes we need not develop the details of this type of approach—although we could, in principle, do so in several ways. The important point to see is that realists have available a strategy that mimics that used by expressivists. This strategy consists in taking the Normative Claim at face value, interpreting it as expressing genuine moral propositional content. It then dictates that we disambiguate the first premise of the Motivation Argument, distinguishing two interpretations—the descriptive reading, on the one hand, and the normative reading, on the other. Under the first interpretation, the claim that moral judgments are intrinsically motivating should be rejected, for it is incompatible with the Normative Claim (at least if the Motivation Argument goes through). Under the second interpretation, the claim that moral judgments are intrinsically motivating is not incompatible with the Normative Claim. Defenders of this strategy then propose to

32. Gibbard (1990), ch. 4. See also Blackburn (1998), 131.

accept both the Normative Claim and the claim that moral judgments are intrinsically motivating, albeit only under the second, normative reading.

For ease of reference, let us call this last combination of claims the *realist pairing*. While there is evidence, I believe, for accepting the realist pairing, accepting it might come at a theoretical price.[33] Perhaps in some respects it is less elegant than the expressivist pairing. If this were right, both the expressivist and the realist pairings would display theoretical imperfections. Be that as it may, the resulting situation with which we are left is this.

The Motivation Argument presents a challenge to moral realism, one which appeals to the intrinsically motivating character of moral judgments. But the argument goes through—and avoids the Moorean-style Objection—only if we accept what I have called the expressivist pairing. This pairing, recall, involves accepting the first premise of the Motivation Argument at face value but the Normative Claim under the deflated reading. However, we have seen that there is another way to approach the argument, which consists in accepting what I have called the realist pairing. This pairing consists in accepting the Normative Claim at face value and the normative reading of the first premise of the Motivation Argument. Accepting the realist pairing allows us to hold that moral judgments are intrinsically motivating without being committed to a view that succumbs to either the Motivation Argument or the Moorean-style Objection.

Which pairing should we accept? The Motivation Argument itself will not settle the issue. If so, this argument is not a reason to accept the mixed view. At this point in the dialectic, we need a new argument for why we should accept the expressivist pairing rather than the realist one.

Let me summarize the objection I have developed. Reflection on ordinary moral thought and practice seems to reveal that:

> Moral judgments are intrinsically motivating: it is conceptually necessary that if an agent judges that she morally ought to act in a certain way, then she is motivated to some degree to act in that way.

33. For some of the evidence, see Roskies (2003).

It also seems to reveal that:

It is wrong to break one's promise simply because one feels like it.

Proponents of the Motivation Argument reject this second claim on the basis of the first. The Moorean-style Objection charges that doing so would be arbitrary. Why, after all, should not we argue the reverse, rejecting the claim that moral judgments are intrinsically motivating on the strength of the Normative Claim?

This charge of arbitrariness could, in principle, be satisfactorily addressed. Friends of the Motivation Argument propose to do so by accepting the expressivist pairing, according to which we accept the claim that moral judgments are intrinsically motivating at face value but offer a deflated reading of the Normative Claim. Realists counter, however, by presenting the realist pairing, according to which we accept the Normative Claim at face value but offer a normative construal of the claim that moral judgments are intrinsically motivating.[34] To generate the results they want, proponents of the Motivation Argument must accept the expressivist pairing. But it is difficult to identify a reason why they should. The Motivation Argument itself offers no support for accepting this pairing. Indeed, in the next chapter, I will argue that there are reasons emanating from the mixed view itself for rejecting it.

In summary

This completes the presentation of the dilemma that I take the mixed view to face. If sound, the argument either throws the existence of practice-based normative features into question or yields the result that some prominent arguments for moral antirealism are infected by methodological arbitrariness. As I mentioned earlier, my aim has not been to consider the full catalogue of arguments offered in favor of moral antirealism, only a sample of the most prominent ones. Still, with a little thought, I believe that the general strategy

---

34. Expressivists could, I believe, accept a normative interpretation of the claim that moral judgments are intrinsically motivating. Blackburn (2001), for example, gestures at such a reading. This reading, however, would not provide any reason to reject realism.

could be extended to other arguments against realism, such as the so-called argument from supervenience and at least some versions of the argument from disagreement.[35]

35. Blackburn (1993), chs. 6 and 7, offer the classic formulations of the Supervenience Argument. One lesson of Enoch (2011), ch. 8, is that identifying a version of the argument from disagreement that has bite but does not depend essentially on key premises from other arguments, such as what I have called the Knowledge Argument, is difficult. Loeb (1998) maintains that the best version of the argument rests on empirical claims about the scope and nature of moral disagreement. Specifically, any such argument would rest on the following pair of claims: first, that moral disagreement is systemic and apparently irresolvable, and second, that this disagreement is not primarily rooted in differences regarding the non-moral facts. I suspect that a version of the argument that rests on these empirical claims would escape the dilemma that I have pressed in this chapter. But, as Loeb himself points out, we do not know whether these empirical claims are true. If so, the empirically based argument from disagreement is inconclusive, as it awaits the type of empirical support it needs to go through.

5
Against the Mixed View
Part II

The Postmaster General has rights, responsibilities, and obligations of various sorts, including the right to hire and fire US postal employees and the obligation to oversee consumer complaints. Those under the Postmaster General's authority—the US postal employees—also have rights, responsibilities, and obligations in virtue of being US postal employees, such as the right to take ten holidays per year and the obligation to submit to regular drug testing. These normative features are a species of what I have called practice-based rights, responsibilities, and obligations, having their home in the modern social practice of delivering and receiving mail.

Of course, practice-based rights, responsibilities, and obligations are not limited to those employed by the US Postal Service and other institutions. You and I, for example, participate in the discursive practices of giving and receiving promises, giving and receiving requests, and performing and responding to assertions. As participants in these practices, we also have rights, responsibilities, and obligations, such as the right to issue assertions about the weather and request the time. What sorts of rights, responsibilities, and obligations are these? Friends of the mixed view maintain that they are not moral, as we have sufficient independent reason to believe that moral facts do not exist. Hence the "mixed" character of the view: while there are all manner of normative facts, there are no moral ones.

In the previous chapter, I argued that we should reject the mixed view, presenting its advocates with a dilemma. Consider, I said, the most prominent arguments for holding that moral facts do not exist.

These arguments, I suggested, fall into two categories. On the one hand, there are those that, if sound, would provide reason to reject apparent truisms such as:

The Normative Claim: It is morally wrong to break one's promise simply because one feels like it.

But these arguments, I contend, would also provide equally good reason to reject the existence of practice-based norms, such as those that attach to the Postmaster General and US postal employees. This is problematic, I claimed, because moral antirealists are naturally understood to embrace the mixed view. While they reject the existence of moral facts, they do not deny that the Postmaster General has the obligation to oversee consumer complaints or that you and I have the legal right to receive a fair trial.

On the other hand, there are those arguments against realism that, if sound, would provide reason to reject propositions such as the Normative Claim but would provide no independent reason to reject practice-based norms. These arguments, I claimed, are subject to what I called the *Moorean-style Objection*, since it is difficult to see why we should accept certain intuitively plausible claims about the moral realm—such as the claim that moral judgments are intrinsically motivating—while rejecting others—such as the Normative Claim. While this charge of arbitrariness could, in principle, be satisfactorily addressed, I have argued that it is not. Since neither rejecting the existence of practice-based norms nor methodological arbitrariness is acceptable, the mixed view should be rejected.

A piece of unfinished business, however, remains. For what emerged from our discussion is that the mixed view can be paired with different understandings of the nature of moral concepts. Many combine the mixed view with concept descriptivism, maintaining that normative thought is representational across the board. Those who defend this position claim that not only do judgments that, say, pertain to legal rights, responsibilities, and obligations function descriptively, but so also do moral ones. For the most part, it is this combination of views on which I have had my eye. However, other philosophers, such as expressivists, combine the mixed view with the thesis that moral thought is not representational. Under the most natural interpretation, these philosophers maintain that normative

thought comes in two distinct kinds. That which pertains to prosaic
normative features, such as legal rights, responsibilities, and obligations is representational, having as its normative representational
content rights, responsibilities, and obligations. By contrast, that
which pertains to morality is not; such thought does not even purport to represent moral reality.

Or so I conjecture. To my knowledge, expressivists have not explicitly addressed the issue of how, according to their view, we should
characterize practice-based normative judgments, such as those that
appear to concern the rights of the Postmaster General. Still, as I
pointed out in the previous chapter, there is reason to believe that
expressivists would not reject important parts of the characterization
of their view that I have offered, if only because their view is not
easily extended to cover practice-based normative judgments. For
suppose that the basic expressivist analysis of moral judgments were
correct: when you judge that you are morally obligated to act in a
certain way, this judgment consists not in your grasping a moral
proposition with normative representational content but in endorsing that way of acting in light of its descriptive features, which
might include its being such as to bring about the best consequences.
Imagine that we were to extend this analysis to, say, legal judgments.
The resulting view would be one according to which, when you judge
that you are legally required to act in a certain way, this judgment
consists not in grasping a proposition with normative representational content—one that purports to represent the fact that you are
legally required to act in that way. Rather, the judgment consists in
endorsing a way of acting in light of certain of its descriptive features, which might include its being such that if you do not perform
it you will likely be punished. There is, however, no plausibility whatsoever to the claim that when you competently judge that you are
legally required to pay a considerable parking fine, your judgment
consists in endorsing paying that fine in light of some cluster of descriptive features, such as those that I just mentioned. For you may
deeply resent being required to pay the fine and be entirely un-
moved to do it.

In this chapter, I want to engage with the expressivist view further.
My reason for doing so is this: there are two ways, I said earlier, to block
the argument from cases offered in Chapter 3. One is to maintain

that, appearances to the contrary, propositions such as the Normative Claim are false. A second way to block the argument, which is embraced by expressivists, is to contest the assumption that moral concepts are descriptive. If this last approach were successful, the argument from cases would collapse. For this argument hinges on the assumption that what best explains the fact that we appeal to moral concepts when categorizing the rights, responsibilities, and obligations of being a speaker is that there are moral features to which those concepts refer.

At the end of the previous chapter, I voiced misgivings with expressivism, contending that the main argument offered in its favor fails. My task in this short chapter is to put more pressure on this view. I want to argue not simply that we have not been given good enough reasons to accept expressivism, but also that we have reason to reject it. If this challenge stands, then so also does the argument from cases.

I Characterizing concept expressivism

There is a traditional view about the nature of concepts, running from Aristotle through Frege, which many philosophers find attractive. Concepts, according to this position, are not mental states, mental images, sentences in the head, or anything of the sort. Rather, they are abstract, sharable, mind-independent ways of thinking about objects and their properties. Take, for example, the concept 'horse.' According to the traditional view, this concept is a way of thinking about horses, a shareable ability or device to refer to them, which you and I can employ in thought and language to think and communicate "horse thoughts" of various kinds. These "horse thoughts" are Fregean *Gedanken* or propositions, which are composed (at least in part) of concepts. As the traditional view has it, then, concepts are the building blocks or sub-components of (at least some) propositions. The proposition *that horses are often skittish,* for example, is (to simplify a bit) constituted by the concepts 'horse' and 'being skittish' bound together by the "predicative tie." If the traditional view of concepts is correct, it is because propositions are constituted by concepts, which are devices for referring, that someone's believing *that horses are often skittish* can be about the kind *horse*, attributing to its instances the property of *being skittish*.

Concept descriptivism—the view that moral concepts function descriptively—is naturally understood along Fregean lines. So understood, moral concepts are ways of thinking about moral features, such as rights, responsibilities, and obligations. These concepts, in turn, constitute our moral thoughts, the moral propositions. Expressivists reject this view, maintaining that moral concepts function not referentially but expressively. What, however, would an expressive concept be? And what would it be to deploy such a thing in moral thought?

For various reasons, these are not easy questions to answer. There are deep feuds about the nature of concepts, and expressivists tend not to explicitly tie their views to particular positions on their nature. Still, I think we cannot go too far wrong if we formulate an expressivist view by appeal to a view regarding moral concepts that borrows from the traditional view of concepts, attributing to expressivists the following position:

> **Concept Expressivism**: Moral concepts are abstract modes of approbation and disapprobation, ways of being for or against actions and persons. As such, moral concepts are abilities that we use not to refer to moral features but to express states of approbation and disapprobation toward actions and persons. When combined with descriptive concepts of various kinds, these expressive concepts form the content of moral judgments.

If this is right, to apply a normative concept such as 'being what one ought to do' to a given action is not to think of it as having a normative property *being what one ought to do*, but rather to express a way of being for that action. We do not have to look far, say concept expressivists, to find analogs to the ways in which moral concepts function. Suppose someone were to look at the boots you are wearing and say "That is a cool pair of boots." According to the expressivist view under consideration, we should resist the inclination to interpret this speech act as one in which an agent thinks that your boots have the property of *coolness*. Better to think of it as one in which an agent, in light of some of the boots' properties, simply expresses approbation or takes up a positive stance of a certain kind toward them, much in the way that an agent expresses gratitude toward you when she says "Thank you."

There are, I believe, important advantages to characterizing expressivism in this way, which I will not detail here.[1] It is enough for present purposes to have a way of thinking about expressivism according to which it is primarily a view about the way normative concepts work that stands in sharp contrast to the position embraced by concept descriptivists.

II Against concept expressivism

In the course of our daily comings and goings, you and I hear people utter all manner of normative sentences, such as:

> "You are required to file an affidavit within 24 hours."
>
> "You ought to use the fourth tone when singing today's sticheron."
>
> "You should never use a water glass to serve wine."
>
> "Unless you really know what you are doing, you should avoid playing a diminished scale against a major seventh chord."
>
> "If the play at second base is close, then the manager has a right to dispute the call."

For ease of reference, call the judgments expressed by sentences such as these "ought thoughts." While there is a considerable variety of ought thoughts, here is a constraint on an adequate metanormative theory about them:

> **Unity**: Other things being equal, if the normative judgments with regard to a domain K are representational, having as their content the

---

1. Thus formulated, concept expressivism is supposed to be structurally isomorphic with concept descriptivism. It implies that moral predicates do not express full-blown attitudes but the modes of approbation and disapprobation ingredient in the contents expressed by these attitudes. Schroeder (2008)—from which I borrow the locution "being for"—also formulates expressivism along these lines, arguing that expressivists can satisfactorily address the Frege/Geach problem(s) only if they understand their view to be committed to something similar to concept expressivism. It should be evident from what I say above that I find broadly Fregean ways of thinking about concepts helpful for understanding what concept descriptivists and expressivists believe. Nevertheless, I should emphasize that I employ Fregeanism primarily for ease of exposition. Both concept descriptivism and expressivism could also be understood using different ways of thinking about the nature of concepts.

putative rights, responsibilities, and obligations that constitute that domain, then the normative judgments with regard to another norma- tive domain K' are also representational, having as their content the putative rights, responsibilities, and obligations that constitute that domain. In a phrase, all else being equal, a metanormative theory should offer a unified account of ought thoughts, especially when these ought thoughts exhibit very similar logical and semantic properties.

Let me explain why I believe that Unity is a plausible thesis.

Unity is, in the first place, not a thesis about normative terms such as "ought." Nor is it (in the first instance) a thesis about normative concepts such as 'ought.' Unity does not rest, then, on the assump- tion that if a certain term or concept makes a semantic contribution of one sort in one context, then we have reason to believe that it makes the same contribution in other contexts.[2] If that assumption were true, then Unity would be much less plausible. We do not have reason to believe, for example, that because gendered pronouns such as "he" and "she" refer to gender properties when we use them to talk about humans, they also refer to gender properties when we use them to talk about hurricanes or bicycles. Hurricanes and bi- cycles do not have any sort of gender, despite what many languages might lead us to suppose.

Unity is instead a thesis about the character of normative judg- ments. Its plausibility rests, in part, on the following three assump- tions. First, a central role of normative judgments, such as those expressed by the sentences offered above, is practical. It is to guide us in action and to aid us in evaluating an action by helping us to determine whether certain activities have been performed well or involve mistakes of certain kinds. When, for example, an agent judges that she ought to use the fourth tone when singing a sticheron, she is not merely employing the "predictive ought" or making a claim about what is statistically normal. Rather, her judgment concerns standards of correctness intrinsic to Byzantine chant that

---

2. Here I do not presuppose what I have called the traditional view of concepts. If the traditional view is correct, it is, I believe, plausible to hold that if a concept makes a semantic contribution of one sort in one context, then we have excellent reason to believe that it makes the same contribution in other contexts.

can be used to guide and evaluate the activity of singing Byzantine chant.

Second, in a large range of cases we determine how to act or to evaluate behavior by forming judgments that represent normative standards that are intrinsic to social practices such as baseball and Byzantine chant. It is in virtue of the fact that an agent's judgment accurately represents the standards of Byzantine chant that she can correctly evaluate the behavior of those singing a sticheron. If this is right, the judgments expressed by the sentences mentioned previously are naturally viewed as having normative representational content.

And third, it is not obvious that central cases of normative judgments, such as legal and moral ones, lack normative representational content. To the contrary, by all appearances, they have such content, as they bear all the earmarks of being ordinary propositions whose constituent concepts play referential roles. In this regard, legal and moral judgments are different from some judgments that are expressed by the use of gendered pronouns, such as those that concern hurricanes and bicycles, since these judgments obviously do not designate gendered properties or objects.

Suppose for these reasons that Unity is a plausible thesis. Concept descriptivism, it is worth noting, satisfies Unity. For, according to this view, normative thoughts have genuine normative representational content. Expressivism, by contrast, does not satisfy Unity. For, to say it again, expressivists are not skeptics about practice-based normativity. Under a natural construal, these philosophers do not deny that there are such things as legal rights, responsibilities, and obligations. Expressivists are, then, plausibly understood to maintain that our thoughts regarding the rights, responsibilities, and obligations that constitute the law or the game of baseball have genuine normative representational content, purporting to represent the rights, responsibilities, and obligations that constitute these domains. Yet these philosophers deny that moral judgments have genuine normative representational content. The challenge is to explain why this should be so—why normative judgments should come in two entirely different varieties, even though they behave, for all intents and purposes, very similarly. Under the further

assumption that expressivists will have to provide a semantics that
reflects this difference in the nature of ought thoughts, expressivists
may have to furnish two entirely different semantics of ought
thoughts: one that is expressivist, another that is not. That would be
a significant theoretical burden. At the very least, it should make us
wary of the claim, which is sometimes made, that expressivist positions are simpler than their cognitivist cousins.[3]

The question that faces expressivists, then, is what it is about moral
ought thoughts that would make it seem plausible to hold that they
lack normative representational content. Here is one possible answer that is available to expressivists:

> The norms that constitute domains such as baseball and Byzantine
> chant are conventional. Arguably, however, conventional normativity
> is unproblematic. We can offer a thoroughly naturalistic account of
> the rights, responsibilities, and obligations that constitute games such
> as baseball and Byzantine chant—one according to which their na-
> ture can be completely specified in terms of conventional rules. Since
> we can do this, it would be unsurprising were judgments concerning
> these domains to have normative representational content. But the
> realm of morality is different. Unlike conventional normativity, mor-
> ality appears to be problematic since, were there moral features, then
> we could not offer a satisfactory naturalistic account of them. Since
> we cannot do this, it would be surprising if moral judgments were to
> have normative representational content; there would, after all, be
> no naturalistically respectable story about how moral judgments
> could represent normative reality. If so, there is reason to believe that
> Unity does not pose a deep challenge to expressivism—a reason for
> believing that, when it comes to moral matters, other things are not
> equal.

I find it difficult to assess this response. The problem is that philosophers operate with widely different understandings of what a
properly naturalistic understanding of normativity would be. Suppose, for example, oughts were to play robust explanatory roles.
Would that be enough to earn them naturalistic credentials? Some
philosophers, including those suspicious of moral naturalism, seem

3. See Gibbard (2003), especially 180–1. Schroeder (2008), ch. 7, argues that expressivists must accept a unified semantics according to which all judgments (not simply the
normative ones) receive an expressivistic treatment. This project, Schroeder maintains, ultimately comes to grief.

to think so.[4] Or suppose, somewhat differently, we were to identify rules of thumb, the conformance to which would allow us to do such things as praise, blame, and coordinate our actions in certain ways, thereby allowing social life to go better for most. Would that render them naturalistically acceptable? Again, some philosophers, such as the moral naturalists, seem to think so. If these philosophers are right, the line of argument articulated above does not go through; there simply is not enough reason to believe that conventional normativity is naturalistically respectable while non-conventional normativity is not. For non-conventional normative features might play robust explanatory roles, including that of being ingredient in count-generation.

But perhaps we can spell out the underlying idea behind the expressivist response somewhat differently by returning to a distinction alluded to in Chapter 1, namely, that between lean (or prosaic) normativity, on the one hand, and robust normativity, on the other. While this distinction is not easy to articulate precisely, the following will do for our purposes.

Let us say that a system of putative rights, responsibilities, and obligations is *normative in the lean sense* just in case it does not necessarily imply reasons such that an agent ought, on the whole, to conform to the rights, responsibilities, and obligations that constitute that system. Examples of such a system would be baseball or Byzantine chant. We do not hold, for example, that the responsibilities that attach to Major League Baseball players necessarily provide conclusive reasons for them to act in certain ways. In fact, we can think of cases—such as when a Major League player no longer cares about playing the game because he has better things to do—in which these responsibilities provide no reason to act at all. By contrast, a system of putative rights, responsibilities, and obligations is *normative in the robust sense* just in case it necessarily (but perhaps defeasibly) implies reasons such that an agent ought, on the whole, to conform to the rights, responsibilities, and obligations that constitute that system. Although there are no uncontroversial examples of such systems, many philosophers hold that the moral domain is normative in the robust sense.

---

4. See Wedgwood (2007), ch. 8, in this regard, which argues that mental facts of certain kinds are causally efficacious in virtue of their normative properties.

Suppose that these philosophers are right: while there are some domains, such as baseball and Byzantine chant, which are normative in the lean sense, there are others, such as morality, which are normative in the robust sense. Were we to grant this, then perhaps there is the sort of disanalogy we are looking for. Perhaps practices such as baseball and Byzantine chant are naturalistically acceptable, since they are normative only in the lean sense, while practices such as morality are not, since they are normative in the robust sense. And perhaps this difference could explain why, according to expressivists, lean normative judgments have normative representational content but moral thoughts do not. Perhaps, that is, there is something about morality's being robustly normative that would explain why morality is naturalistically problematic and, hence, why moral thought lacks normative representational content.

Of course, expressivists and realists will disagree about how to understand robust normativity and what it is for someone to form judgments with regard to a robustly normative domain such as morality. Realists ordinarily hold that when an agent competent with normative concepts judges that she is morally required to act in a certain way, she will presuppose or take it for granted that this requirement has the property of favoring or justifying her acting in a certain way. (As I noted in the previous chapter, this thesis is compatible with the view that all moral reasons are Humean. In that case, these presuppositions would be false.) Expressivists, by contrast, will reject such an account. They will say that when an agent forms such a judgment, she does not presuppose or take it for granted that there is an obligation that has the property of favoring or justifying the action.[5] Rather, according to expressivists, when an agent forms such a judgment she is doing something else, such as commending or endorsing that action.

There is, then, a deep difference between the ways that realists and expressivists think of robust normativity. For present purposes, however, we can remain neutral regarding the best way to under-

---

5. This is not quite accurate, as I indicate in the discussion of deflationism in the next chapter. For now, however, I bracket the various ways in which expressivists can accommodate talk of moral properties, noting that such talk is the final layer added to the expressivist project of explaining how the content of moral judgments could so closely mimic ordinary representational content.

stand it, focusing instead on this question: If morality were a robustly normative domain, would that explain why moral thoughts—or at least a certain range of them—lack normative representational content?

The best way to address this question, I believe, is to distinguish two types of expressivism regarding a domain R that is robustly normative. Call the first view *comprehensive expressivism*. Comprehensive expressivists hold that R-normative judgments—judgments that pertain to some robustly normative domain—have no normative representational content. For example, according to this view, the judgment expressed by the sentence "I am obligated to Φ" has no normative representational content, as it does not purport to be about an obligation. Rather, it expresses endorsement of Φing or an endorsement of Φing inasmuch as it bears one or another relation to some other non-normative property, which might include its being such as to maximize happiness. Let us call the second view *restricted expressivism*. Restricted expressivists accept a more nuanced position. They maintain that some R-judgments have genuine normative representation content, namely, those that concern the rights, responsibilities, and obligations that constitute robustly normative systems. They deny, however, that other normative judgments have such content, namely, those that pertain to the reasons implied by the rights, responsibilities, and obligations that constitute such systems—what we can call the *robust reasons*.

Neither of these views, I believe, offers a satisfactory response to Unity. Begin with comprehensive expressivism. Suppose that I form the R-normative moral judgment that:

I am obligated to Φ.

Suppose, further, that this judgment necessarily implies that I have a robust reason to Φ. It would not follow from this, however, that:

The content of my judgment that I am obligated to Φ lacks normative representational content, as it does not purport to represent a moral obligation.

For the fact that a judgment is robust reason-implying is not itself a reason to believe that that judgment itself is devoid of normative representational content, failing to represent an obligation.

We can, I believe, throw this last point into sharper relief by re-calling how expressivists think of reason judgments. Roughly put, expressivists tell us that, for an agent to judge that she has a reason to Φ, is for her to endorse Φing. Now suppose, once again, that I form the R-normative judgment that:

I am obligated to Φ.

Suppose, also, that competence with the normative concepts in ques-tion requires that I endorse Φing. It would not follow from this last claim that my judgment that I am obligated to Φ lacks normative representational content, failing to represent an obligation. Indeed, as far as I can see, it provides no reason whatsoever to believe this. If this is right, the fact that certain R-normative judgments (the true ones) imply robust reasons does not provide any reason to believe that those judgments themselves are devoid of normative represen-tational content, failing to represent rights, responsibilities, and obligations.

Let me reiterate, finally, that there appears to be no special epis-temological mystery that we must countenance if we allow that moral judgments have genuine normative representational content. For, presumably, any story we tell about how we grasp rights, responsibil-ities, and obligations of the lean sort, we can also tell about how we could grasp rights, responsibilities, and obligations of the robust reason-implying sort. For example, as I will suggest in Chapter 7, we might get a cognitive grip on both sorts of normative feature by spe-cifying the explanatory roles they play and the conceptual relations they bear to one another.

Let us now consider restricted expressivism, which implies that some R-normative judgments have normative representational content. Specifically, restrictive expressivists hold that those judg-ments concerning the rights, responsibilities, and obligations that constitute robust normative systems, such as the moral system, have genuine normative representational content. Nonetheless, they deny that other R-normative judgments have similar content. They deny, for example, that those normative judgments that concern robust reasons or oughts, which are implied by the rights, respon-sibilities, and obligations that constitute robustly normative do-mains, have normative representational content.

What should we say about this position? Well, suppose, once again, I form the R-normative judgment that:

I am obligated to Φ.

Suppose, also, that this judgment is reason-implying, committing the agent to robust reasons. The fact that this judgment is robust reason-implying would not itself, however, imply that:

> The content of any robust-reason judgment I might form or take for granted upon judging that I am obligated to Φ—such as the judgment expressed by the sentence "I thereby have a decisive reason to Φ"— lacks normative representational content.

For the fact that a judgment is robust reason-implying is not itself a reason to believe that judgments regarding those reasons themselves are devoid of normative representational content.

In his earlier work, Gibbard developed an expressivist view according to which there are systems of norms that allow, forbid, and require actions of various sorts.[6] When Gibbard's talk of systems of norms is taken at face value, his view is plausibly understood to be a version of restricted expressivism. Those judgments that pertain to what is allowed, forbidden, and required have normative representational content, while those that concern robust reasons do not. But why, according to Gibbard, would judgments that pertain to robust reasons lack normative representational content? Gibbard offers an answer in the following well-known passage:

> What, though, of the special element that makes normative thought and language normative? There is such an element, I am claiming, and it involves a kind of endorsement—an endorsement that any descriptivistic analysis treats inadequately. The problem is not merely that every time one loophole in the analysis is closed, others remain. It is that a single loophole remains unpluggable by descriptivistic analysis.[7]

---

6. Gibbard (1990). I find Gibbard's own characterization of these norms elusive, as he simply says that they are imperatives or "linguistically encoded" precepts (46, 57, 70). Under the most natural construal, imperatives are not sentences but speech act types. Presumably, though, the norms in question are neither speech act types nor determined thereby.

7. Gibbard (1990), 33. See also 10.

This reply, however, would not establish that robust reason judgments—genuinely "normative" judgments, to use Gibbard's terminology—lack normative representational content. It establishes merely that they must involve endorsement. In principle, such judgments could involve both. This last position is defended by hybrid expressivists of certain kinds.[8]

In his later work, Gibbard supplements this last line of argument, writing that ought thoughts are not "beliefs about a special property, a property of *to-be-doneness* or of being the thing to do."[9] The reason is that a property such as *being what one ought to do* would not help to explain the choices we make or the ways we act. If this is true, Gibbard says, then there is no need to say that when an agent judges that she ought on the whole to act in a certain way she thereby grasps the property *being what she ought to do*. However, once this property drops out, then—the claim is—so also does the need to appeal to normative representational content regarding robust reasons.[10]

We should not, I believe, be moved by this argument. For consider, once again, normative judgments that pertain to rights, responsibilities, and obligations. By all appearances, these judgments play an explanatory role, as they help to guide and evaluate behavior. By determining that I have a legal obligation to submit an affidavit in the next 24 hours, for example, I can decide what to do. Now consider judgments regarding robust reasons. Were concept descriptivism regarding robust reason judgments true, these judgments would also guide and evaluate behavior by registering where the balance of reasons lies. If I ascertain, for example, that my colleague has a decisive reason to file an affidavit in the next 24 hours, I can determine whether he is liable to correction or blame if he fails to do so. If this is right, we should not deny that robust reason judgments lack normative representational content because such content would not explain why we act in the ways that we do.

---

8. See, for example, Copp (2001); Hare (2003); Boisvert (2008), and Schroeder (2009).
9. Gibbard (2003), 50. Gibbard qualifies his claim by maintaining that "at the outset" we do not want to explain ought thoughts as beliefs with normative representational content.
10. See Gibbard (2003), especially 10, 50, and 180–1. See also Blackburn (1998), 87.

III Summary

The argument from cases rests on the assumption that moral concepts function descriptively, purporting to represent moral reality. Expressivists reject this understanding of moral concepts, contending that moral concepts are abilities or devices that we use not to refer to moral features but to express states of approbation and disapprobation toward actions and persons. In this chapter and the previous, I have offered a two-pronged case against this view. The first prong, which I developed toward the end of the last chapter, has been to argue that the main argument offered in favor of expressivism—the Motivation Argument—fails. The second prong, which I have presented in this chapter, has been to pose a challenge to expressivism, charging that the view fails to satisfy Unity. According to this challenge, there is nothing about the nature of naturalism or robust normativity that should lead us to believe that ought thoughts come in two radically different sorts: those with normative representational content and those without such content. I conclude that, all else being equal, we should reject concept expressivism in favor of concept descriptivism. We should not, then, reject the argument from cases offered in the previous chapter because this argument presupposes an understanding of concepts that expressivists reject.

6

Three Antirealist Views

A judge utters the phrase "Guilty!" and your future looks much different than it did a moment ago. A colleague sends you a note that reads "Would you read the most recent draft of my paper on health-care reform?" and you now owe her a prompt response. A friend begins a sentence with the preface "I have never told anyone this before…" and you now must negotiate a delicate situation. In the blink of an eye, the performance of the seemingly innocuous action of uttering an ordinary English sentence completely alters our world. How could this be so?

The answer, I have argued, does not merely reside in the fact that by performing linguistic acts we exert causal influence over one another by doing such things as angering or delighting each other. Rather, I have claimed, it also consists in the fact that by performing such acts we alter our normative position with respect to one another, generating rights, responsibilities, and obligations that were not present prior to their performance. When, for example, a judge utters the phrase "Guilty!" under normal conditions, he has not only exercised his standing power to render verdicts, laying himself open to correction if things are not as he presents them. He has also brought it about that you no longer have rights that you did prior to his pronouncement. In this and many other ways, speech is normatively transformative; our world is changed by the introduction of new rights, responsibilities, and obligations into our lives. The central aim of my discussion has been to build a case for moral realism by deploying this insight.

The case proceeds in three stages. In the first stage (Chapters 1 and 2), I argued for the normative theory of speech, maintaining that having the rights, responsibilities, and obligations of being a speaker is ingredient in the count-generation of speech. In the second stage (Chapter 3), I claimed that a wide range of these rights, responsibilities, and obligations is plausibly viewed as being moral. The argument for this claim, recall, is one to the best explanation. What best explains the fact that a perspicuous account of the normative features ingredient in speech requires appeal to moral concepts, I argued, is that there are moral features that satisfy these concepts. This argument to the best explanation could be blocked, however, if we had independent reason to believe that there are no moral facts or that moral concepts do not function descriptively. In the argument's third stage (Chapters 4 and 5), I maintained that the most prominent arguments to reject the existence of moral facts fail and that we have good reason to believe that moral concepts are descriptive.

My project in this chapter is to explore the implications of this three-stage argument for moral antirealism. My strategy for doing so is to divide antirealist positions into three kinds: error theory, expressivism, and constructivism—particular versions of moral antirealism being such as to belong to at most one of these kinds. I begin by stating the challenge that the argument developed so far poses to each of these views. I then consider various ways that proponents of these antirealist views might respond. This strategy has the advantage of addressing two gaps in the discussion. First, it addresses the possibility that the phenomenon I have called speech is considerably different from how I have described it, since it is not normative in any interesting sense. And second, it speaks to the concern that the Speech Act Argument—at least to the extent that I have presented it—does not imply that moral features should be understood as realists believe. Both of these concerns, I contend, can be satisfactorily addressed.

I Error theories

Widely regarded as the most radical version of moral antirealism, error-theoretic views about morality accept the following two claims:

There are no moral facts (in the realist's sense or in any other).

Ordinary moral thought and discourse purport to represent moral facts but fail to do so, since there are none.[1]

The second of these claims is that in virtue of which the error theory earns its name: inasmuch as ordinary moral thought and discourse purport to represent moral reality but fail, they are, say error theorists, deeply and systematically mistaken. The character of the mistake is variously described. According to some error theorists, the failure of ordinary moral thought and discourse to represent moral reality implies that their content is, by and large, false. According to others, the failure consists not in the fact that the content of such thought and discourse is by and large false, but that it fails to refer (and, thus, is neither true nor false). Either way, the claim is that moral thought and discourse are systematically mistaken. Neither achieves its aim of accurately representing moral reality.

The objection I would like to put to the error theory directly falls out of the argumentation I have offered thus far. It runs as follows: suppose we say that an agent can speak just in case she can, in ordinary speech situations, perform a wide range of speech acts, such as asserting, promising, commanding, requesting, adjourning, entreating, and so on. All of us (ordinary adults in ordinary speech situations) speak. But if so, then we have the rights, responsibilities, and requirements of being a speaker. However, if we have these rights, responsibilities, and obligations, then moral facts exist, for a significant range of these rights, responsibilities, and obligations is moral. If an error-theoretic view of morality were true, however, then there would be no moral features and, so, no moral facts. And, thus, we could not speak. But we do speak. So, error-theoretic views are false.

I believe this objection to be decisive against error-theoretic views. But the moves it makes are swift—perhaps too swift to generate conviction. So, let me consider two strategies to which error theorists might appeal in reply. The first strategy, which I will call the "soft-line reply," maintains that error theorists can satisfactorily reply to the

---

1. See, for example, Mackie (1977), ch. 1; Joyce (2001) and (2006); and Olson (2011b). Joyce combines his view with a fictionalist account of moral discourse, about which I will have something to say shortly. I am using the term "represent" as a success term; to represent is to do so accurately.

Speech Act Argument by accepting a close enough approximation to the normative theory. Although the soft-line reply is supposed to vindicate the claim that we speak, philosophers who advocate this position deny that speaking requires that agents have rights, responsibilities, and obligations. By contrast, the second strategy, which I will call the "hard-line reply," offers a response that rejects the normative theory full stop, maintaining that we do not speak. Both these replies imply that the phenomenon that I have called speech is very different from how I have described it.

The soft-line reply

Let us begin with the soft-line reply. Proponents of this position wish to preserve some of what the normative theory says about speech without committing themselves to the claim that normative features are ingredient in its count-generation. How might they do that? Well, suppose normative theorists were to assemble a list of conditions necessary and sufficient for the performance of a speech act such as promising. This list would include the claims that, when promising, an agent takes responsibility for states of affairs such as

   his intending to do as he says he will,

and

   his having the standing power to lay an obligation of the relevant sort on himself.

Different versions of the normative theory will include different items on their list. But all will emphasize that it is the phenomenon of taking responsibility for a state of affairs that lies at the heart of speech.

   Now suppose proponents of the soft-line reply were to compile a similar list of conditions. They could include on it many of the claims included on the normative theorists' list. But proponents of the soft-line reply could not include on their list the claim that an agent takes responsibility for states of affairs such as those mentioned above. For that—at least if the argument offered in Chapters 2 and 3 is correct—would commit them to there being moral rights, responsibilities, and obligations, which would be tantamount to surrendering their view. These philosophers could, however, include on their list the claim that an agent *takes himself* or *intends* to take responsibility for various states of affairs, such as his having an intention to do what he says he will. In doing so, advocates of the soft-line reply would simply be applying the following general strategy: when the normative theorist appeals to the phenomenon of an agent's taking responsibility for a state of affairs to account for the performance of a speech act, appeal instead to the phenomenon of an agent's taking himself to take responsibility for a state of affairs to account for the performance of that speech act. In their response to Searle's famous article "How to Derive Ought from Is," some philosophers have recommended something like this position. Parfit, for example, maintains that Searle was wrong to assume that laying an obligation on oneself is constitutive of promising. To promise, Parfit has suggested, one need only intend or take oneself to do so—provided, of course, that other relevant conditions for promising hold.[2]

Is the phenomenon of taking oneself to take responsibility for a state of affairs the sort of thing that could count-generate speech? I doubt it. Consider a case in which I sign a loan document from a bank. Presumably, given our present legal arrangements, by signing this document I thereby take responsibility for satisfying the conditions specified in the document, such as paying back the loan at a given interest rate. In doing so, I gain the standing of being a loan holder, complete with its constitutive legal rights, responsibilities, and obligations. By all appearances, though, I acquire this standing and its constitutive rights, responsibilities, and obligations not merely by taking myself to take responsibility for a state of affairs but by actually doing so. Advocates of the soft-line reply would, I imagine, agree with this. They do not deny that we can acquire legal standings by doing such things as signing loan documents.

Could I have acquired the status of being a loan holder merely by taking myself to take responsibility for satisfying the conditions specified on the document? Given our present legal arrangements, it is difficult to see how. To acquire the status of being a loan holder, I have to actually take responsibility for these conditions, leaving myself liable if I fail to satisfy them. (With proponents of the soft-line

2. See, for example, Parfit (2011), Vol. II, 311–12.

reply, I assume that taking oneself to take responsibility for a state of affairs does not imply actually taking responsibility for that state of affairs.) But if so, then it is difficult to see why we should believe that things would go any differently when it comes to speech. That is, it is difficult to see how gaining the status of being a loan holder is accomplished only by taking responsibility for a state of affairs, while acquiring the status of being a speaker is accomplished merely by taking oneself to take responsibility for a state of affairs. The proponent of the soft-line reply owes a plausible explanation of how there could be this difference. I, however, fail to see what that explanation could be.[3]

But suppose, for the sake of argument, that things are different when it comes to speech. Suppose, that is, that taking oneself to take responsibility for a state of affairs is the sort of thing that could count-generate speech. Then it is worth asking whether a strategy that appeals to this idea yields a satisfactory account of speech. While I know of no general criterion that specifies what counts as a satisfactory account of speech, the following strikes me as a plausible proposal: any minimally adequate account of speech should not only be compatible with our being able to perform the full range of speech acts—including what I earlier called assertives, directives, commissives, and exercitives—but should also ensure that the speech acts we perform are not deeply and systematically malformed. The soft-line reply, I believe, fails this criterion of minimal adequacy.

We can see why by distinguishing (in a somewhat rough and ready fashion) various ways in which a speech act can be malformed. One such way is when a speech act does not bear a well-formed relation to the way the world is. Jake, for example, may assert something that is false, promise to do something that is in fact impossible, request something that has already been done, and so forth. Another mode of malformation is when a speech act does not bear a well-formed relation to the conditions necessary for its performance. When Jake's speech acts suffer from a malformation of this sort, he may attempt to promise or command what he has no right to because he lacks the relevant sort of standing power. If the soft-line reply were true, I want

3. The auction case mentioned in Chapter 2 suggests a different problem, which is that taking oneself to take responsibility for a state of affairs is not even necessary to speak.

now to suggest, ordinary cases of promising would be ones that inevitably suffer from malformations of both kinds.

Consider the first type of malformation just mentioned. Suppose, in ordinary speech conditions, Jake utters the sentence "I promise to lead you in a performance of *Mack the Knife* late in the first set." In doing so, he not only intends to lay an obligation on himself to act in this way, but also takes it for granted that he can do as he intends. That is, in the ordinary case, Jake takes it for granted that he not only can lay an obligation on himself by uttering such a sentence, but also that in doing so he has thereby promised the Big Band that he will act in a certain way. Arguably, moreover, Jake assumes more than this. Jake also assumes that he is liable to correction if he fails (when promising) to intend to do as he says he will, since he is a competent participant in our practices of speech. Suppose that the error theory were true, however. Then the content of these presuppositions would be false; they would fail to bear a well-formed relation to the world. If so, the account of promising offered by advocates of the soft-line reply is not one that vindicates, on error-theoretic assumptions, the reality of our performing well-formed promises. At best, it explains how we perform deeply *malformed* promises. But this is not what we were looking for. We were interested in seeing whether it is possible for agents, on error-theoretic assumptions, to perform ordinary, well-formed promises. If the soft-line reply were true, however, we could not perform speech acts of this variety.

Consider now the second, more severe type of malformation. According to the normative theory, when Jake promises to lead the Big Band in a performance of *Mack the Knife*, he does not simply take responsibility for intending to act as he says he will. He also takes responsibility for such things as

> his having the standing power to lay an obligation of the relevant sort on himself.

If the normative theory is true, in taking responsibility for his having the relevant sort of standing power, Jake thereby leaves himself open to appropriate correction if he lacks this standing power. This, in part, is what accounts for his having promised anything to the Big Band. Now suppose, once again, that the error theory were true. If it were, then Jake could not take responsibility for his having the standing power to lay the relevant sort of obligation on himself. For were he to do so, then his audience would have a right to hold him responsible were he to lack this standing power. But, error theorists say, it is impossible for his audience to have this right—there being no moral features of this sort. At most, Jake could intend or take himself to take responsibility for his having the relevant sort of standing power.

Advocates of the soft-line reply now face a choice. They could simply deny that Jake can perform speech acts such as promising, while acknowledging that he can perform speech acts of other sorts such as asserting. Or they could maintain that Jake succeeds in promising simply in virtue of his taking himself to have the relevant sort of standing power regardless of whether or not he in fact has that power. Or, finally, they could maintain that Jake succeeds in promising only if he both takes himself to have the relevant standing power and he has that power, even if he cannot take responsibility for his having it. None of these options is satisfactory.

The first option is unsatisfactory, since it fails to satisfy the condition that an adequate account of speech should be compatible with our being able to perform the full range of speech acts, including promising. The second option fails for a similar reason. Merely taking oneself to have a standing power of some sort is clearly not sufficient (even when other relevant conditions are in place) for performing a well-formed speech act. Suppose—to advert to an earlier example—you are a visiting police officer, and I sincerely utter the sentence "I promise you at least a three-percent pay raise." The mere fact that I take myself to have the standing power to promise this is not sufficient for me to succeed in performing a well-formed promise. Since I lack the relevant sort of authority to promise anything of this sort, my speech act misfires; I have either failed to promise anything or my promise is radically malformed. The third option, admittedly, is not vulnerable to exactly this complaint. Like the normative theory, it implies that for an agent to perform a speech act such as promising, he must have the relevant sort of standing power. But this option is not genuinely available to error theorists, at least if the argument in Chapter 3 is correct. For to have a standing power is to possess a cluster of rights, responsibilities, and obligations, including the permission-right to alter the world in some way specified by that power and a claim-right against others that they not try to prevent you from bringing about that alteration. Part of the purpose of Chapter 3 was to argue that some of these rights, responsibilities, and obligations are moral, which is incompatible with the error theory.

Promising is, however, not unique in the fact that it requires an agent to have the relevant sort of standing power. Directives such as commanding and exercitives such as pronouncements of certain types are identical in this regard. If I lack the relevant sort of standing power, I cannot command you to declare a national state of emergency. Likewise, if I lack the relevant standing power I cannot pronounce you to be legally married. The point made against the soft-line reply in the last paragraph, then, holds for a wide range of speech acts: merely taking oneself to have a standing power to perform a speech act of a given kind is not sufficient (even when other relevant conditions hold) for performing a well-formed speech act of that kind. Indeed, pronouncing a person to be married or declaring a batter out are vivid cases of types of speech act whose performance requires that one actually have the relevant sort of standing power to perform them.

In sum: defenders of the soft-line reply maintain that error theorists can avoid the objection that, if error theory were true, then we would not be able to speak, claiming that the error theory is compatible with an account of speech that is good enough. I have argued that this is mistaken. The account of speech suggested by the soft-line reply is not good enough. This is not simply because it is doubtful whether taking oneself to take responsibility for a state of affairs could generate speech. It is also because a theory that excises the normative dimensions of speech cannot account for our being able to perform both well-formed speech acts and the full range of speech acts. Granted, if this reply is correct, it would not spell the end for the error theory. For advocates of the error theory can avail themselves of what I referred to earlier as the hard-line reply.

The hard-line reply

Defenders of the hard-line reply hold that there is no way to reconcile anything like the normative theory of speech with the error theory; something has to give. So, they reject the normative theory of speech. Advocates of the hard-line response, it should be noted, do not reject the normative theory in favor of some other theory of speech, such as the perlocutionary-intention view, which also implies that speakers acquire rights, responsibilities, and obligations of various kinds. Rather, advocates of the hard-line reply maintain that we do not speak. We do not perform such actions as asserting, commanding, promising, requesting, and the like. At best, we perform actions that are easily mistaken for them. This, defenders of the hard-line reply emphasize, does not imply that we fail to communicate information to each other by doing such things as uttering and writing sentences. Nor does it preclude our exercising causal influence over one another by using language. To the contrary, say defenders of the view, we succeed in performing these activities all the time. Nonetheless, defenders of the hard-line reply maintain that these communicative acts are not count-generated in virtue of our having rights, responsibilities, or obligations of any sort. Communication is a wholly non-normative phenomenon, even if we mistakenly believe otherwise.

In what follows, it will be helpful to have a neutral term that picks out that phenomenon that advocates of the normative theory call speech and what defenders of the hard-line reply call communication. Let us use the term "discourse" to fill this role. Discourse, thus understood, includes actions that appear to be ones in which we take responsibility for things being as we present them, such as promises, commands, requests, and the like. I believe that advocates of the hard-line reply are correct to recognize that we cannot reconcile the error theory with anything like the normative theory of speech. But toeing the hard-line reply also seems to me deeply unattractive. Let me illustrate why.

Suppose one were charged with the task of offering a more or less comprehensive description of a game such as baseball. While the description would have to be complex, it could not leave out the fact that the game is essentially a norm-governed practice. Were one to describe the norms that govern the practice of Major League Baseball, one would presumably begin by identifying various arrangements for playing the game, such as the following: the game is divided into increments that are called innings, nine of which constitute a game in the standard case; pitches are to be designated by the umpire as either balls or strikes; if during an at-bat a batter has four balls called by an umpire, then he is awarded a walk; if during an at-bat a batter has three strikes called by an umpire, then he is out; and so forth.

This would be the first step. The next step would be to describe the normative standings that the participants—that is, the players, coaches, and officials of the game—enjoy in virtue of the fact that these arrangements are in effect. As is often the case, the best way to identify the character of these normative standings and their constitutive rights, responsibilities, and obligations, is to consider cases in which things do not go well.

To that end, imagine a case in which a batter has four balls thrown against him while batting. The rules of baseball dictate that he has a right to a walk. Accordingly, the team who is in the field has the obligation to allow him to take first base. Imagine, however, that the batter to whom four balls is thrown were not awarded the walk by the home-plate umpire. Rather than award the walk, the umpire interrupts the game to confer with the opposing manager about the issue of whether a walk should be awarded. If this were to occur, something would have gone wrong—so wrong, in fact, that it would be appropriate to complain to the commissioner of Major League Baseball that, in this game, the umpires had not properly enforced the rules of baseball. The commissioner, in turn, would have sufficient grounds to censure the home-plate umpire, or more drastically, suspend or fire him. Were one to probe further as to why this is so, one would discover further facts about how the rights, responsibilities, and obligations that attach to the participants in the game of baseball are distributed. The rules tell us, for example, that during an official game only the umpires who are officiating that game have the right to declare a pitch a ball or award a walk. The players and coaches involved in that game have no such right. Similarly, while only the umpires have this standing right, their rights are limited. They do not, for example, have the right to do such things as determine who will be the starting pitcher for a team or who will hit in the lead-off position. Only the coaches have such rights.

Anyone familiar with the game of baseball will recognize that I have offered a fairly stark description of some of its normative dimensions. Were we to complete the description, we would have to articulate layer upon layer of (both written and unwritten) rules with their correspondent rights, responsibilities, and obligations. Although it could be complained that the description offered is substantially incomplete, it is much more difficult to understand how it could be said to be inaccurate. Baseball is, by all appearances, essentially a rule-governed practice and its participants possess normative standings of various kinds. Moreover, certain events can transpire in an official game of Major League Baseball—such as a batter's being called out—if and only if the participants exercise their rights and conform to the responsibilities and obligations that are constitutive of the normative standings they enjoy in virtue of being participants in the game.

Let us bracket, for the time being, the issue of the ontological status of the putative rights, responsibilities, and obligations that attach to the participants in the game of baseball. Let us likewise bracket the related issue of the ontological status of the putative rights, responsibilities, and obligations that attach to those who engage in discourse.[4] The complaint against the hard-line reply that I would like to press is this: their position is no better than one that attempts to offer an entirely non-normative description of baseball, according to which its participants fail to have normative standings with their constitutive rights, responsibilities, and obligations.[5] However, if what I have said is correct, the prospect of offering a decent description of the game of baseball that is completely non-normative is bleak. If one had tried to describe the game, but completely omitted reference to the rules that govern it and the rights, responsibilities, and obligations enjoyed by its participants, one would have failed to offer anything approaching a decent description of baseball. But if a non-normative description of baseball is as bleak as it seems, then the prospect of offering a decent non-normative description of discourse appears no better. Discourse is

---

4. In Chapter 3, it will be recalled, I pointed to some of their relevant differences.
5. I do not wish to deny that there could be such descriptions. Perhaps video games that simulate baseball games are cases of such descriptions. But these games are *simulations* of baseball; they do not describe the game as we know it, since they omit important elements of the game, such as the fact that when an umpire fails to call a balk, he has failed to do his job.

at least as normatively laden as baseball. It is for this reason that we should, I believe, reject the hard-line reply. The view is descriptively inadequate.[6]

Before we move forward, it may prove worthwhile to make one final observation about the error theory. Some recent proponents of the view, such as Richard Joyce, have wished to couple it with a fictionalist account of moral thought and discourse. According to this approach, while ordinary moral thought and discourse are in massive error, we should attempt to revise them in such a way that, when ordinary agents engage in them, they do not attempt to represent moral reality. Rather, they merely pretend to do so.[7] One might, however, hold that the revision is not necessary. For one might maintain, as does Mark Kalderon in his book *Moral Fictionalism*, that ordinary moral thought and discourse are already fictionalist in orientation. If Kalderon is right, what Joyce describes as the aim of the revision of moral thought and discourse is in fact the reality. Ordinary moral discourse is already fictionalist in character. This position is what Kalderon calls hermeneutic fictionalism.[8]

Hermeneutic fictionalism would attempt to explain apparent reference to the rights, responsibilities, and obligations that attach to participants in baseball and speech along fictionalist lines. But the attempt would, I believe, soon reach a dead end. As Joyce points out

---

6. By arguing that the hard-line approach fails to describe what we are doing when we engage in discourse, I do not thereby mean to rule out the possibility that normative facts reduce to natural or descriptive facts. Perhaps a reduction of this sort is available; perhaps not. I note only that there is an uneasy fit between the combination of the error theory and the hard-line reply, on the one hand, and normative reductionism, on the other. For if I understand the error theory, it is driven (in part) by the following argument: were moral facts to exist, then they would be irreducibly normative. But nothing could be irreducibly normative; so there are no such facts. But now suppose the conclusion of the arguments offered in Chapters 3 and 4 is true: some of the rights, responsibilities, and obligations that are ingredient in the count-generation of speech are moral. According to the error theory, these facts would have to be irreducibly normative. But if that is right, then error theorists who tout the hard-line reply will not have available an argument for the conclusion that the normative dimensions of discourse are merely natural or descriptive facts. For, to say it again, given the arguments of Chapters 3 and 4, error theorists would have to say that at least some of the normative features that are ingredient in the count-generation of speech cannot be reduced to mere descriptive or natural facts.

7. Joyce (2001). Joyce distinguishes different ways in which one can develop a fictionalist account of discourse. For my purposes, these distinctions will not matter.

8. Kalderon (2005), it is worth noting, offers several models of what it is to engage in a fiction.

in his defense of moral fictionalism, a tell-tale mark of an agent's engaging in a fiction with respect to some domain of entities, the Ks, is that, in critical contexts in which she is undistracted, reflective, and candid, she is prepared to disavow that she believes in the Ks. Our discourse about "creatures of the holidays" such as Santa Claus and the Easter Bunny clearly exhibits this feature. Many of us, for example, remember being sat down by our parents only to be told that there is no Santa. As a result, we are now inclined in critical contexts to back off any apparent commitment to his existence, even though in other contexts—such as when we play with children—we freely speak of his comings and goings.

Our discourse about the normative dimensions of baseball and speech is different. None of us, I trust, were told by our parents that the rules of baseball are mythical; we were not told that umpires lack the right to call a pitch a strike. Nor were we told anything similar about speech. None of us, I imagine, were told that everyone lacks the authority to make promises. And this is not because it was assumed to be so obvious as to not merit mention that umpires really do not have the right to call a pitch a strike. Nor is it because it was assumed to be equally obvious that no one has the authority to issue a promise (or correct someone who has inadvertently uttered a falsehood). The issue of whether ordinary thought about baseball and speech are a species of make-believe simply never arose. It may be, then, that hermeneutic fictionalism offers us the right account of our thought and discourse about creatures of the holidays, such as Santa Claus. But, by all appearances, it does not offer a descriptively adequate account of our thought and discourse about the normative standings that attach to the participants in both baseball and speech.[9]

In sum: I have argued that the error theory has implications that no one should be happy to accept. For if anything like the normative theory of speech is true, then advocates of the error theory face the charge that, according to their view, we cannot speak. I identified two ways in which error theorists might respond to this charge: the soft-line reply and the hard-line reply. I have claimed that neither

9. Cuneo and Christy (2011) presents a more elaborate defense of this claim. Among other things, our essay engages with the possibility, which Kalderon defends, that we unwittingly engage in the moral fiction. The paper argues that this is not a coherent option.

response is adequate. I should emphasize that, when engaging with these views, my argument has not been that it would be impossible to engage in discourse (understood in the broad sense introduced above) were we to lack the rights, responsibilities, and obligations of being a speaker. Rather, it has been that we have inadequate reason to suppose that discourse is as proponents of the soft- and hard-line replies maintain. Practices such as law and baseball, I observed, are constituted by rights, responsibilities, and obligations. Since they are, we should believe that the same is true of our discursive practices. This, however, implies that we have insufficient reason to believe that discourse is non-normative, as proponents of the soft- and hard-line replies maintain. (A parallel: realists about the external world need not claim that it is impossible that phenomenalism be correct. They might simply maintain that, given what else we know about the world, we do not have good enough reason to accept it.) At any rate, the best option for error theorists, I believe, is to admit that we speak but to deny that the rights, responsibilities, and obligations that attach to speakers are moral. This is a variant of the position that I have called the mixed view.[10] At this point, however, I have nothing new to say about the mixed view. In the preceding two chapters, I offered my reasons for rejecting it.

II Expressivism

Some philosophers hold that we can adopt the error theorist's ontology without committing ordinary agents to massively mistaken moral beliefs. Traditional expressivists are such philosophers. They contend that we should embrace the following two claims:

---

10. What I am calling the "best option" for error theorists would resemble the normative theory in three respects. Like the normative theory, the position would imply that (i) when engaging in discourse, agents take responsibility for states of affairs, (ii) rights, responsibilities, and obligations are ingredient in the count-generation of speech, and (iii) the performance of well-formed speech acts requires that agents have moral rights, responsibilities, and obligations. Unlike the normative theory, however, this position would deny that any of the rights, responsibilities, and obligations ingredient in the count-generation of discourse are moral. An implication of this last claim is that, if this view were true, agents could perform only deeply malformed speech acts or—if it is true that having moral rights, responsibilities, and obligations is constitutive of performing speech acts—ersatz speech acts.

There are no moral facts (in the realist's sense in or any other).

Ordinary moral thought and discourse do not purport to represent moral reality, but express attitudes of approval, disapproval, and so forth toward non-moral reality.[11]

According to its proponents, traditional expressivism is an attractive via media between moral realism and the error theory. Expressivists maintain that, unlike realism, their ontological commitments are minimal, since their view relieves us from commitment to the existence of highly controversial entities such as moral facts. Unlike the error theory, however, expressivism—so its proponents claim—does not imply that ordinary moral thought and discourse are massively in error. Since neither is even in the business of representing moral facts, there is no sense in which they purport to do so but fail.

Those not sympathetic with expressivism sometimes find themselves exasperated by the view. The primary problem with expressivism, it is said, is that it falls into a trap similar to that which Bishop Berkeley did when defending idealism. Berkeley, you will recall, claimed to be speaking with the vulgar, maintaining that his idealism is perfectly consistent with common sense. After all, Berkeley reminds us, were his view true, we would make no mistake when we talk about there being such things as mountains, trees, and chairs. Most, however, have thought that Berkeley was mistaken about the compatibility of his view with common sense. For fundamental to common sense, Berkeley's critics have maintained, is the assumption that when we talk about mountains, trees, and chairs, we endeavor to talk not about mental ideas but spatially located physical objects. One cannot reconcile idealism with common sense by simply reinterpreting what ordinary people are saying when they claim that there are mountains, trees, and chairs, as Berkeley did.

Moral realists have lodged similar complaints about expressivism. Expressivists have tended to claim that their views are entirely consonant with ordinary moral thinking. But fundamental to ordinary moral thought, say moral realists, is the assumption that there are moral truths that we can know. Excellent evidence of this is the fact

11. Ayer (1936), Gibbard (1990), and Bennett (1993) among others, defend traditional expressivism. In the previous chapter, I distinguished *comprehensive* from *restricted* expressivism. In this chapter, I will have my eye on comprehensive expressivism.

that when we disagree about moral matters, we assume that there is normally a fact of the matter about which of our conflicting moral judgments is correct. Expressivists, it is charged, cannot make sense of this; there is no interesting sense in which the expression of an attitude could be correct if their view were true. If so, expressivism, it is said, is no more compatible with common sense than is Berkeleyan idealism. One cannot reconcile expressivism with common sense by simply reinterpreting what ordinary people are saying when they claim, for example, that it is wrong to lie.[12]

While I have sympathies with this complaint, the objection I wish to press against traditional expressivism is not a variant of it. I want to argue not that expressivism offers us a wrong account of moral discourse. Rather, I contend that if the view were true, we could not engage in moral discourse—or any sort of discourse, for that matter—at all.

For suppose we say, once again, that an agent can speak just in case she can, in ordinary speech situations, perform a substantial range of speech acts, such as asserting, promising, commanding, requesting, entreating, extolling, and so on. In our day-to-day lives, all of us (ordinary adults in standard conditions) speak. But if so, then we have the rights, responsibilities, and obligations of being a speaker. If we have these rights, responsibilities, and obligations, however, then moral facts exist, for many of these rights, responsibilities, and obligations are moral. If traditional expressivism were true, however, then there would be no moral facts. And, thus, we could not speak. But we do speak. So, traditional expressivist views are false. I might add that this objection is compatible with expressivism's offering a more or less correct account of the way in which large tracts of moral thought and discourse actually work. If it did, then traditional expressivism would have the paradoxical implication that if it were true, then it would be incompatible with the very thing that it is purports to explain, namely, the workings of ordinary moral thought and discourse.

12. Cuneo (2006), Egan (2007), Enoch (2011), ch. 2, FitzPatrick (2011), and Parfit (2011), Vol. II, ch. 28, develop arguments along these lines. Note that the claim advanced against expressivists is not that they lack a workable account of what it is to *say* that something is correct or true; it is rather that they have no plausible account of what it *is* for a claim to be correct or true.

I suspect that this objection will strike many as not cutting to the heart of the expressivist project. This is primarily because, although traditional expressivism has exercised considerable influence in contemporary metaethics, it is increasingly difficult to find contemporary advocates of it. The position has evolved. Perhaps the most important respect in which it has evolved is that, unlike its more traditional predecessors, sophisticated expressivism does not categorically deny that there are moral features of any sort. Rather, its advocates maintain that it is legitimate to at once embrace expressivism and talk of there being moral facts, properties, truths, propositions, and so forth.

Granted, it is not always easy to know what to make of such talk. Expressivists such as Blackburn and Mark Timmons, for example, maintain that from the "engaged" or "internal" perspective it is appropriate to talk of moral facts. But philosophers such as Blackburn sometimes claim that such talk consists simply in our valuing certain aspects of the world—this valuing being such that, from the "external" perspective, it carries no commitments to there being moral facts. (Indeed, at various points, both Blackburn and Timmons explicitly say that from the external perspective there are no moral facts.[13]) In other places, however, philosophers such as Blackburn and Gibbard talk not of perspectives from which it is legitimate to talk of moral facts but of there being moral facts. Typically, they are quick to indicate that the existence of such facts does not come to much, for they exist in only a deflationary sense (or, alternatively, that they are simply offering accounts of what it is to say that moral facts exist).[14] In still other places, philosophers such as Gibbard claim that what realists call normative features are not deflated properties but are (or are constituted by) ordinary natural features to which normative concepts "pertain."[15]

These positions do not fit together well. For it is difficult to understand how it could be that moral facts do not exist from the external perspective, exist in a merely deflationary sense, and are also naturalistic features of the world (or are constituted by such features).

13. See Blackburn (1993), 173; and Timmons (1999), 153.
14. See Blackburn (1998), ch. 3, (1999); and Gibbard (2003), 18.
15. See Gibbard (2002) and (2003), 7, ch. 6.

However, I propose not to enter into the thicket of expressivist exegesis in order to make sense of the various things that expressivists say. For present purposes, it is enough to note that those versions of expressivism that affirm the existence of moral features in some non-realist, deflationary sense may have the resources to respond to the objection I have been pressing, as they claim that there are moral features. But to do so, expressivists of this sort will have to offer an account of these features that yields the result that they are the right sort of things to be ingredient in the count-generation of speech. Is such an account available?

It is hard to tell. As I noted in Chapter 1, it is not easy to say what it is for something to be a deflated property or fact; those sympathetic with deflationism appeal to metaphors when presenting their views, claiming that moral features are "shadows" that "come for free" with the assertoric cast of moral discourse.[16] If we are to make progress on the issue before us, however, we need to move beyond appeal to these metaphors. We need to have a better idea of what these philosophers have in mind when they say that, in their view, there are moral facts but only of the deflated variety.

The best way to do that, I propose, is by tightening our focus for a moment. We can do this, I suggest, by taking a closer look at what philosophers have said about deflationary accounts of truth. For this is the arena from which expressivists seem to have drawn much inspiration and in which deflationary views have been most carefully worked out.[17] In what follows, then, I want to say just enough about deflationism regarding truth to explain why I believe an appeal to deflated moral facts does not represent an adequate reply to the Speech Act Argument.

Before I begin, however, a caveat. The phrase "deflationism regarding truth" means different things in the mouths of different philosophers. In this section I will present not a composite portrait, but simply a sketch of a prominent version of deflationism. In the back of my mind is the supposition that sophisticated expressivists accept something like this understanding of deflationism, applying it to the cases of moral properties and facts. I recognize that I might

16. See Blackburn (1998), 80.
17. This is explicit in Blackburn (1998), 75.

be wrong about this last claim. Perhaps there is no view or cluster of views that expressivists have in mind when they avail themselves of deflationism. Or perhaps—as I have heard suggested—when expressivists talk of there being moral truths, they do not wish their pronouncements to have genuine ontological import. Perhaps they mean only to advance a metalinguistic thesis about what it is that we are doing when *say* that there are such truths—this thesis being compatible with there being no such truths in any sense. These, as I say, are possibilities that I cannot rule out. However, they are views, I believe, that are vulnerable to the objection that I have pressed against versions of traditional expressivism.[18]

Deflationism

Lying at the core of deflationism about truth is a commitment to the slogan that "truth has no nature"—this slogan being a somewhat cryptic way of advancing a pair of related ideas. The first idea is that there is a truth property but there is nothing informative to say about its nature. Or, more precisely, the claim is that there is a truth property such that there is nothing informative to say about its nature beyond that which is revealed by the schema:

TS: the proposition p is true if and only if p.

18. Some expressivists understand so-called thick normative concepts such as 'being cruel' or 'being chaste' in the following way: these concepts divide into a descriptive and an expressive component. To competently deploy a concept such as 'being cruel' on a given occasion requires both that its user believe that its object has certain descriptive properties and condemn (or be disposed to condemn) that object in virtue of its having those properties. In principle, expressivists could understand illocutionary act concepts such as 'being an assertion' or 'being a promise' in the same way. The idea would be that to competently deploy a concept such as 'being an assertion' on a given occasion requires both that its user believe that someone has performed a locutionary act and to correct or admonish the speaker (or be disposed to engage in these actions) if things are not as she presents them. In principle, expressivists could say that these requirements, which apply to users of these concepts, are ingredient in the count-generation of speech. Given the assumption that, all else being equal, a failure to conform to some of these requirements implies that one suffers from a moral demerit, expressivists could also say that they are moral.

I am not going to give this view full consideration. My reason is this: the requirements in question will be either of the realist, constructivist, or deflationist variety. If they are of the realist or constructivist variety, then this view is not a version of expressivism as I understand it. If the requirements are of the deflationary variety, then what I say in this section addresses this view.

The underlying thought is that schema TS expresses our ordinary truth concept and that this concept gives us more or less full insight into the nature of truth. Deflationists, of course, do not deny that we can rightfully say things such as:

A proposition is true just in case it corresponds to a correlative fact.

This last claim might appear to tell us something informative about truth, namely, that it consists in the correspondence between a proposition and correlative fact. Deflationists insist, however, that it does not. The correspondence claim stated above, deflationists claim, is simply a more elaborate way of stating schema TS, which is a trivial analytic truth.[19]

The second, related idea expressed by the slogan that truth has no nature is that the truth property plays no significant explanatory roles. For, presumably, if it did play such roles, then there would be interesting and informative facts to discover about the nature of truth, which, according to deflationists, there is not. When they make pronouncements such as these, deflationists such as Paul Horwich do not specify exactly what they have in mind when they use the phrase a "significant explanatory role." But it is clear from the examples they use that, in their view, something plays a significant explanatory role if it figures in ordinary scientific explanations, such as ones in which we appeal to a thing's real essence to explain its superficial properties or to account for causal happenings in the world.[20]

Under a natural reading, however, deflationists wish to cast their net wider than this. For there appear to be ways in which something could play a significant explanatory role other than those just mentioned. Most obviously, a feature might play an important explanatory role in accounting for phenomena that not scientists but

---

19. For the record, this last claim strikes me as false. TS is, after all, a *schema*; as such, it cannot be true or false. The claim that a proposition is true just in case it corresponds to the facts is, by contrast, truth-evaluable. If so, the claim that a proposition is true just in case it corresponds to the facts cannot be just a longwinded way of stating schema TS.

20. Horwich's views seem to have shifted over the years. In his (1998) he works with a contrast between substantial properties versus deflated ones. In his later (2010), ch. 12, he maintains that there is no such distinction available. My understanding of deflationism owes a debt to Lynch (2009).

philosophers wonder about. Consider modal attributions as an example. Suppose a person were to say that time travel is impossible or that the property *being rational* belongs to the essence of being human. Philosophers wonder: What it is for something to be impossible or belong to a thing's essence? Some propose that possible worlds hold the answer. If these philosophers are right, for example, what it is for a state of affairs to be impossible is for there to be no possible world at which it obtains. If they are correct about this, then we have good reason to believe that possible worlds do important explanatory work; they help to explain deeply puzzling issues, such as the character of modal attributions.

Suppose, then, we think of deflationism about truth as incorporating the thesis that, while there is a truth property, it has no nature, playing no significant explanatory roles. Sophisticated expressivists have assumed that we can readily apply this broadly deflationary approach to the moral domain. Blackburn, for example, writes that G. E. Moore was right when he said that there is "almost nothing to say" about goodness. Goodness, writes Blackburn, "will indeed resist analysis, resist any account of empirical or causal access, and bear a relation of supervenience to other properties." As with truth, Blackburn continues, we can say "that there is a property there, if properties are just the semantic shadows of predicates. But there is no topic there, no residual mystery, therefore, about how we get our hooks into it nor why we should want to do so."[21]

Elsewhere I have argued that this way of thinking rests on a mistake. Despite the appearances, deflationism and expressivism do not sit well together. If deflationism about moral features were true, after all, then there would be nothing informative to say about the nature of moral features, nothing informative to say about that necessarily in virtue of which actions are right or wrong. That, however, would make it impossible to engage in normative ethics, which offer us substantive proposals about that in which rightness and wrongness consist. Since no decent metaethical theory that affirms the existence of moral facts (and holds that normative theorizing is not irredeemably diseased) should have this implication, we cannot plausibly combine

---

21. Blackburn (2010), 310–11.

expressivism with deflationism.[22] On this occasion, however, my purpose is not to argue that deflationism and expressivism are incompatible. Rather, it is to explore the issue of whether expressivists
could plausibly maintain that moral features, as they understand
them, could account for the performance of speech acts. It seems to
me that it could not; deflated moral properties or facts are not the
right sort of thing to be ingredient in the count-generation of speech.

To see this, bring to mind the central deflationary thesis. According to this thesis, deflated properties or facts have no nature;
not only is there nothing in which these properties or facts consist,
they are also not the sorts of things that play any sort of significant
explanatory role. As such, they are not the sorts of things that figure
in the explanations that scientists or philosophers offer when attempting to account for one or another puzzling phenomenon.

Now consider speech. An agent, let us say, utters a sentence. In so
doing, he thereby performs an illocutionary act, such as asserting.
This, I have stressed, is puzzling. The two acts are not, after all, identical. Nor does the first act logically imply or cause the second. What,
then, explains how it is that a sentence utterance generates an illocutionary act such as an asserting? The Speech Act Argument tells us
that moral facts explain this, at least in part. They are that which
bind together locutionary and illocutionary acts. If this is right, then
moral facts play an indispensible explanatory role in our everyday
lives, as they are ingredient in what count-generates speech acts.
Were there no facts of this sort, then we would not be able to perform such acts as promising a friend to help or declaring a person
guilty—acts, I have emphasized, that alter our world in remarkable
and sometimes unpredictable ways. If this were true, then moral
facts are not of the deflated variety. And, so, they are not as sophisticated expressivists claim. For they play significant explanatory
roles—roles, I might add, that are not revealed by moral concepts as
expressivists understand them.

It might be worth noting that philosophers such as Wright, who
are not expressivists, allow that there are moral facts but deny that

22. Cuneo (2013) develops the argument. Rosen (1998) and Dreier (2004) press a dif-
    ferent objection, which is that when we combine deflationism with expressivism, the
    latter becomes indistinguishable from realism.

they are as realists or deflationists ordinarily describe them.[23] Wright, recall, allows that moral facts may play an explanatory role but not a *wide* explanatory role. Were moral facts to explain anything, in Wright's view, it is only in virtue of the fact that they are "mediated" by or represented in our propositional attitudes. To return to an earlier example, suppose the Big Band were to confront Jake after their concert, since he failed to keep his promise to lead it in a rendition of *Mack the Knife*. Were the fact *that the Big Band has a moral right to hold Jake accountable* to explain why its members confronted Jake, according to Wright, this fact would do so only because agents believe it. And, in this respect, Wright holds, moral facts differ from ordinary natural facts. The fact *that the stove is hot*—to stay with our example from the previous chapter—is such that it can explain all sorts of happenings in the natural world (such as the boiling of water) without its being mediated by our propositional attitudes.

There might be conceptual space, then, for a view that allows moral facts to play a more significant role than deflationists allow but a less significant role than realists typically defend. Still, if the normative theory of speech is correct, there is good reason to reject views such as Wright's, according to which moral facts play only a very limited explanatory role. After all, central to the normative theory is the thesis that it is an agent's having the rights, responsibilities, and obligations of being a speaker that is ingredient in the count-generation of speech. For these normative features to play this explanatory role, it need not be the case that they are mediated by or represented in our propositional attitudes. All that needs to be the case is that an agent in fact has these rights, responsibilities, and obligations. To be sure, there is ordinarily ample reason for us to keep track of these normative features. That is how we can hold each other accountable when speaking. So, in the ordinary case, many of the normative features that are ingredient in the count-generation of speech will form the content of our propositional attitudes. But, to say it again, speech is not generated by the fact that these normative features are mediated by our propositional attitudes. If so, the

---

23. See Wright (1992), ch. 6. In principle, one could go deflationary about explanation itself. While I know of no philosopher who endorses this position, Zangwill (1992) discusses it (only to reject it).

Speech Act Argument implies that moral facts earn their explanatory keep, as they play a robust and wide explanatory role. Indeed, in the next chapter, I will argue that the scope of their explanatory role is even wider than I have indicated here.

Let us take stock. Expressivism, I have emphasized, is primarily a thesis about the character of moral thought and discourse. In both its traditional and more sophisticated forms, it tells us that moral thought and discourse are not in the business of representing moral reality, at least in any substantive sense. In this chapter, I have conceded that expressivists might offer us a correct account of how much of ordinary moral thought and discourse actually works. But, I have maintained, expressivism is incompatible with our best theory of how we speak. In its traditional guise, expressivism denies that there are moral features of any sort. This exposes the view to the objection leveled earlier against the error theory, namely, that were it true, we would not be able to speak. In its more sophisticated versions, expressivism allows that there are moral facts, albeit only of the deflated variety. I have argued that deflated moral facts could not be ingredient in the count-generation of speech, for their deflationary status bars them from playing any significant explanatory role, such as explaining the hook-up between locutionary and illocutionary acts.

Let me add a final point. In *Thinking How to Live*, Gibbard writes that expressivism covers "any account of meanings that follows this indirect path: to explain the meaning of a term, explain what states of mind the term can be used to express."[24] Later in his discussion, Gibbard concedes that once expressivists have explained the meaning of normative terms, the resulting view may be virtually indistinguishable from realism. Any difference between the two views will lie in the fact that expressivists will have explained crucial features of moral thought and discourse that realists have left unexplained, such as why normative concepts supervene on natural ones.[25] This explanatory advantage, Gibbard argues, is an important reason for us to prefer expressivism to realism.

An implication of the Speech Act Argument is that this cannot be right. Expressivists *might* be able to explain the meaning of norma-

24. Gibbard (2003), 7.
25. Gibbard (2003), 20, 184.

tive terms such as the all-things-considered "ought" without invoking normative properties; that will depend, in part, on whether the meaning of a term gets explained in terms of its use in speech. But explaining the meaning of a term is one thing; explaining how it is we speak is another. If the Speech Act Argument is correct, to explain the latter, both realists and expressivists will have to appeal to moral features of the non-deflated variety. In this respect, the views are identical.[26]

III Constructivism

There is a world of difference between moral constructivism and the two antirealist views that we have considered so far. The difference lies in the fact that constructivists, unlike both error theorists and expressivists, ordinarily believe that there are moral facts (and not just of the deflationary variety). Often, moreover, they hold that these facts are objective, waiting for us to discover them. In these respects, there is considerable common ground between constructivism and realism. But, as I pointed out in Chapter 1, this does not imply that constructivism is a form of moral realism—at least not in the sense of "realism" that I introduced there. (I am happy to admit that there are other legitimate uses of the term, some of which imply that some versions of constructivism qualify as forms of realism.) In that discussion, I illustrated the difference between the two views as follows.

Suppose, I suggested, we use the phrase "a recognitional stance" to stand for a host of attitudes or actions that an agent could take toward something, such as declaring it to be F, taking it to be F, wanting it to be F, valuing (or disvaluing) it as F, or the like. Agents

---

26. Chrisman (2008) proposes that expressivists deploy an "inferentialist" account of meaning, according to which a sentence or term has its meaning in virtue of the inferential roles it plays. The type of inferentialist view to which Chrisman appeals is Brandom's, which has much in common with the normative theory of speech. According to this position, inferential roles are to be understood in normative terms. If what I have argued here is correct, however, this maneuver is unavailable to expressivists (or other non-descriptivist positions, such as that presented in Chrisman (2011)). For it would imply that normative properties do important explanatory work, since they account for why sentences have the meanings they do.

of certain kinds—whom I called "conferring agents"—can confer properties on things simply in virtue of taking recognitional stances of certain types toward them. Ordinary people, for example, can confer the property of *being esteemed* on a rock star simply by esteeming her. Given that the proper conditions hold, a judge can confer the property of *being guilty* (before the law) on a person simply by declaring him guilty. Call a fact that x is F *recognition-dependent* just in case x has the property of being F simply in virtue of the fact that a conferring agent takes (or would take) one or another recognitional stance toward x. Some normative facts, I said, are recognition-dependent. The fact *that Major League managers are prohibited from ejecting umpires* is such a fact. This fact is recognition-dependent, since baseball managers are prohibited from ejecting umpires simply because a conferring agent has declared that anyone who occupies the role of being a manager is subject to that prohibition.

Now consider a moral fact such as:

that it is wrong to torture someone simply because she has inconvenienced you.

Realists claim that this fact is not recognition-dependent. They deny, then, that the moral status of torture is determined by any recognitional stance that conferring agents actually have toward it. They also deny that its wrongness is determined by the recognitional stance that an agent would have toward it, even under idealized conditions. According to realists, even if a perfectly rational agent would disapprove of torture, this is not what renders torture wrong; it is wrong independent of any such disapproval.

Constructivists see things differently, holding that moral facts such as the one mentioned above are recognition-dependent. The moral status of torture, according to constructivists, is determined by the attitudes that actual human agents either have toward it or would have toward it in idealized conditions.

This gives one a sense of how realism differs from constructivism. Now, however, we need to draw a further distinction. For, strictly speaking, realists need not hold that all moral facts are recognition-independent. And constructivists need not hold that all moral facts are recognition-dependent. The way to distinguish the two views, I suggested earlier, is to assume that moral properties of certain types are explanatorily basic. Something is an explanatorily basic moral property, I said, just in case if something exemplifies it, then there is a range of circumstances such that no other moral property accounts for this. Consider, for example, the property *being wrong*, which is an ingredient in the moral fact mentioned above. This property is explanatorily basic just in case there is a range of circumstances such that there is no other type of moral feature that accounts for the fact that actions are wrong. Actions are not wrong because a virtuous agent would not perform them, or because we have most moral reason not to perform them, and so on.

If this is right, we can specify more exactly what the difference is between realism and constructivism. Realists hold that there are explanatorily basic moral facts that are not recognition-dependent. Constructivists deny this. They claim that all explanatorily basic moral facts are recognition-dependent.

We are now in a position to formulate an adequacy condition on any constructivist position. Begin by noting that all constructivist positions have the following tripartite structure. There is, first, a conferring agent who takes (or would take) recognitional stances toward things, such as desiring or valuing them.[27] Second, there are the outputs of an agent's taking (or being such that she would take) a recognitional stance toward some object. These outputs are often the explanatorily basic moral facts. Finally, there is the determination base of these outputs, which includes the conferring agent's taking a recognitional stance toward an object, the objects of these stances, the information that she takes into account when taking up these stances, and any reasoning in which she might engage that determines which recognitional stances she has (or would have).

To illustrate, consider a crude subjectivist view about moral value. According to this position, there is, first, a conferring agent who disapproves of actions of certain types. Second, there is the output of her expressing attitudes of disapproval, namely, that the actions of which she disapproves have the property of *being morally bad*. Finally, the fact that these actions are bad has a determination base, which includes the information that she takes into account when disapproving

---

27. Recall that I use the term "agent" broadly. In principle, a conferring agent could be a community of individual agents.

of them—such as the fact that when agents engage in these actions, they tend to eventuate in states of pain and embarrassment for those she cares about.

With the structure of constructivist positions in hand, let me introduce one last piece of conceptual apparatus. Suppose we say that *moralized facts* are either the moral facts themselves or those facts that are themselves determined by moral facts. The moralized facts, then, will include not only the fact *that torture is wrong* but also *that an agent knows that torture is wrong*—the last being itself not a moral fact but constituted by one. Importantly for my purposes, provided that the Speech Act Argument is correct, the moralized facts will also include facts that consist in the performance of one or another speech act, as they too are constituted by moral features. The adequacy condition that any constructivist position must satisfy, I want to suggest, is what I shall call:

> **No Moralization**: Whenever the output of a construction procedure is an explanatorily basic moral fact, then moralized facts cannot belong to the determination base of this output.[28]

As it happens, this thesis is an implication of what it is for something to be an explanatorily basic moral fact. For, as I described them, an explanatorily basic moral fact might be grounded in other facts. But, by hypothesis, these other facts cannot themselves be or be determined by moral facts.

Constructivism has enjoyed a surge of popularity among philosophers in recent years.[29] And understandably so: it promises to deliver much of what one could want from a metaethical view. Like realism, constructivism (in its most plausible forms, at least) purports to vindicate a fairly robust account of moral reality, one according to which we cannot simply make up the moral facts as we please. However, like more radical versions of antirealism, it

---

28. What is the nature of the determination relation? On this matter, I remain relatively agnostic. I will assume only that it is a species of what, in Chapter 1, I called the generating relation, which might come in different varieties.

29. See, for example, Firth (1952); Lewis (1989); Copp (1995); Milo (1995); Korsgaard (1996); Carson (2000); James (2007); and Street (2008a). I should add that many philosophers take themselves to defend constructivism only with respect to a certain type of moral or evaluative property (or concept) and do not explicitly identify that property (or concept) as explanatorily basic. See, for example, Smith (1994); Scanlon (1998); Rawls (1999); and Street (2008a). Attempts to work out versions of fully comprehensive metaethical constructivism are rare.

promises to avoid objectionable ontological commitments, since it does not posit brute moral facts, but endeavors to account for their existence and nature by grounding them in philosophically unproblematic features of reality, such as the recognitional stances of human agents. In this way, its proponents claim, constructivism demystifies moral reality.

Despite its considerable attractions, I maintain that constructivism should be rejected. The argument I will press is that constructivists cannot satisfactorily accommodate No Moralization. For if the Speech Act Argument is sound, I claim, there is no satisfactory way to specify the determination base of the explanatorily basic moral facts without recourse to moralized facts, such as the performance of speech acts. The case I will present for this conclusion will be selective. I will present, first, a version of so-called non-idealized constructivism. Then I will explore a more sophisticated idealized version of the position. The fundamental problem that these positions face, I will contend, is endemic to constructivism. Nothing hangs on the details of any particular constructivist view.

Non-idealized constructivism

Sharon Street's version of "metaethical constructivism" can be viewed as a variant of non-idealized constructivism.[30] Street proposes that it is an agent's taking something to be a reason that accounts, in part, for its being a reason for that agent. What needs to be added is that an agent's taking something to be a reason generates a reason for that agent only if it withstands scrutiny in the sense of being "fully in line" with her other normative judgments.[31] Since an agent's other normative judgments might not in fact cohere with what she takes to be reasons, Street acknowledges that agents "can be mistaken about what those reasons are."[32] Still, Street forthrightly admits that this position, in her view, implies a version of relativism. Unlike Michael

---

30. See Street (2008a), 223.
31. Street (2008a), 216. In her (2006), Street says that "evaluative truth is a function of how all the evaluative judgements...stand up to scrutiny in terms of each other; it is a function of what would emerge from those evaluative judgements in reflective equilibrium" (154).
32. Street (2008a), 224.

Smith's or Christine Korsgaard's view, constructivism of this variety "is strongly Humean in that it accepts that practical reason as such commits us to no particular substantive conclusions about our reasons; depending on one's starting set of values, one could in principle have a reason for anything."[33] Street's version of constructivism, then, cuts loose any commitment to the claim that some reasons are non-relative or agent-neutral in character—a commitment, as we will see in a moment, that constructivists such as Smith, Korsgaard, and Ronald Milo believe is crucial to defend.

There is a lot left unspecified in Street's presentation of metaethical constructivism. Although it is officially labeled a version of metaethical constructivism, it is largely silent about the nature of moral reality. It says nothing, for example, about what grounds moral facts, offering instead a view about the nature of practical reasons or oughts. For present purposes, I am not going to speculate about what Street's actual views on the nature of moral reality are; the issue (as I will point out in the next chapter) is complicated. I will simply assume that we can model a version of metaethical constructivism on Street's position. Call this position *Humean constructivism.* Humean constructivists reject the realist view that the explanatorily basic moral facts are attitude-independent. Instead, they identify a type of explanatorily basic normative feature—in this case a moral reason—and endeavor to explain moral reality in terms of this feature. Humean constructivism, I am going to contend, fails to respond satisfactorily to the charge that it fails No Moralization.

Let me build a case for this last claim by identifying a recipe for generating a type of problematic case for constructivists. Here is the recipe: we begin by identifying a candidate for being an explanatorily basic moral feature. In the case at hand, our candidate is *being a moral reason.* We assume, next, that these reasons have determination bases. If what I said earlier about constructivism is correct, they include such things as an agent's taking one or another recognitional stance toward some object, the object of such an attitude itself, and whatever practical deliberation in which she engages that results in her taking up such a stance. (Conceivably, there might be all sorts of facts that are modally necessary for an agent to have moral reasons but do not

33. Street (2008a), 244. Although, see what Street says on 225.

belong to their determination base. That the Law of Simplification holds, for example, might be modally necessary for us to have moral reasons. But, arguably, it does not belong to the determination base of most of our moral reasons.) Finally, we devise cases in which an agent has a moral reason to act, and the determination base of that agent's having that reason includes moralized facts, such as the fact that an agent has performed a speech act. If there were such cases, they would represent the first step toward establishing that constructivist views cannot satisfactorily accommodate No Moralization, for moralized facts would belong to the determination base of the putatively explanatorily basic moral facts. Are there such cases?

There are indeed. Imagine that your spouse has repeatedly promised you to stop indulging an annoying habit but, since promising, has shown no intention to do so. Suppose that you are aware of his insincerity. Do you have a moral reason to condemn his behavior? Presumably, yes. This, after all, is not a difficult case in which it is indeterminate whether you have a moral reason to be against his behavior. What determines whether you have a moral reason to condemn his behavior? According to Humean constructivism, it is (in part) the fact that you take yourself to have a reason to condemn his behavior and your attitude's being such that it is fully in line with your other normative judgments. Suppose, for argument's sake, that your taking yourself to have a reason is, in this case, fully in line with your other judgments. If so, you have a moral reason to condemn your spouse's behavior (the reason, of course, need not be decisive). However, in this case, it is the fact that your spouse has performed a speech act that is the object of your recognitional stance. And, so, this moralized fact is part of the determination base of your having a reason to condemn your spouse's behavior, which violates No Moralization. Nothing about this case, it should be added, depends on the fact that moral reasons are assumed to be explanatorily basic. The same result could be generated if Humean constructivists were to offer views that took moral values, fittingness relations, or the like to be explanatorily basic.

This is the first step toward establishing that Humean constructivism cannot satisfactorily accommodate No Moralization. The reason it is only a first step is that, in any given situation, moral considerations can come in layers. Moral reasons might be determined by rights, responsibilities, and obligations, as they are in the case just described. But, in principle, these rights, responsibilities, and obligations could be determined by other moral reasons. Defenders of Humean constructivism, then, could concede that some moral reasons are determined by the rights, responsibilities, and obligations ingredient in the count-generation of speech. But these philosophers might also maintain that these rights, responsibilities, and obligations are themselves determined by moral reasons—where these reasons are understood to be those that are explanatorily basic.

Is this position defensible? I doubt it. To see why, call to mind the conditional moral rights, which we considered in Chapter 3, that attach to you and your audience upon your asserting a proposition p. They include:

> You have the right against your audience to its taking you at your word if you know that p.
>
> Your audience has a right to admonish you for being dishonest if you believe that p is false.

And:

> Your audience has a right to reproach you for exhibiting disrespect toward them if you fail to believe that p, although p happens to be true.

Suppose, for simplicity's sake, we grant that these rights supervene on moral reasons. If Humean constructivism were true, these reasons themselves would be determined (in part) by a speaker or his audience taking there to be reasons. In any given case of asserting, then, it would have to be true that:

> You take your audience to have a (moral) reason to take you at your word if you know that p.
>
> Your audience takes itself to have a (moral) reason to admonish you for being dishonest if you believe that p is false.

And:

> Your audience takes itself to have a (moral) reason to reproach you for exhibiting disrespect toward it if you fail to believe that p, although p happens to be true.

For these takings to actually determine that you have (or your audience has) reasons, then they would also have to be fully in line with your (or your audience's) other normative judgments.

Is it true that, when asserting occurs, speakers and their audience must take themselves to have such reasons? Not so far as I can tell. Some people, after all, do not believe or take there to be any moral reasons. And yet they speak. Other people believe that there are such reasons but their takings are not fully in line with their other normative judgments. And yet they also speak. But if they do, then the moral rights, responsibilities, and obligations that are ingredient in the count-generation of their speech acts are not determined by what they take to be reasons. It follows that Humean constructivism either fails No Moralization or implies that some of us fail to speak in cases in which we clearly do.

Humean constructivism is, of course, only one version of non-idealized constructivism. If we liked, we could give the view a Kantian twist. With Korsgaard, for example, we might maintain that practical agency has (non-moral) value in virtue of the fact that all practically rational agents must value it. For it is this fact about ourselves, says Korsgaard, which "places us under moral obligations."[34] For these obligations to be moral, however, they cannot simply be requirements for each person to value her own rational agency. Rather, they must be obligations to value the rational agency of each and every person. How, though, do we move from the fact that we are obligated to value our own rational agency to the claim that we must value that of others? "The solution" to this problem, says Korsgaard, "must be to show that reasons are not private, but public in their very essence."[35] The public character of reasons, Korsgaard continues, "is indeed created by the reciprocal exchange, the sharing, of the reasons of individuals."[36]

Korsgaard offers an explanation of how self-regarding, agent-relative reasons are converted into other-regarding, agent-neutral reasons. This conversion can occur, Korsgaard says, only in virtue of our discoursing with one another. If this is right, however, then Kantian versions of constructivism also fail No Moralization. For it

34. Korsgaard (1996), 132.
35. Korsgaard (1996), 135.
36. Korsgaard (1996). See also Korsgaard (2008), where she writes that agent-neutral reasons are "things that emerge in the interaction between people;" in particular, the possibility of their "shared deliberation" (191). Korsgaard uses the terms "private" and "agent-relative," on the one hand, and "public" and "agent-neutral," on the other, interchangeably.

cannot be the case that if moral reasons are explanatorily basic, then something is a moral reason for an agent S to act in a certain way if and only if and because agents, such as S or the members of S's community, have the rights, responsibilities and obligations of being speakers, some of which are moral.

Idealized constructivism

I have argued that non-idealized versions of constructivism, whether they be of the Humean or Kantian variety, either fail No Moralization or imply that we do not speak. Let us now turn to idealized versions of constructivism. Of the various versions of idealized constructivism on offer, I am going to consider the ideal adviser view, as it is widely thought to be the most powerful version of constructivism. Like the non-idealized position that we modeled on Street's position, ideal adviser views also identify moral reasons as being explanatorily basic. These views then offer us an account of what makes it the case that an agent has a moral reason to act. They tell us that an ordinary agent has a moral reason to perform an action in circumstances of a certain kind just in case and because an idealized version of that agent—what I have called a "conferring agent"—would want him to perform that action in those circumstances. Three aspects of these positions merit special mention.

First, the conferring agent is idealized: that is, she exhibits no defects in practical or theoretical reasoning, her cognitive faculties are working well, and she exhibits no gaps in the knowledge relevant for her being able to advise her non-idealized self how to act. There are good reasons for thinking that conferring agents must be idealized. For were it denied, constructivists would have difficulty honoring what appear to be certain conceptual constraints on what counts as a moral fact. If such an agent, for example, were ignorant of important contours of the nature of human well-being, she might prize the performance of an act-type wholly inimical to the well-being of others. And, thus, the performance of such an act-type might be, according to the position, (objectively) morally right, which sits poorly with the idea that a conceptual constraint on (objectively) right actions is that they promote, foster, or honor genuine human flourishing (or the participation in the goods that constitute human well-being, such as being the object of appropriate respect).[37]

Second, the conferring agent is an idealized version of the agent whom she advises.[38] As such, she is—to use Aristotle's terminology—a friend, an extension of the self. There also appear to be good reasons for accepting this claim. For were it rejected, constructivists would be subject to the following concern: suppose, as some have held, that a conferring agent were simply an idealized individual not bearing any particularly intimate relation to those she advises. You might rightly wonder: "Why should I care about what this agent advises me to do? And why should I trust her advice?" For all we reasonably believe, such an agent might care little about you and share few of your desires; she may have little interest in your well-being. But it is considerably less tempting to raise such questions about a perfected version of one's self. For in this case, the conferring agent is an extension of you and, as such, shares your desires or has desires that have evolved through a process of idealization from your desires. It is—so the thought goes—unlikely that such an agent would be "alienated" from her non-idealized self.

Third, idealization has an ineliminable social dimension. In his development of the ideal adviser theory, Michael Smith specifically draws attention to this aspect of the view. An ideal agent, Smith supposes, must be fully rational. Full rationality, Smith proposes, can be thought of as comprising these three features:

> The agent must have no false beliefs.
> The agent must have all relevant true beliefs.
> The agent must deliberate correctly.[39]

---

37. Milo (1995), 197, is a constructivist who recognizes the importance of conceptual constraints of this kind. Although I did not draw attention to it, what I called Humean constructivism would be vulnerable to the complaint that they fail to honor such constraints.

38. This is, admittedly, a misleading way of stating the view. As will become apparent, according to ideal adviser views, ideal advisers do not engage in advising—actual or counterfactual—of any sort.

39. Smith (1994), 156. I am using Smith's position to specify what idealized constructivists say about the social dimension of idealization. I doubt, however, that Smith's position is a version of constructivism, as I understand it, since he does not fashion his view as one regarding explanatorily basic moral facts.

In specifying these features as being constitutive of full rationality, Smith borrows from Bernard Williams. Yet Smith finds Williams' own understanding of full rationality unsatisfactory. The problem, says Smith, is with the third condition. Williams works with a thin account of practical rationality, according to which correct deliberation primarily consists in correct instrumental reasoning and exercise of the "imagination." But, Smith rightly points out, one could deliberate correctly in Williams' sense and still suffer from "compulsions, addictions, emotional disturbances, and the like."[40]

This, however, is unacceptable. No plausible view tells us that normative reasons are determined by the desires of an agent who, for all we reasonably believe, suffers from such maladies. To handle this problem, Smith proposes that we think of correct deliberation in a more substantive fashion. Correct deliberation, Smith suggests, is a process by which we try to find out whether our desires are "systematically justifiable"—this being a state in which our desires and other propositional attitudes achieve a state of coherence. Engaging in a process whose aim is to achieve this, says Smith, "creates new desires and destroys old" ones.[41] To which it should be added that, given Smith's aims, full rationality must consist not in simply trying to bring about such a state but also actually *succeeding* in doing so. Fully rational desires are the product of rational deliberation that has been successfully executed.

But how does one go about achieving coherence between one's desires and other propositional attitudes? According to Smith, by engaging in the social practice of advancing reasons in favor of having certain desires and commitments and subjecting these reasons to the critical scrutiny of others. Engaging in this social practice is crucial for two reasons. In the first place, it is the appropriate response to the recognition that none of us "has any special epistemic gifts that would justify us in privileging our own desires and judgements" over those of others.[42] Moreover, Smith claims, were idealized agents to engage in the practice of rational dialogue, then they could achieve substantive convergence among their desires and

40. Smith (1994), 158.
41. Smith (1994), 160.
42. Smith (1994), 177.

those of other ideal advisers. This, says Smith, is critical to any plausible version of an ideal adviser view, for the notion of a normative
reason is "stubbornly non-relative."[43] Generally speaking, reasons are
not reasons for me or reasons for you. Rather, they are reasons for
anyone situated as I am or you are. For an ideal adviser view to vindicate such a non-relative account of reasons, however, "the truth of a
normative reason claim requires a convergence in the desires of fully
rational agents." And, once again, that is possible only insofar as we
"converse and argue" about the reasons we have.[44] Smith, I might
add, is not alone in this conviction. In his version of constructivism,
Milo maintains that the explanatorily basic moral features are the
outcome "of a process of construction in which rational agents,
under idealized conditions, seek to reach an agreement on principles for regulating their relationships and behavior toward one
another."[45] The thought, apparently, is that were moral obligations
or reasons to exist, then some must be agent-neutral. Agent-neutral-
ity, however, requires convergence among idealized agents.

We now have before us the outlines of a prominent type of constructivist position. According to this position, all ordinary agents
have moral reasons of various sorts. Some of these reasons, moreover, are "non-relative." What moral reasons an ordinary agent has
are determined by those desires of his that would survive a process of
critical reflection in idealized conditions. The critical reflection, in
turn, is ineliminably social. Desires are rational to the extent they
would survive the process of giving and assessing reasons among
similarly idealized agents in what Smith calls the "evaluating world."[46]

Critics sometimes allege that philosophers who defend idealized
constructivism must walk a conceptual tightrope.[47] On the one hand,
they must incorporate into their account of idealization various substantive commitments about that in which idealization consists. For
only by doing so can they avoid the charge that their view fails to
honor certain conceptual constraints on what counts as a moral

43. Smith (1994), 172.
44. Smith (1994), 173.
45. Milo (1995), 183.
46. Smith (1994), 151.
47. Shafer-Landau (2003), ch. 2, for example, raises this challenge. Enoch (2005) raises
    related issues.

reason, such as the claim that moral reasons generally concern the well-being of human agents and are non-relative in nature. On the other hand, those who defend these positions must avoid incorporating into their account of idealization substantive commitments to entities whose existence and nature they are trying to explain, such as moral rights, responsibilities, and obligations. Many suspect that constructivists fail to navigate this challenge. I believe that they are correct.

Let me explain why by returning to a case introduced earlier. Suppose, once again, that your spouse has repeatedly promised you to stop indulging an annoying habit. His promises are, however, insincere, as he has no intention—and never has had an intention—to change his ways. Do you have a moral reason to condemn his behavior? Presumably, yes (although, of course, the reason need not be decisive). This, after all, is not a difficult case in which it is indeterminate whether you have a moral reason to be against his behavior. What accounts for your having a reason to condemn his behavior? According to ideal adviser views, at least two factors.

The first factor is the relevant information of which your ideal adviser is aware. That information includes facts regarding speech. More specifically, it includes information that your spouse has altered his normative position with regard to you by taking responsibility for his intending to act a certain way, even though he has no intention to act that way. This normative fact, according to normative theorists, is ingredient in the count-generation of your spouse's speech acts. The second determining factor is that whatever desire your ideal adviser has with regard to you, it is the result of her having engaged in rational deliberation with her idealized peers in the evaluating world. In this sense, the verdict your adviser forms is not simply her own; it represents the will of the ideal community.

With this noted, let us suppose that your ideal adviser renders the following verdict regarding your spouse: she wants you, her ordinary self, to want to condemn your spouse's behavior. It follows that, according to idealized adviser views, you have a moral reason to condemn your spouse's behavior (although, once again, this reason need not be decisive). It also follows that this moral reason is determined by moralized facts. For the determination base of your having a reason to condemn your spouse's behavior includes the rights, responsibilities, and obligations ingredient in the count-generation of speech. Nothing about this case, it should be added, depends on the fact that moral reasons are taken to be explanatorily basic. The same result could be generated if ideal adviser views were to take moral values, fittingness relations, or the like to be explanatorily basic.

This would be the first step toward establishing that ideal adviser views cannot satisfactorily accommodate No Moralization. But, as we noted earlier, another step is required. For advocates of ideal adviser views can remind us that often there are layers of determination relations. Moral reasons can be determined by rights, responsibilities, and obligations, as they are in the case just described. But these normative features could, in principle, be determined by other moral reasons that are explanatorily basic. The challenge, then, is for constructivists to identify a class of explanatorily basic moral features such that these features either determine the rights, responsibilities, and obligations that account for speech or are identical with these rights, responsibilities, and obligations.

Idealized constructivists could try to meet this challenge in the following way. Call to mind, once again, the rights that attach to assertors and their audiences, such as:

> You have the right against your audience to their taking you at your word if you know that p.
>
> Your audience has a right to admonish you for being dishonest if you believe that p is false.

And:

> Your audience has a right to reproach you for exhibiting disrespect toward them if you fail to believe that p, although p happens to be true.

Suppose we grant, for argument's sake, that these rights supervene on moral reasons. If ideal adviser views were true, these reasons themselves would be determined by what ideal advisers would want their ordinary selves to want. In any given case of asserting, then, it would have to be true that:

Your ideal adviser wants you to want your audience to take you at your word if you know that p. All other ideal advisers have the same want for the right reasons.

Your audience's ideal advisers want them to want to admonish you for being dishonest if you believe that p is false. All other ideal advisers have the same want for the right reasons.

And:

Your audience's ideal advisers want them to want to reproach you for exhibiting disrespect toward them if you fail to believe that p, although p happens to be true. All other ideal advisers have the same want for the right reasons.

Call these claims the *idealized conditionals*. If the idealized conditionals were true, and their determination bases did not include moralized facts, then ideal adviser views would be well along to having established that their position does not fail No Moralization.

A crucial issue remains to be determined, however. That issue is whether we have sufficient reason to believe that the idealized conditionals are true under the assumption that their determination bases do not include moralized facts. The way to make headway on this matter, I suggest, is to distinguish between different types of idealized conditions.

Let us say that an agent occupies *minimally ideal conditions* just in case she has no false beliefs, has all relevant true beliefs, and is perfectly instrumentally rational—with this caveat: the determination conditions for any output that may issue from these conditions include no moralized facts, as these outputs are explanatorily basic moral facts. The relevant information of which a minimally idealized agent is aware, then, does not include any information regarding the rights, responsibilities, and obligations of speakers. Nor are the outputs from minimally ideal conditions determined by facts about ideal agents engaging in discourse wherein they present and respond to reasons. In contrast to this, let us say that an agent occupies *maximally ideal conditions* when and only when she is in minimally ideal conditions and also subjects her desires to the scrutiny of her idealized peers by engaging in the discursive activity of offering and responding to reasons. Unlike minimally ideal conditions, the relevant information of which a maximally ideal agent is aware can (and often does) include moralized facts, such as the rights, responsibilities, and obligations of speakers.

If the normative theory of speech is correct, proponents of the ideal adviser view can maintain that their position does not fail No Moralization. But they can plausibly maintain this only if the idealized conditionals are true under the assumption that the idealized agents to whom these conditionals refer are only minimally ideal. For only then will it be the case that the determination bases of the idealized conditionals do not include moralized facts. Our question is whether these conditionals are true under this assumption.

The best way to answer this question is to raise some questions of our own about the idealized conditionals, such as:

> In minimally ideal conditions, would your ideal adviser and those of every other ordinary agent, want your audience to want to admonish you for being dishonest if you believe that p is false, want your audience to want to reproach you if you fail to believe p, and so forth?

And:

> In maximally ideal conditions, would your ideal adviser and those of every other ordinary agent, want your audience to want to admonish you for being dishonest if you believe that p is false, want your audience to want to reproach you if you fail to believe p, and so forth?

Critics of the ideal adviser theory are skeptical about whether we should answer Yes to the second question. These critics maintain that even in maximally ideal conditions we should not expect the desires of ideal agents to converge.[48] Be that as it may, both friends and critics of ideal adviser views agree that we have no reason to answer Yes to the first question. After all, as Smith points out, for all we reasonably believe, minimally ideal agents could suffer from all manner of maladies including compulsions, addictions, and emotional disturbances.[49]

To illustrate, imagine a gambling addict. When this person becomes a minimally ideal agent, we can suppose, his zest for gambling diminishes not a bit. Accordingly, in minimally ideal conditions, he has all sorts of desires regarding gambling. One such desire is that his ordinary self

48. See Joyce (2001), ch. 4, for example.
49. Smith (1994), 158.

succeed spectacularly at gambling, even if such success requires that his ordinary self repeatedly dissembles to win. For example, when his ordinary self presents himself as believing propositions that he knows are false, then his idealized self does *not* want his ordinary self's audience to want to reproach his ordinary self. Likewise, when his ordinary self presents himself as intending to act in a certain way but has no intention of doing so, then his idealized self does not want his ordinary self's audience to want to admonish his ordinary self. And when his ordinary self presents himself as having the authority to lay obligations on others even when he knows he lacks this authority, then his idealized self does not want his ordinary self's audience to want to blame his ordinary self. At least this is true when being insincere in these ways is a good strategy for his ordinary self to be a successful gambler.

It is because of possibilities such as this that philosophers such as Smith and Milo introduce the notion of maximally ideal conditions. These conditions are supposed to function as the corrective mechanism by which maladies such as gambling addictions are removed. The Speech Act Argument, in effect, blocks this maneuver. For it prevents ideal adviser theorists from appealing to moralized facts, including facts about speech in which idealized agents exchange reasons, when offering an account of what determines the explanatorily basic moral facts. If the Speech Act Argument is sound, defenders of idealized constructivism can appeal only to minimally ideal conditions when fashioning their view. But that, all parties agree, is insufficient. For we have no reason to believe that in minimally ideal conditions, the idealized conditionals are true.

Here, in summary, is the argument that I have just presented. When offering an account of the explanatorily basic moral features, defenders of ideal adviser views could appeal to either maximally or minimally ideal conditions. If they appeal to conditions of the former sort, then these views fail No Moralization. If they appeal only to conditions of the latter sort, then, by their own lights, we have no reason to accept the idealized conditionals, which are ingredient in the count-generation of speech. Either way, their view ought not to be accepted.

Like error theorists, constructivists could maintain that the rights, responsibilities, and obligations ingredient in the count-generation of speech are non-moral, defending a position close to the mixed view. It is worth noting, however, that constructivists are not in a good position to defend such a view. Unlike error theorists, constructivists believe that there are moral facts. But, if so, they cannot hold that we have good reason to believe that the rights, responsibilities, and obligations ingredient in the count-generation of speech are non-moral because we have sufficient independent reason to believe that there are no moral facts. Constructivists would have to adduce some other reason to believe that the normative features that account for speech are not moral, all the while maintaining that the appearance that they are moral systematically misleads. The obvious worry about any such strategy is that it would backfire, providing reason to believe that there are no moral facts. That conclusion, however, is something that all constructivists wish to avoid.

IV Conclusion

In Chapter 1, we began our discussion by considering a dispute between Hobbes and Clarke. This dispute, it turns out, reveals deep differences between how philosophers think of the nature of morality. According to the broadly Hobbesian approach, morality is a relative newcomer to the world, emerging only upon the formation of a social contract between self-interested agents. Elizabeth Anderson voices something like this position when she writes that "moral rules spring from our practices of reciprocal claim making, in which we work out together the kinds of considerations that count as reasons that all of us must heed, and thereby devise rules for living together peacefully and cooperatively, on a basis of mutual accountability."[50] For Clarke, by contrast, morality does not emerge with the formation of any social contract or practices of reciprocal claim making, but lies deep in the structure of reality—so deep, in fact, that the types of speech acts that Hobbes believes generate morality would not be possible were there not moral facts that are ingredient in count-generating them. Many philosophers are sympathetic with the broadly Hobbesian conviction that morality, so to speak,

50. Anderson (2007), 228.

arrived late on the scene. I have, however, defended something similar to Clarke's position, maintaining that if the normative theory of speech is true, then among the features that account for speech are moral ones. If this view is right, then error-theoretic and expressivist views, which reject the existence of moral facts, are false. So also are constructivist views, which in many ways stand in the lineage of Hobbes. For all I have said, morality may have emerged in one way or another from human activity. But it did not do so because we first began speaking to one another.

7
Epistemic Implications

In Chapter 1, I presented the Speech Act Argument for moral realism, formulating it as follows:

(1) Agents perform illocutionary acts such as asserting, promising, and commanding.

(2) Illocutionary acts are count-generated by locutionary acts. But locutionary acts are not sufficient for the count-generation to occur; there must be something else that explains why it occurs.

(3) It is an agent's having the rights, responsibilities, and obligations of being a speaker that explains (at least in part) why the count-generation of illocutionary acts occurs.

(4) So, agents have the rights, responsibilities, and obligations of being a speaker.

(5) If an agent has the rights, responsibilities, and obligations of being a speaker, then moral facts exist.

(6) So, moral facts exist.

In the preceding chapters, I have focused my attention on premises (3) and (5) of this argument. Chapter 2 offered a defense of premise (3) both by developing a case for the normative theory of speech and defending it against its most prominent rival, the perlocution-ary-intention view. Chapters 3, 4, 5, and 6 presented a multi-pronged defense of premise (5). I claimed that not only are some of the normative dimensions of speech moral in character, but also that they are best understood as realists believe. In the course of that discussion, I indicated why, rather than conclude that we do not speak at all, we should also accept the argument's first premise.

If the Speech Act Argument succeeds, it provides good reason to accept a substantive and contested philosophical position—one which many believe it is important to defend. Arguments for substantive philosophical conclusions, however, fall into two broad types. Some arguments purport to provide evidence for believing a substantive philosophical position without furnishing the resources to reply to important objections to it. Consider, for example, the cosmological argument. Conceivably, a sophisticated version of this argument could provide evidence for theism. But if it did, it would shed little light on how to address the most pressing challenges to theism, such as the problem of evil or the problem of religious diversity. Even in its most powerful guise, the cosmological argument would be a case of an argument for a substantive philosophical position that fails to provide the means to answer important objections to that position.

Other arguments, in contrast, not only purport to provide evidence for believing a substantive philosophical position but also make available resources to reply to objections to it. The Speech Act Argument, I maintain, is an argument of this type. The argument provides not only good reasons to accept moral realism, but also the resources to address persistent worries about it. Which persistent worries? In principle, several. In this chapter, however, I will have my eye on only one such concern—what I will call the *epistemological challenge* to moral realism. The central concern expressed by this objection, which I touched upon in Chapter 4, is that moral realists have no plausible account of how we could reliably grasp moral facts. According to some recent critics, this challenge exposes realism at its weakest point, highlighting one respect in which it is explanatorily deficient.[1]

Not all versions of realism are equally vulnerable to the epistemological challenge. Versions of moral naturalism, which tell us that moral facts are ordinary natural facts, are widely viewed as being

---

1. The critics include Gibbard (2003), 263–5; Joyce (2006), ch. 6; Street (2006), (2008b), and (forthcoming); Bedke (2009); and Lynch (2009), ch. 8. Oddie (2005); Wielenberg (2010); Enoch (2011), ch. 7; Parfit (2011) Vol. II, chs. 32–3; Shafer-Landau (2012), and FitzPatrick (forthcoming) address the challenge. All the philosophers included in this second group, I should note, locate themselves in the non-naturalist realist tradition. Among them, Oddie alone maintains that moral facts are causally efficacious.

immune to the challenge. After all, according to moral naturalism, moral facts are causally efficacious; as such, its proponents claim, there is no special problem as to how we could know them.[2] Versions of non-naturalism which deny that moral facts enter into the causal nexus are a different story. They—or so it is often alleged—especially struggle to articulate in what sense our moral judgments could reliably track the moral facts. How, after all, could we get a cognitive grip on the properties that constitute these facts in the first place? And how would our normative judgments track these facts if they were causally inert? These are difficult questions to answer well. Nonetheless, in this chapter, I propose to grasp the nettle and offer a response to them on behalf of moral non-naturalists. My primary rationale for doing so is this: if the version of realism most vulnerable to the epistemological challenge can mount a respectable response to it, then that is a very positive sign for realism. We will have succeeded in shining light in one of the darker corners of the view.

I Stating the challenge

Philosophers have long suspected that non-naturalist realists—"realists" for short—have nothing particularly informative to say about how we acquire moral knowledge. Many suspect that the realist's appeal to "moral intuitions" is simply an avoidance tactic—an attempt not to admit that realists have nothing enlightening to say about the topic. In recent years, however, this suspicion has been sharpened into an articulate objection. This objection hinges on what I will call:

> **The Remarkable Coincidence**: It is remarkable that our moral judgments reliably track the moral facts. For had we been born into a different culture, lived in a different millennium, or been the product of a different evolutionary history, we would have made very different normative judgments from the ones we now make.[3]

---

2. Notably, Street (2006) disagrees. Copp (2008) responds on behalf of the naturalists. There are, however, other sorts of challenges to naturalism in the vicinity—most notably, the Moral Twin Earth Argument developed by Horgan and Timmons (1991).

3. Two points: first, I shall understand the reliability of a faculty or a method to consist in its yielding not simply a preponderance of true beliefs with respect to a field of propositions, but also non-accidentally true beliefs in the following sense: these beliefs do not

Sharon Street, who more than anyone has emphasized just how re-markable the coincidence is, maintains that the coincidence is one about which realists should worry. She contends that not only have realists not tried to explain the coincidence, they also have no good explanation of it. However, moral antirealists of a certain type—the so-called Humean constructivists—do. They can explain the coinci-dence. This, Street argues, is a powerful reason to reject realism in favor of constructivism of this sort.[4]

Later I will touch upon the issue of why, according to Street, Humean constructivists can explain the Remarkable Coincidence. For now, it is important to emphasize that this argument's conclu-sion is explicitly comparative: it says that constructivism does a better job accounting for the Remarkable Coincidence than realism. If true, this claim itself does not imply that realism is false. Nor does it imply that realism does a worse job accounting for the Remarkable Coincidence than other antirealist views, such as those we considered in the previous chapter. Rather, the argument's conclusion concerns how realism stacks up to one of its more prominent rivals with re-gard to one important issue.[5]

I want to emphasize this last point because philosophers some-times proceed as if the realist's inability to explain the Remarkable Coincidence is crippling. But it is not. Bring to mind the three types of moral antirealist view that we evaluated in the last chapter. Error theorists do not explain the Remarkable Coincidence better than

---

issue from a source, such as an evil demon or systemic hallucinations, which prevents them from being cases of knowledge. Second, I am not using "tracking" to mean to causally track. I assume that the term can be understood in a non-causal way, such as when beliefs of a certain kind tend to correspond to or represent facts of a given sort.

4. See Street (2006), (2008b), and (forthcoming). My formulation of the Remarkable Coincidence draws upon Street (forthcoming), 10. In section III, I will explain what Street means by Humean constructivism. It might be worth noting that Street's chal-lenge hangs on the implicit assumption that, according to realists, some moral facts are not determined by such things as cultural facts, where we are located in history, or our particular evolutionary history.

5. There are other ways of formulating the argument—such as the way in which I did in Chapter 4—that are not comparative. According to one such formulation, a necessary condition of having reason to accept realism is realism's having an adequate explan-ation of the Remarkable Coincidence. Such a premise is, however, more difficult to defend than the comparative claims that I attribute to realism's critics here. That noted, I believe that when modified, the points I make concerning the comparative version of the argument would apply also to the non-comparative version.

realists. Their view, after all, implies that there is nothing to explain, as we have no moral knowledge. Is this any reason to believe that, when it comes to the epistemology of moral belief, the error theory is superior to its rivals? Not obviously. No one thinks, for example, that when it comes to the epistemology of perception, radical solipsism is superior to rival views because it relieves itself of having to explain knowledge of the external world. Better, we think, to have a position according to which we have such knowledge even if that position struggles to explain how we gain it. Arguably, something similar is true of moral knowledge. After all, were the error theory true, we could not know apparently obvious moral truths, such as that it is wrong to engage in recreational slaughter. That is not a virtue of the position.

Or consider sophisticated expressivists. Their position also implies that the Remarkable Coincidence calls for no explanation. For, in their view, while there are deflated moral facts, they are not the sort of thing that can be reliably tracked. As Blackburn puts the point in one place, deflated moral facts are simply not the sort of thing that "answer to" our moral judgments.[6] When it comes to the epistemology of moral belief, is this better than a position according to which our moral judgments can track the moral facts, even if we have yet to successfully explain the relation? Not obviously. It is not clearly preferable to accept a position according to which moral judgments could not track the moral facts (or according to which there is little informative to say about the tracking relation) than one according to which there is, in principle, a substantive story to be told about the tracking relation although we have yet to articulate it.

Or consider, finally, those who favor idealized versions of constructivism, holding that the moral facts are fixed by the attitudes of idealized agents. Unlike error theorists and sophisticated expressivists, these philosophers endeavor to explain the Remarkable Coinci-

---

6. Blackburn (1999), 216. In other places, Blackburn is happy to say that moral judgments represent the moral facts, provided we work with a deflated understanding of the facts and the representation relation (see Blackburn (1998), ch. 2). In this case, the view is that while the moral facts can be tracked, there is nothing informative to say about that in which the tracking relation consists. I discuss these issues at more length in Cuneo (2008).

dence. Is this view better placed to explain it than realists? Not obviously. It is not at all evident that our present culture, time, and evolutionary history have placed us in a favorable position to grasp what idealized agents would care about. Idealized constructivists, after all, do not operate with any analog to special revelation in which we, like Moses on Mount Sinai, receive the moral law.

If this is right, the epistemological challenge to realism is best understood as having limited ambitions. To say it again, it is supposed to provide reasons for rejecting realism in favor of a particular type of antirealist position, namely, Humean constructivism. Although modest in aspiration, the argument is, I believe, important. For realists would very much like to have interesting and informative things to say about how we might reliably track the moral facts.[7] Were they to have nothing to say, that would be a liability—perhaps not a crippling one, but a liability nonetheless. In what follows, I am going to argue that realists can say interesting and informative things about how we can track the moral facts. I am going to contend, moreover, that the Speech Act Argument can help realists to say these things. Before I turn to these matters, however, I should first make an observation about the epistemological challenge itself.

The Remarkable Coincidence states that there is a reliable tracking relation between the moral facts and our beliefs. It assumes that we can cognitively access these facts; they are there available for thought. In what follows, I propose to pull apart two related issues that the argument runs together. The first concerns how we could gain epistemic access to moral properties, how it is that they are available for thought and attention. The second concerns how, having grasped these properties, we might reliably track the facts of which they are constituents. A moment's reflection reveals that an answer to the first issue need not provide an answer to the second. And *vice versa.*

---

7. McGinn (1993), chs. 6–7, offers a different approach to these issues, not considered by Street. McGinn notes that significant stretches of moral knowledge are *a priori*. While it is plausible to suppose, McGinn argues, that we have some knowledge of this sort, it has to be conceded that we have no good explanation of how we gain it. But this, McGinn hypothesizes, may simply be a function of the fact that the correct explanation of such knowledge is "cognitively closed" to us; we are constitutionally unable to discern it, given the limited power of our cognitive faculties. While I have some sympathy with what McGinn says, I am going to try to say more about moral knowledge than McGinn thinks we can.

One could, after all, supply an account of how we grasp moral properties without having supplied an account of how it is that we reliably refer to moral facts. For example, to claim that we grasp moral properties by something akin to Russellian acquaintance would not thereby establish how we reliably track them. Conversely, one could offer an account of the Remarkable Coincidence without having shed much light on how we apprehend moral properties. For an explanation of how we track these facts might tell us little about how we get the properties that constitute these facts in mind in the first place. Think of mathematics as an analog: by all appearances, we can reliably track numbers and their relations by mastering mathematical theorems and proofs. Arguably, however, this sheds little light on how we can apprehend numbers and the relations they bear to one another.

Yet both issues are of interest. Moreover, providing an answer to one may illuminate how we can answer the other. The Speech Act Argument, I believe, can help us address each issue. So, I am going to tackle these two issues—how we might apprehend and refer to moral properties, and how we can reliably track the moral facts—separately. However, it is worth emphasizing that, in addressing these issues, I will be painting with fairly broad strokes. I am not going to fill in many of the details that a full-scale treatment of them would. My primary aim is to lay out a type of strategy that could be developed at greater length.

My discussion falls into three parts. In the first, I offer one account of how we might apprehend moral properties, which draws upon the Speech Act Argument. In the second, I address Street's challenge that moral realists cannot account for how we might reliably track the moral facts, arguing that it can be met. In the third, I present a positive reason for thinking that we could reliably apprehend such facts, which also draws upon the Speech Act Argument.

II Having things in mind

Let me begin with some preliminary remarks about how I will understand the phenomenon of apprehending or getting a mental grip on something. In what follows, I will operate with a distinction between *having something in mind*, on the one hand, and *reference*, on the other.[8] As I understand it, for a person to have something in mind or apprehend it is simply for her to have a cognitive grip on that thing sufficient for her to form a range of *de re*/predicative thoughts about it. When, then, I say that an agent apprehends a moral property, I will mean that that property is there, available to her for thought as a potential referent; she has it well enough in mind to do such things as predicate it of various things, reflect upon it, discern some of its conceptual and explanatory relations with other properties, and so forth. In contrast, for a person to refer to something is, I will assume, for that person to pick out that thing on some occasion by the use of a concept or linguistic expression. So, for example, I might apprehend the property *being wrong*, since I can form various *de re*/predicative thoughts about it, recognizing (among other things) that while it can be predicated of actions, it cannot be predicated of people. On a given occasion I might also refer to this property by the use of the concept 'being wrong,' such as when I form the judgment that your having lied to your employer about your criminal record is wrong.

Not all philosophers, I realize, operate with a distinction between having something in mind and reference. And among those who do recognize this distinction, not all would understand it in the way that I do. Let me, then, say a little more about how I understand each notion and how they are related, since doing so will be helpful for setting up the argument I want to present in this section.

Begin with the notion of having something in mind. An agent, I assume, can get something in mind in different ways. I could, for example, get Mount Rainier in mind by seeing it, being told about it, or viewing a representation of it on a map. Not only can an agent get something in mind in different ways, she can also *have* it in mind in different ways, having different cognitive perspectives or "takes" on it. When hiking on Mount Rainier, for example, I could have the thought about a tent in the distance that *that tent is on fire*. This

---

8. In the contemporary discussion, the phrase "having in mind" traces back to Donnellan (1966). My use of the concept expressed by this phrase, I believe, is similar to but not identical with Donnellan's. For if Kaplan (2012) is right, having in mind is for Donnellan a primitive non-descriptive cognitive relation; as will be evident shortly, I do not assume this.

thought is importantly different from the thought, about the very same tent, that *my tent is on fire*, if only because the latter thought is connected with action dispositions that the former is not.

What this last example illustrates is that while having something in mind is closely related to both possessing a concept and to referring to something, it is identical with neither. Having something in mind is not the same as possessing a concept, since an agent could possess a concept that fails to stand for anything. Having something in mind is not identical with referring to something, since an agent could have something in mind and fail to refer to it because she makes no attempt to do so.[9] I hasten to add that having something in mind can bear all sorts of interesting relations to referring, among which is guiding us when we refer, such as when my seeing Mount Rainier on the horizon guides me when I refer to it by, say, pointing at it.

I turn now to reference, about which I can be even briefer. While I assume that we can refer to things, I do not assume that any particular *theory* of reference is correct—where a theory of reference offers a more or less complete account of how we refer to various things in the world by the use of names, natural kind concepts, indexicals, descriptions, mass terms, and the like. This is mostly because I doubt that we presently have any such theory that is satisfactory. The two most prominent options—broadly descriptivist and broadly causal views of reference—each have their fair share of problems.[10] Nonetheless, I will not turn my back on these theories, since each has important insights to contribute, even if it does not supply the whole story about reference. Let me add that the assumptions that inform my discussion will not suppose that an adequate account of reference to moral reality must incorporate other constraints, such as explaining how we can over time reliably grasp moral properties or why we are necessarily motivated upon grasping them, which realists such as Richard Boyd and Ralph Wedgwood accept.[11]

These preliminary matters having been noted, I can now offer the argument that interests me. The argument is one from parallel cases. It first presents a case in which most of us agree that an agent both

9. Another difference: as my comments above suggest, having in mind comes in degrees. Arguably, though, reference does not.
10. Johnston (2007) offers a succinct review of them.
11. See Boyd (1988), 195 and (2003), 515–19; and Wedgwood (2007), chs. 2 and 3.

has in mind and has referred to something that is not a normative property. It then offers a second, parallel case that shares relevant similarities with the first except that an agent appears to have in mind and refer to a normative property. Given that we agree that the agent has succeeded in having something in mind and securing reference in the first case, we should also agree that she has done so in the second case.[12]

Here is the first case, which is inspired by Gilbert Harman. The case, ironically, is one that Harman employs to argue that moral facts do not play interesting explanatory roles.

> **Lab**: A physicist sits in her lab. She peers into a cloud chamber, observing a vapor trail. Upon observing the vapor trail, she forms the judgment *there goes a proton.*[13]

Let us agree that, in this case, our protagonist already has the kind *proton* in mind and upon forming her judgment she thereupon refers to a proton. Harman himself emphasizes that cognitive acts such as observing and judging are theory-laden, as much of a physicist's thinking about protons presupposes an extensive network of background beliefs and dispositions, including the employment of models about the nature and behavior of protons. Of course, some of these beliefs are probably false. Those knowledgeable about physics, moreover, acknowledge that the models employed to theorize about such things as protons are often highly misleading. (If philosophers of science are right, atomic and subatomic entities, such as protons, are not at all similar to miniscule billiard balls that bounce against one another. But, apparently, models that present them as such are, in many ways, helpful for thinking about the nature and behavior of these "denizens of the theoretical deep."[14]) Nevertheless, we know that these models can help us think about things such as protons. If this is right, we often apprehend and refer to entities such as protons

---

12. The argument I am presenting, then, is not one that attempts to show that normative features explain observations or judgments in the way that non-normative features do. Rather, it *supposes* that normative features play the explanatory role of being ingredient in the count-generation of speech. This assumption having been made, the argument endeavors to establish that we can grasp normative features in much the same way that we grasp non-normative features of certain kinds.

13. Harman (1977), ch. 1.

14. I borrow this phrase from Steve Wykstra.

even when we hold false beliefs about them or think about them (often self-consciously) in misleading ways. I shall return to this point later.

Protons and other subatomic entities, we can assume, enter into causal relations. Still, when physicists refer to entities of this sort they do not do so by directly perceiving them, say, in the way that we can directly perceive a nugget of gold by feeling or seeing it. Protons are not part of our manifest environment; they are unobservables. We observe them only by the effects that they have on our environment. But if so, how do physicists manage to get them in mind? And how do they manage to refer to them?

Let me address the first question. In this case, a natural suggestion is that they get them in mind by way of the apprehensive use of singular (or descriptive) concepts, which specify that these entities bring about one or another effect in our environment, such as vapor trails, or play some explanatory role in our best theories, such as unifying otherwise disparate phenomena. Or to state this natural suggestion more precisely: physicists get these entities in mind by way of the apprehensive use of singular concepts or by standing in some suitable relation to someone who has used these concepts in this way.[15] If one likes to think of these unobservables as being entities that are endowed with causal powers of certain kinds, then another way to put the matter is that we get these unobservables in mind by apprehending the effects of the manifestation of their powers or by standing in some suitable relation to someone who has. In such cases, we designate the entities in question as being the sort of thing that has powers to bring about such and such effects in a given environment.

Call a singular concept that denotes an entity in virtue of that entity's playing one or another explanatory role a *role-designating* concept.[16]

---

15. I assume that singular (or descriptive) concepts can be used in at least two different ways: to apprehend an entity (as when these concepts are used in the subject position) or to predicate something of that entity (as when these concepts are used in the predicate position). It is the apprehensive use of concepts on which I focus. Donnellan (1966) is the inspiration for the distinction, although what I say does not neatly map onto what Donnellan says but more nearly approximates some of the points made in Strawson (1950) about how descriptions work.

16. The term "role-designating concept," I realize, is not entirely felicitous, since what gets designated by such a concept is not a role but an object that plays a role. So long as we keep this in mind, using this term should not create confusion.

Taken on their own, role-designating concepts are often superficial, as they often tell us relatively little about the nature of the entities they denote. But, when employed in thought and investigation, they can also be extraordinarily illuminating. A role-designating concept often allows us to get in mind an object that plays an explanatory role, linking together various phenomena that we did not know were linked or that we knew to be linked but were unsure in what way. (One of the great triumphs of Newtonian science, we are told, is that it understood the concept of gravity in such a way that allowed us to link apparently disparate phenomena such as the orbit of the moon and the tidal forces.) Moreover, having gotten some entity in mind by the use of a role-designating concept, we can often discover other important things about it, such as the conceptual and explanatory relations the thing designated bears to other entities, including its being such as to unify otherwise disparate phenomena. Finally, when things go especially well, we can discern that a thing with a certain kind of nature best satisfies a role specified by a role-designating concept. In that case, we employ what we might call a *role-revealing* concept—a concept that reveals the nature of that which plays one or another explanatory role specified by some role-designating concept.

Thus understood, role-designating concepts function descriptively. A person apprehends some entity by the apprehensive use of some role-designating concept in virtue of there being something that satisfies (or satisfies to some sufficient degree) the description it expresses. In a case similar to Lab, for example, it might be that an agent gets the kind *proton* in mind by the apprehensive use of some role-designating concept. With more exploration, she could then discover more about protons, such as whether they are fundamental entities and the relations they bear to atoms and other subatomic entities such as neutrons and quarks. There are, presumably, ways to apprehend reality other than this; not every case of getting an entity in mind is a matter of its satisfying some concept that expresses an explanatory role of a certain kind. Apprehending that one is dizzy, for example, does not involve the employment of a role-designating concept. The state of being dizzy is simply there, present to consciousness. Still, one of the relationships between mind and world that brings about our having some thing in mind, I assume, is that thing's being such as to sat-isfy a role-designating concept.[17]

As our earlier distinction between having something in mind and reference will have indicated, when the physicist in Lab refers to the proton in her lab environment, she already has the kind *proton* in mind. If recent work in the philosophy of language is any guide, this opens conceptual space for two possibilities. The first possibility, which draws upon Saul Kripke's insights, is that the way we get some indi-vidual, property, or kind in mind may differ from how we refer to that individual, property or kind. Suppose, for example, that physicists have used a role-designating concept to get the kind *proton* in mind. It might be that when you and I refer to this kind, it is not because we use the same descriptive concept but that we stand in the right sort of causal and epistemic relations to the initial or expert employments of one or another concept that allowed us to get a cognitive grip on this kind. In this way, there is reference preservation.[18] The second possi-bility, stressed by philosophers such as Keith Donnellan (at least under Kripke's interpretation), is that when we have something in mind, we often succeed in referring to it even when the concepts we employ (or our employment of these concepts) are defective.[19] For example, I might have you in mind by seeing you in the room and succeed in referring to you, even when I use a defective description, such as 'the man speaking Dutch' when you were speaking Norwegian.[20]

17. Many philosophers doubt that something's satisfying an agent's apprehensive use of a role-designating concept is sufficient for her to have that thing in mind well enough to form *de re*/predicative thoughts about it. I confess to not sharing these doubts. In my view, getting an entity in mind by the apprehensive use of a role-desig-nating concept is, when all goes well, sufficient for being able to form *de re*/predica-tive thoughts about that thing. That said, it may be that we need to identify parameters for when "all goes well." For example, if I introduce a blind description such as 'the first person to be born in the twenty-first century,' I might succeed in referring to this person. But given the paucity of information I have about him or her, I might not be able to get him or her in mind, since I fail to bear any sort of evi-dential or epistemic connections with him or her.
18. Kripke (1980), Lecture III.
19. See Kripke (1977).
20. Donnellan (1966). Kaplan (2012), 147–9, makes other suggestive remarks about how we can transmit the state of having something in mind even when initially offered a faulty description. In a conversation, I might say something like "I am looking forward to having you meet Smith's wife." You thereby get Smith's wife in mind even when a half hour later I privately reveal to you that she and Smith never officially married.

Our first case, then, is one in which we get a theoretical entity in mind by way of the use of a role-designating concept or stand in some suitable relation to someone who does. Let us now turn to the second case, which I term:

> **Mistrial**: A judge is presiding over a trial. During the course of the trial she discovers that a juror has engaged in gross misconduct that interferes with due process. In the presence of the court she utters the sentence, "I hereby declare this trial a mistrial." Upon hearing this utterance, you immediately form the judgment that the judge has the authority to do this.

Let us agree that Mistrial resembles Lab in the following two respects: by all appearances, you already have the property *the authority to declare a mistrial* in mind and upon forming your judgment you refer to this property. Still, the power to which you refer is no more part of our manifest environment than a proton—it not being the sort of thing that we can directly perceive or point to simply by using the naked eye. How, then, do we apprehend this power? And how do we refer to it?

Begin with the first question. One way that we might do so is by the apprehensive use of a role-designating concept or standing in some suitable relation to someone who has employed the concept in this way. If this were correct, we could apprehend the power by latching onto its explanatory role: it is that power the exercise of which (under favorable conditions) simultaneously brings it about both that a judge's performing a locutionary act counts as her having declared that an event is a mistrial and that that event is, as a matter of fact, a mistrial. As such, a judge's exercising this power is what (at least in part) accounts for the hook-up between her uttering a sentence and the world's being altered in two significant respects. Of course, to grasp a standing power in this way we would need extensive conceptual expertise and background beliefs, including beliefs about various conventions that are in effect and the ways in which our social institutions function. And it may be that some of these beliefs are mistaken. One might falsely believe, for example, that judicial authority is hereditary. But this would not as such prohibit one from apprehending (or referring to) standing powers. As with the physicist in Lab, holding mistaken beliefs and employing mistaken models need not derail getting something in mind (or referring to it).

Standing powers are not, however, causal powers. They are *normative* powers, incorporating rights of a certain sort. In Chapter 2, I suggested that a judge's having a standing power consists in her having the permission-right to alter the world in certain ways, such as altering what requirements her audience has, and a claim-right against others that they not prevent her from exercising this permission-right. Still, for present purposes, it may be helpful to think of both causal and normative powers as belonging to the common genus *explanatory power*. Etymology in this case may prove illuminating. Latin, for example, has two words that are translated as "power" in English: *potentia* and *potestas*.[21] This way of using language meshes nicely with the two cases I have presented. In Lab, theoretical entities are available for thought because they manifest a *potentia*, a causal power or disposition. We can apprehend such entities by latching onto the exercise of their *potentiae* (or by standing in suitable relations to those that do). In Mistrial, normative features are available for thought because they are themselves a type of *potestas*, or normative power that persons bear. We can apprehend such entities by latching onto their explanatory roles (or standing in suitable relations to those that do). Far from being explanatorily inert, then, normative powers do extraordinary explanatory work in the world. In fact, we have barely touched upon the various explanatory roles they play. That an agent has been declared guilty; that someone has been fired from his job; that a couple has recently married; that a boat has been christened; that a motion has been passed; that a promise has been made; that a mistrial has occurred—these are just a few of the facts that the exercise of normative powers brings about.

Suppose, then, that we can get things in mind by latching onto their explanatory roles in the way that I have described. These things are now available as objects of thought and attention. As objects of thought and attention, we can then engage in the project of discerning various types of conceptual or explanatory relations that these powers might bear to other things. To return to Mistrial: judges, we have noted, possess the standing power to declare something a mistrial. In ordinary conditions, a standing right of this sort is accompanied by standing obligations. Among them is the requirement

---

21. I borrow this observation about Latin from Wolterstorff (2008), 57.

upon those participating in a given trial to acknowledge that if that trial has been competently declared a mistrial by someone with the relevant standing power, then it is a mistrial.

If we like, we could extend these insights to other speech acts, including commands and assertions. In the case of commands, one sort of standing power is available for thought under the description of that power the exercise of which brings it about that by performing a locutionary act an agent has thereby (directly) laid an obligation on another to perform one or another action. Once again, we can employ a role-designating concept to get this normative power in mind. And with a little reflection we can see that the standing right to issue a command is accompanied by standing obligations of various sorts on the part of its recipients—among them being the obligation to perform that action which is commanded, at least when the command is not malformed. Assertions, we saw earlier, are different. In the case of assertions, it is not the exercise of a power that is explanatorily central, but our being liable to correction, admonishment, or blame if things are not as we present them. Even so, we also seem able to apprehend this type of liability by employing a role-designating concept. At a first approximation, the relevant sort of normative feature might be available for thought as that liability of an agent the possession of which is that in virtue of which his performing a locutionary act counts as an assertion.[22]

With this much in mind, we could also reflect on cases in which things do not go well—cases in which agents perform malformed speech acts. We could, for example, reflect on that case in which an agent performs the locutionary act of uttering the sentence that something is a mistrial but lacks the standing power to do so. Or we could reflect on that case in which the content of an assertion fails to bear a proper relation to the mental states of the speaker, such as when he does not believe what he says. Were we to do so, then some of the moral dimensions of these speech acts would come to light. In the case of assertion just described, for example, the liability is moral. The agent is liable to blame for being dishonest if the sort of

22. Our earlier discussion of assertives revealed that that for which an agent is liable is not merely facts about the speaker but the world. Tanesini (2005) argues that in this way, assertives appear to differ from other illocutionary act types such as exercitives.

malformation alluded to occurs. Something similar is true of that case in which, under ordinary conditions, a judge purports to declare something a mistrial while being aware that she lacks the relevant standing power to do so (since the case does not fall under her jurisdiction). Not only does the trial not count as a mistrial, she is also (at least in standard cases) liable to blame or admonition for having misrepresented her normative standing.

Moral features appear to play a dual explanatory role in cases such as these. They explain, in the first place, why some speech acts are malformed, and why normative powers are not explanatorily efficacious in bringing about one or another state of affairs. Recall the case offered in Chapter 3 in which a Quisling official orders you to publish an anti-Semitic tract. Under one understanding of this case, the official fails to order you to do anything, since no one has the standing power to command someone to do what is morally impermissible. If this is right, moral features play a role parallel to that of causal inhibitors; they block normative powers of certain kinds from being exercised (or from being exercised in such a way that a commander's audience has an obligation laid on her). In the second place, the presence of these features accounts for the count-generation of speech itself. If the argument of Chapter 3 is correct, an agent asserts a proposition in virtue of there being a range of not only standing rights, responsibilities, and obligations but also generated rights, responsibilities, and obligations that attach to him. If the argument offered there is correct, some of these normative features are moral. Here I will not repeat the arguments for this claim.

Let me now add a caveat similar to that offered when reflecting upon Lab: by distinguishing having something in mind from reference, we will have opened conceptual space for two possibilities. The first is that the way in which an agent has some normative property in mind may differ from how we refer to it. Suppose, for example, that some have used a role-designating concept to get in mind the property *the authority to declare* a *mistrial*. It might be, however, that when you and I refer to this property by forming a judgment about a judge's powers, it is not because we use this concept but because we stand in the right sort of causal and epistemic relations to the initial or expert employments of this concept. If this is right, although someone in the referential chain might have used a role-designating concept to get a normative property in mind, it may be that we do not. The second possibility is that when we have a property in mind, we can succeed in referring to it even when the concepts we employ (or our employment of these concepts) are defective. For example, I might attempt to refer to a judge's standing power by using the description 'that authority with which God has endowed judges' but succeed in referring to the property nonetheless because I already have the property sufficiently in mind.

Suppose the line of argument that I have developed is correct, and we can apprehend entities by the use of role-designating concepts. If we can do so in cases similar to Lab, then, I claim, we can also do so in cases similar to Mistral. If we think of these types of cases as ones in which powers of certain kinds are at work, then they are very similar indeed. We apprehend these powers by latching onto their explanatory roles. In this regard, the view I have sketched is hospitable to broadly naturalist approaches to reference—not simply because reference is a matter of latching onto the explanatory roles that entities of various sorts play, but also because it is compatible with the use of moral terms being "causally regulated" by moral properties. For when philosophers such as Richard Boyd defend the view that when an agent succeeds in referring to a moral feature F by the use of some term because F causally regulates his use of that term, these philosophers do not necessarily mean that F causes us to acquire the concept which that term expresses.[23] Rather, they often mean (roughly) that F features in a feedback loop according to which, over time, we (or the experts) become increasingly more reliable with regard to our views about F because (among other things) we stand in new causal relations to F, each other, or our environment. For example, you might gain a better understanding of F's nature because you now stand in certain causal relations to those who have investigated the nature of F in which they correct

---

23. Here is one reason why, offered by Tyler Burge: "A martian scientist could refer to H_2O even though he or she bore no causal relation to H_2O...Suppose that the scientist has causal relations to oxygen and hydrogen and, despite lacking any experimental causal relation to the particular sort of bonding connection between them, guesses or hypothesizes—near enough—the correct bonding relation. Then the object of the idea, H_2O, is not the explanatory cause of either the representational content or the mental event" ((2007), 437). I have found van Roojen (2006) helpful for thinking through Boyd's view.

certain misunderstandings you have had about the nature of F. It should be apparent that (when modified slightly) what I have said is compatible with this dimension of Boyd's view, since our grasping a normative property by the use of a role-designating concept is perfectly compatible with that property's causally regulating our use of moral terms in the sense just identified. Suppose, for example, I mistakenly claim an agent's holding a certain kind of office implies that he has a standing power of a certain type. You correct me about this. Insofar as you have a reasonably accurate understanding of the power in question, that power's being a certain way is implicated in a feedback loop, which (if all goes well) will eventuate in my having a better grasp of the nature of the power. Incorporating these points would represent the beginnings of naturalistic-style semantics for non-naturalists.[24]

Of course, I do not wish to deny that there are important differences between the two cases I have presented. We posit the existence of theoretical entities such as protons simply because of the explanatory roles they play. We do not, by contrast, posit the existence of rights, responsibilities, and obligations simply because of the count-generating roles they play. Moreover, in Lab, a person needs extensive conceptual expertise and background beliefs to apprehend or refer to theoretical entities. But this expertise and these background beliefs do not, in the first instance, pertain to the conventional arrangements that are in place. The opposite is true in Mistrial; we apprehend normative powers only if we have conceptual expertise and extensive background beliefs about our social practices, including which conventional arrangements are in place. Finally, while we cannot directly perceive protons in the way in which we can other features of our manifest environment, we can perceive their causal effects. That is not obviously so in Mistrial. We do not perceive declarations and mistrials, at least in any direct sense.

All true. These differences do not, however, undercut the relevant parallels between the two types of cases. The fact that we introduce

---

24. I have said that, having gotten some entity in mind by the use of a role-designating concept, we can get other things in mind by noting their conceptual relations to it. Certain things that Boyd says indicate that he would disagree with this ((2003), 509). But the apparent disagreement may not run deep, as Boyd is happy to speak of things bearing quasi-analytic relations to other things (see 520).

theoretical entities into our best theories simply because of their explanatory power does not cast doubt on whether we can apprehend
them (or their powers) by employing role-designating concepts.
Moreover, the fact that the types of required conceptual expertise
and background knowledge in both cases are very different does
nothing to suggest that the role-designating concepts employed operate in importantly different ways. As for the role of causality in
Lab, this, admittedly, is a difference between it and Mistral that
many philosophers would think important. Take, for example, what
Michael P. Lynch says toward the end of his fine book *Truth as One
and Many*. Representation, says Lynch, requires responsiveness. A
mental state is responsive to some entity, Lynch further claims, only
if it bears one or another causal connection to it. (Lynch does not
specify what sort of causal connection he has in mind.) But moral
facts do not causally explain our moral judgments. And, Lynch
writes, it is difficult to see what else they could causally explain. This
is presented as problematic because a thing's entering into a "nexus
of causal connections is part of what convinces us there is something
to which we are responding."[25]

The line of argument that Lynch offers strikes me as suspect.
It might be that certain kinds of representation relations, such as Russellian acquaintance, require us to be responsive to and, thus, stand
in causal relations to what is represented. But other types of representation relations, such as Russellian denotation, do not. Without being
in any way responsive to the closest star never seen by a human being,
I can denote and, hence, represent this star by the apprehensive use
of the singular concept 'the closest star never seen by a human
being.'[26] What is more, it would be a mistake to claim that all explanatory relations are causal, for among the explanatory relations, I have
argued, is the count-generation relation. It is because moral features
are ingredient in such explanations that they are excellent candidates
for being the sort of things that non-causally account for a rich variety
of phenomena, including the performance of speech acts and the
social facts that these speech acts themselves generate. It is their

25. Lynch (2009), 162. For additional reasons to be dubious of Lynch's claims, see the
    quotation from Burge in note 23, as well as his comments about simple indexicals,
    cases of self-knowledge, and future actions in Burge (2009).
26. Russell (1956), ch. 2.

doing this sort of explanatory work—or so I have suggested—that allows us to latch onto them by the use of role-designating concepts. And that, I claim, is sufficient for our mental states being responsive to their explanatory activity in the world. I should add that there is nothing about what I have said that prohibits normative features from being taken up into the causal flow of nature. Perhaps when we apprehend them and form judgments and intentions on the basis of them, this is exactly what happens. Perhaps moral features are introduced into the causal flow by proxy, thanks to their being that which individuates the contents of mental states that themselves cause behavior in virtue of their having those contents. If this is right, my belief that an act is morally required is what (in part) causes me to perform it. But this mental state is the belief it is and has the explanatory profile it does in virtue of its having the content it does. If so, the differences between Lab and Mistrial recede from view.

Lab and Mistrial highlight important similarities between how we might get powers of different kinds in mind. Nevertheless, I realize that puzzles remain. Specifically, I realize that there are puzzles regarding how role-designating concepts could successfully allow us to get things in mind or denote when they fail to accurately (or uniquely) describe that which they purport to describe. Given their difficulty, I cannot hope to try to address these puzzles on this occasion. I offer the argument in this section, then, in a speculative spirit—one which attempts to specify how we might apprehend and refer to normative reality. The best way, then, to understand the argument in this section is this: it is plausible to hold that we can get such things as protons (and their powers) in mind—arguably, by the apprehensive use of role-designating concepts. It is also plausible to hold that we can get normative powers in mind—also, arguably, by the apprehensive use of role-designating concepts. If this were correct, getting normative features of certain kinds in mind would be no more problematic than getting such things as protons (and their powers) in mind. This conclusion is, however, compatible with the further claim that getting something in mind by the use of role-designating concepts is, in important respects, problematic.[27]

---

27. Strevens (forthcoming) articulates some of the challenges facing broadly descriptivist views.

III Reliability

To sketch one way that we might apprehend normative reality is not, however, to lay the epistemological challenge to rest. For, recall, the challenge turns on the Remarkable Coincidence, which presents realists with a challenge. The challenge is, in effect, to harmonize judgments made from two perspectives.[28] There is, on the one hand, how things look from the morally engaged, practical perspective. From this perspective, we assume that some of our moral beliefs reliably track the moral facts. There is, on the other hand, how things look from the theoretical perspective—the vantage point of someone who has stepped back to critically assess her moral beliefs. From this perspective—or so the challenge runs—we recognize that had we been born into a different culture, lived in a different millennium, or been the product of a different evolutionary history, we would have made very different moral judgments from the ones we now make. An account of how we might apprehend and refer to moral facts, such as the one just offered, will not itself harmonize the judgments made from these two perspectives.

Some philosophers, such as Street, argue that we cannot harmonize the deliverances from these two perspectives, at least if we are realists. Since Street's is the most vigorous and developed version of this charge, I propose to lay it out in more detail. Before I do so, I should note that Street's challenge is pressed not against moral realism in particular but against normative realism in general (that is, realism about epistemic reasons, prudential reasons, aesthetic reasons, and so on). I, however, shall be interested in the charge that it poses to moral realism in particular, by which I have in mind *non-naturalist* realism. At the end of this section, however, I will touch upon its implications for normative realism more broadly understood.

Street's challenge

Imagine yourself in a situation in which you believe that you have won the New York State Lottery but have no reason to think you won

28. Street (forthcoming), 10, calls this the *practical/theoretical puzzle.*

apart from the fact that you entered it. Your belief in this case, we agree, would be deeply defective. Now imagine a situation in which there is vast domain of incompatible moral systems, only one of which is correct. Imagine further that we take ourselves to have "landed" near the correct moral system, even though our capacities for normative judgment have been shaped by cultural and evolutionary forces that in no sense have directed us toward that system. What we have imagined, says Street, is what realists believe:

> The realist thinks that there is a fact of the matter about how to live that holds in a way that is robustly independent of his own evaluative attitudes and what follows from within the standpoint constituted by them. This is like thinking that there is a winning lottery ticket that has been selected by a procedure that is neutral with respect to the fact that it is your ticket (as will be true in any fair lottery). The realist also thinks, as part of his substantive normative view, that there are countlessly many ways of going wrong with respect to the independent normative truth he posits... This is like thinking that there are countlessly many losing tickets in the lottery one has entered. Finally... the realist has no non-trivially-question-begging reason to think that the causal forces that gave rise to his own starting fund of evaluative attitudes would have "landed" those attitudes anywhere near the robustly independent normative truth that he himself posits. This is like having no non-trivially-question-begging reason to think that you won a fair lottery.[29]

Nevertheless, say realists, we have won the moral lottery.

Is the admission that, remarkably enough, we have won the moral lottery really as bad as it seems? Ronald Dworkin seems to think not. "We are forced," writes Dworkin,

> to choose between the following two propositions. (1) Human beings have a special though sometimes fallible faculty of judgment that enables us to decide which moral claims to accept or reject, a capacity whose malfunctioning may sometimes result only in moral misjudgment with no spillover impairment of other cognitive activity. (2) There is no moral objection to exterminating an ethnic group or enslaving a race or torturing a young child, just for fun, in front of its captive mother. Which should we abandon?[30]

29. Street (forthcoming), 18.
30. Quoted in Street (forthcoming), 31.

In this passage, Dworkin is ringing changes on a theme introduced at the outset of this chapter: theory evaluation is always comparative. It is true, Dworkin seems to admit, that realists may have little illuminating to say about the Remarkable Coincidence. Maybe this is like assuming one has won a fair lottery without special evidence. But that is certainly no worse than having to admit that "there is no moral objection to exterminating an ethnic group or enslaving a race or torturing a young child, just for fun, in front of its captive mother."

Not so, says Street. Dworkin's menu of options is flawed. The realist's relevant comparison class, Street claims, is Humean constructivism. Like realists, Humean constructivists tell us that things have value and that we have reasons to act. Unlike realists, however, they claim that a thing has value for an agent only because he values it, and that an agent has reasons to act only because he takes them to be reasons to act. This position, according to Street, dissolves any mystery accompanying the Remarkable Coincidence. For had our personal, cultural, and evolutionary histories been different, then we would have found different things to be valuable and, thus, different things would have been valuable.[31] There is, then, no question of calibrating our views to an independent normative standard, which is not set by our contingent personal, cultural, and evolutionary histories. Instead, discovering normative standards is not much more complicated than figuring out what we happen to value and care about and whether these attitudes cohere with one another.

That said, we human beings share common cultural and evolutionary histories. We tend, accordingly, to converge on what we most care about. If this is right, Street contends, the real choice is not that which Dworkin offers but is

> between the following two propositions: (1') I am in all likelihood hopeless at grasping the normative truth; and (2') some conceivable agents have reason to exterminate an ethnic group or enslave a race or torture a young child for fun in front of its captive mother, but most real life human beings have no such reasons, and if we ever encounter any who do, then we...have reason to band together against them, lock them up, and throw away the key.[32]

31. Street (2006), 154.
32. Street (forthcoming), 32.

It follows from this that realists are in a considerably worse position than Dworkin thinks. They—so Street suggests—have a defeater of a certain kind for all their normative beliefs. Realists should hold that we are in all likelihood hopeless at grasping the normative truth.

Or so it would seem. As it happens, Street pulls back from this conclusion, offering a crucial qualification to her assessment of the realist's predicament. Here is the qualification:

> Dworkin's proposition (2) is couched not in terms of normative reasons in general, but in terms of what there is or is not "moral objection to." Straight off, this is unfair to the antirealist, for one might think that it is a conceptual truth or near conceptual truth that there is "some moral objection" to torturing a child for fun – such that any "morality" that denied this would not be recognizable as a brand of *morality* at all. Because it denies such a fundamental moral platitude, proposition (2) sounds almost crazy. But morality/reasons externalism [that is, Humeanism about reasons], according to which we may not always have *reason* to do what we morally ought to do, is a well-known option that the antirealist can adopt regarding such a case. In other words, the antirealist might grant that it is morally objectionable to torture a child for fun, but then deny that all agents always have reason to be moral. To avoid prejudicing the debate against the antirealist with an implicit appeal to platitudes associated with the concept of morality, then, the claim in question should be couched in terms of reasons.[33]

Street's challenge to realists has now come into sharper focus. It is one that concerns how we track not the moral facts as such but those categorical reasons that realists claim are necessarily correlated with them. The charge is that even if realists accept the existence of categorical reasons, they have no account of how we could reliably track them.

My response to this charge comes in two parts. Before I offer this response, however, let me make an observation about how Street has framed the issues. According to her official account, normative antirealism "is the view that there are *no* normative facts or truths that hold independently of all our evaluative attitudes...such that an agent can have normative reason to X even though the conclusion that she has this reason in no way follows...from her own practical

---

33. Street (forthcoming), 33.

point of view."[34] Elsewhere, she indicates that the view is committed to the thesis that something's having value depends on an agent's valuing it.[35] Understood expansively, then, constructivism is a claim about the nature of evaluative or normative facts *tout court*: roughly, evaluative or normative facts fail to hold independently of our evaluative attitudes. Elsewhere, such as in the passage just quoted, Street seems to understand the view more narrowly. Understood restrictively, it is a thesis about only one category of normative facts, namely, those that are or incorporate reasons. Reasons, according to this understanding, fail to hold independently of our evaluative attitudes.

It is not entirely clear to me which position Street wishes to defend. In the last passage quoted, she says only that a constructivist *can* accept what I have called the restricted understanding. However that may be, it is constructivism restrictively understood with which I will engage, at least initially. It will be noticed that this position might be compatible with realism as I defined it in Chapter 1, for realism thus understood is not committed to the existence of categorical reasons.[36] Constructivism restrictively understood might even be compatible with non-naturalist realism, since non-naturalists are not committed to the existence of categorical reasons (although most non-naturalists tend to think that some reasons are categorical). You might wonder why it is worth polemicizing with a view that might be compatible with realism broadly understood. The answer is the one I offered earlier. Not only is non-naturalist realism of this variety an influential position—Street herself thinks it is the only version of realism worth fighting for—but a satisfactory defense of it would also be a boon for the realist program. Even those most vulnerable to the epistemological challenge will have emerged as having plausible things to say in response to it. However, I need to emphasize that realism (in the broad sense in which I defined it) does not stand or fall with the success of this defense. In

34. Street (forthcoming), 2.
35. Street (2008a), 223.
36. Whether it is will turn on how Street wishes to understand the nature of facts such as *that it is wrong to torture simply for fun*. She might defend a broadly constructivist account of the nature of such facts, which would not be compatible with realism as I understand it.

fact, a failed defense might simply count as a defense of naturalistic realism. For understood restrictively, it may be difficult to see how Street's own position differs from naturalistic realism, at least as it is understood by its proponents.[37]

IV The first response

As a first pass, let us say that a *moral system* is a reasonably comprehensive and consistent body of moral propositions that concerns beings like us in a world such as ours. Call such a system *minimally eccentric* just in case it does not incorporate eccentric empirical assumptions about us and the world, such as the assumptions that we tend to like pain or that upon death we are immediately bodily resurrected to enjoy eternal bliss. At various points in our discussion, I have appealed to apparently obvious moral truths—truths that are constitutive of any such system. Let us call these propositions the *moral fixed points*. The moral fixed points include propositions such as

> It is wrong to break one's promise simply because one feels like it.
> It is wrong to torture for the mere fun of it.

And:

> It is wrong to kill someone simply because she has inconvenienced you.

Let me engage Street's argument by working with one such proposition—the one which specifies that recreational torture is wrong. In principle, we could pick another such proposition—it does not

---

37. In her (2008b), 223, Street specifies what she has in mind by naturalistic realism. Her specification implies that naturalistic realists reject Humeanism about reasons. Nearly every prominent version of naturalistic realism of which I am aware, however, embraces Humeanism about reasons (see Railton (1986); Boyd (1988); and Brink (1989)). It seems to me, then, that the view she identifies as naturalistic realism fails to mesh with the views actually defended by naturalistic realists. That said, naturalistic moral realism can be interpreted as incorporating a thesis not about what it takes for something to be a reason but the *weight* of reasons. According to this understanding, it may be that, in the eyes of naturalists, the wrongness of an action counts against performing it. But the weight of such a reason is determined by the agent's own commitments. For something to be a decisive reason for an agent to act, it must be that the agent has commitments of certain kinds.

matter which. What matters is that we work with propositions of this sort. The reason is that realists do not hold that our moral beliefs reliably track the moral facts across the board. Ethical issues are simply too difficult to plausibly maintain that. Rather, they maintain that paradigmatic moral beliefs, such as those that concern the moral fixed points and a range of their applications to particular cases, reliably track the moral facts.

Suppose we use the phrase "it is a remarkable coincidence that p" to express the thought that it would be highly surprising to discover that p, given what we know about other aspects of the world. Suppose, further, that the "we" in question are creatures like us in a world such as ours. We can then distinguish three claims about the moral fixed points:

(i)   It is a remarkable coincidence that we have reliably grasped that it is wrong to torture for the mere fun of it.

(ii) It is a remarkable coincidence that, having grasped that an action such as torturing for the mere fun of it is wrong (and that it wrongs its victim), we have also reliably discerned that, necessarily, this counts in favor of not performing it.

(iii) It is a remarkable coincidence that having grasped that an action such as torturing for the mere fun of it is wrong (and that it wrongs its victim), we have also reliably discerned that this decisively counts in favor of not performing it.

The thrust of the previous passage quoted from Street is that she does not affirm the claim expressed in (i). In that passage, she says that it sounds almost crazy to deny that it is wrong to torture simply for fun.[38]

---

38. I am unsure whether this represents a shift in Street's views. But it sits uneasily with the argument she offers in her (2006), 124, wherein she claims that it is no use to appeal to rational reflection as a way to correct the distorting influence of evolution since "the fund of evaluative judgments with which human reflection began was thoroughly contaminated with illegitimate influence." Because of this "the tools of rational reflection were equally contaminated." But if some moral beliefs express the moral fixed points, which are a species of conceptual truth constitutive of moral thinking, then they are not contaminated in the way that Street claims evaluative thought is. In principle, then, they could be the means by which to correct some of evolution's distorting influences. FitzPatrick (forthcoming) addresses this aspect of Street's argument. Cuneo and Shafer-Landau (2014) develop the view that the moral fixed points are a species of conceptual truth.

Now recall a key move in Street's argument. This move consists in inferring that since there are "countlessly many internally consistent evaluative systems," it would be a miracle if we happened to land on the right one, given our deeply contingent personal, social, and evolutionary backgrounds.[39] But, it turns out, this is not the right way to think about moral systems. For while it might be that there are countlessly many moral systems, these systems are not ones that could fail to incorporate the moral fixed points, provided that these systems are minimally eccentric. That is because nothing is a moral system (in this sense) that fails to incorporate the moral fixed points.[40] Provided, then, that we engage in moral thinking, it is not remarkable that we reliably grasp propositions such as *that it is wrong to engage in recreational torture.* In fact, provided that we are adults competent with a sufficiently wide range of moral concepts who do not accept eccentric empirical beliefs, we could not fail to do so.

Under the present interpretation, then, Street does not endorse the claim expressed in (i). The claims expressed by both (ii) and (iii), however, are different; these, she argues, should be accepted— at least if we assume that realism is true. For while there might not be countlessly many incompatible moral systems, there are countlessly many incompatible *reason-systems.* Some of these systems maintain that wronging someone by recreationally torturing her does not count in the least against the torturing. Others maintain that the wrongness of the torturing provides a decisive reason *to* engage in it. And so forth. Suppose, for argument's sake, that this is correct, and there are countlessly many incompatible reason-systems. This allows us to state Street's argument more precisely yet. The argument, in effect, issues a challenge to realists: explain why, given that we know that torturing for fun is wrong and wrongs its victim, we can also reliably grasp the fact that we necessarily have reason not to engage in it. If realists simply insist that we do in fact grasp these reasons, then they have offered no explanation as to why our moral judgments have "hooked up" with the correct reason-system.

---

39. Street (forthcoming), 19.
40. Or claims very close to them, such as propositions which tell us that there is weighty moral reason not to torture for laughs.

Does realism succumb to this charge? I doubt it. Let us begin by noting common ground between realists and Street. Both agree that it would be almost crazy to deny that:

> If an agent were to torture another merely for fun, then he would have wronged her.

For this is an apparent truism constitutive of competent moral thinking. Realists will, however, point out that it is difficult to see why it would be any less crazy to deny that:

> If an agent were to wrong another by torturing her for fun, then that counts in favor of that agent's not engaging in the torturing.

And:

> If an agent were to wrong another by torturing her for fun, then that counts decisively in favor of that agent's not engaging in the torturing.

After all, say realists, if there were *nothing* to be said against the torturing, then it is very hard to see how it could be wrong. An action's being wrong and its being such as to wrong someone, according to realists, are (at least in part) a matter of there being considerations that count against it. Were a person sincerely to claim otherwise—claiming that his wronging another by torturing her for fun does not at all favor his not doing it—that would be strong evidence that he suffers from a serious deficiency; something has inhibited him from affirming this claim about torturing, such as his lacking the concept of wronging, his being in the grip of a bad theory, his having had a terrible moral education, his suffering from a remarkable moral blind spot, or the like. To wrong someone is, after all, not simply to break a rule. In paradigmatic cases, it is to *degrade* someone. We can easily imagine rules that an agent has no reason to refrain from breaking; some believe that some of the rules of etiquette are like this. It is much more difficult, however, to imagine a case in which a person has no reason to refrain from degrading another by doing something like torturing her for the mere pleasure of it.

It should be added that realists have typically not dropped the matter at this point. They have employed other strategies to vindicate the claims embedded in (ii) and (iii), such as the claim that having grasped that torturing for the mere fun of it is wrong (and that it wrongs its victim), we can also reliably discern that, necessarily, this counts in favor of not performing actions of this type. Russ Shafer-Landau, for example, calls our attention to the fact that the recreational torturer is blameworthy. If he is blameworthy, Shafer-Landau argues, then the torturer has a reason not to engage in his grisly business—regardless of whether he finds it delicious. Indeed, this agent has decisive reasons to not torture, since it would make no sense to blame someone for failing to act on the basis of reasons that are defeated by other considerations.[41] If this is so, the fact that, necessarily, an agent is blameworthy for torturing another simply for recreation implies that there are decisive reasons. It is worth noting, however, that realists do not thereby commit themselves to the claim that moral considerations inevitably provide decisive reasons to act. They need only claim that they do so in a range of paradigmatic cases, such as ones in which we seriously wrong other people.

If realism (of the sort under consideration) is true, then the fact that you would wrong someone by torturing her for fun is necessarily a reason for you not to torture her. It could not be otherwise; there are no other options that are compatible with realism. Yes, there are ways to form mistaken views about the relation between wronging and reasons. A person can make conceptual mistakes, be of unsound mind, be the victim of a terrible moral education, or be in the grip of a bad theory. It might be that the particular ways in which we can be mistaken about the relation between wronging and reasons are countless. This, however, hardly suffices to render it a miracle that we reliably track the moral reasons on the assumption that realism is true.

Humean constructivism, after all, is in a similar predicament. It also allows that agents can make mistakes about their reasons; they might fail to discern what they care about, fail to weight their cares properly, fail to see what these cares imply, or employ normative concepts sloppily. Indeed, if Humean constructivism were correct,

---

41. In this and the previous paragraph I draw upon Shafer-Landau (2009). In this essay, Shafer-Landau responds to the objection that the reasons in question need not be the agent's own but only those who have an interest in blaming him, which Street mentions when defending her view from Dworkin's objection.

agents would regularly go wrong by forming moral judgments—such as the judgment that we have reason not to engage in recreational torture no matter what—that comport badly with the claim that all reasons are Humean. If so, there is no less reason to believe that, according to Humean constructivism, the particular ways in which an agent can go wrong are also countless. There is, then, nothing unique about realism and constructivism in this regard. Every view worth its salt has to wrestle with the possibility that we can make many mistakes about our reasons.

Nonetheless, there remains an important difference between realism and Humean constructivism. The two positions incorporate very different accounts of how moral concepts function. To focus on realism for the moment: fundamental to realism of the sort under consideration is the conviction that if an agent were to deny that torturing for mere fun wrongs its victim, she would suffer from a conceptual deficiency, such as lacking the concept 'wrong,' having an inadequate grasp of this concept, or failing to acknowledge its manifest implications. The same holds true of wronging and reasons. All else being equal, if an agent were to deny that wronging by torturing provides some reason not to do it, she would also suffer from a conceptual deficiency, such as lacking the concepts 'wrong' or 'reason,' having an inadequate grasp of these concepts, or failing to acknowledge their manifest implications. Of course, realists might be mistaken about this. They might hold mistaken views about the nature of moral concepts and what competence with them requires.[42] But that was not, under the present interpretation, the charge leveled against them by Street. The charge, recall, was this: if their view were true, then realists would have no explanation of how we could reliably discern that categorical reasons are necessarily correlated with moral facts of certain types. The realist reply to this charge is that there is no mystery. If you understand why recreational torture

---

42. Cuneo and Shafer-Landau (2014) address the force of this "might." It will be recalled that in Chapter 4, I suggested that Humean realists should be error theorists about reasons. They should acknowledge that our ordinary concept of a reason is as most non-naturalists believe: it is non-Humean. But they should also hold that ordinary agents are mistaken about the nature of reasons, since all reasons are, in reality, Humean. This point, incidentally, is why the argument in this chapter is compatible with that offered in Chapter 4.

wrongs its victim, then you understand why wronging by recreational torturing provides reasons not to do it. Since we understand the former, we also understand the latter.

Let me now draw out an implication of this response. As I noted earlier, Street's original challenge, under the present interpretation, is directed not simply at moral realism but also at normative realism— where normative realism concerns (among other things) the broad question of how one ought to live (the *ought* in question being, presumably, the all-things-considered ought.) Call a system of rights, responsibilities, and obligations that purports to offer a more or less complete guide on how one ought to live a *normative system.* The universe of possible normative systems, like the universe of reason-systems, is huge.[43] Some will fail to incorporate the moral fixed points; others will tell us that it is permissible to torture for mere pleasure; still others will tell us that it is recommendable to engage in torture of this sort, and so forth.

Now suppose moral realism were true. And suppose we know various moral fixed points. Suppose, finally, there is a finite range of normative systems that are reasonably close approximations of the correct normative system. Would it be a remarkable coincidence if we were to find ourselves accepting some member of this range? Well, suppose a system were to fail to incorporate the moral fixed points. Then realists would say the system ought to be rejected; it is incomplete. Or suppose it were to license or recommend activities such as recreational torture. Then these systems, realists would say, also ought to be rejected; all of them incorporate false moral claims. Or suppose a system were to say that recreational torture is wrong but one might have decisive reason to engage in it nonetheless if doing so satisfied one's deepest desires. Realists would say that such a view is also mistaken, for it incorporates a false view about the relation of moral features to reasons whose falsity we can ascertain by reflecting upon what it is to wrong a person. Admittedly, when using such an evaluative process, it would require an extraordinary stroke of luck to hit upon the one uniquely correct moral system. Ethical issues are simply too difficult to suppose anything else. Still, engaging in an evaluative process

43. Street (2006), 133.

such as I have just described would allow us to reduce the range of legitimate normative systems considerably.

Distinguish, then, these two questions: Were realism true, would it be a remarkable coincidence if we were to reliably track the moral reasons, at least of a certain range? And, were realism true, would it be a remarkable coincidence if we were to reliably hit upon a close enough approximation of the correct normative system? I have said that the answer to the first question is No. But if it is, then the answer to the second question is also No.

V The second response

My project in section IV was to remove one reason for thinking that realists cannot account for the Remarkable Coincidence.[44] While engaged in this project, I said relatively little about how our moral judgments might reliably track the moral facts beyond noting that, provided that we do not suffer from one or another conceptual deficiency, we could not fail to grasp that we have reasons of certain kinds. Such a reply is, in principle, compatible with numerous views about what it is to be conceptually deficient. Rather than defend a particular view about that in which such deficiencies consists, I think it is more important for present purposes to highlight an ambiguity that our discussion revealed.[45]

There are two ways to understand the Remarkable Coincidence. According to the first, it is supposed to be remarkable that our moral judgments reliably track the moral facts, where these facts

---

44. This reason is not, I should add, the only one for thinking that realists cannot account for the Remarkable Coincidence. Some philosophers, such as Clarke-Doane (2012), suggest that we might have reason to believe that we do not reliably track the moral facts, since even if (per impossible) recreational torture were not wrong, we would still believe it to be wrong. My own view is that it is exceedingly difficult to assess the evidential value of true counterpossibles such as *were recreational torture not wrong, we would nonetheless believe it to be wrong*. In some cases, they might provide evidence for the fact that we are insensitive to features of the world. But in other cases, they seem to provide no such evidence. We can, after all, formulate counterpossibles regarding what we would believe regarding a wide range of necessary truths, such as logical or modal truths. The mere fact that we can formulate true counterpossibles of this sort, however, goes no distance toward establishing that our beliefs about logic or modality are systematically unreliable.

45. Cuneo and Shafer-Landau (2014) address the matter at greater length.

include what I have called the moral fixed points. According to the second understanding, it is supposed to be remarkable that, having grasped a certain range of moral facts, such as that acts of certain kinds wrong others, we reliably track the reasons that are necessarily correlated with them. I have focused my attention on the second understanding, as this seems to be the one that philosophers such as Street are most interested in defending. If realism were true, I have said, there is indeed a coincidence to be explained. But it is not remarkable. At least it is no more remarkable than the coincidence between our judging that recreational torture wrongs its victim, on the one hand, and recreational torture's being such that it wrongs its victim, on the other.

This leaves us with the first understanding of the Remarkable Coincidence. Is it of philosophical interest? It is indeed. As I mentioned earlier, realists should very much like to have a plausible account of how we have managed to reliably track the moral facts given that our cognitive abilities were not selected by cultural or evolutionary mechanisms to do so. Since it would be a liability if realists lacked any such explanation, their task is to identify what that explanation might be.

At this point in our discussion, however, our understanding of this task will have been altered. In the first place, it should be especially apparent that a failure to meet the epistemological challenge need not imply that realism compares unfavorably to Humean constructivism. For bring to mind Street's presentation of Humean constructivism once again. Humean constructivists do not deny that there are moral truths. Indeed, in her reply to Dworkin, Street indicates that Humean constructivists might believe that some moral truths are necessary in a robust sense. But if they do believe this, it follows that, according to Humean constructivists, the moral status of recreational torture is not determined by the attitudes we have (or might have) toward it.[46] For we might have had many different conflicting attitudes toward recreational torture, including indifference, revulsion, pleasure, and so forth. Were these attitudes to determine the moral status of recreational torture, it would follow that

---

46. At least this is so if they reject the claim that these truths are somehow implied by the attitudes that all agents, of necessity, share. Street (2008a) rejects this view. There are, I realize, other options available to constructivists, such as those in which we rigidify the attitudes of some privileged set of agents.

recreational torture could also have many different moral statuses. But it cannot. It follows that, thus understood, Humean constructivism and realism share the same task: both views need to explain how we have managed to reliably track moral truths that are not themselves determined by our attitudes. The realists' failure to meet the epistemological challenge would also be the Humean constructivists' failure.

Second, we know that accounting for the Remarkable Coincidence does not require realists to say that our moral beliefs, on the whole, track the moral facts. Realism is compatible with significant stretches of these beliefs being mistaken not simply because they are false but also because they incorporate or depend on mistaken assumptions about the nature of the world or moral reality. In his discussion of these issues, Boyd points out that many of our moral beliefs have incorporated, presupposed, or been shaped by false religious views.[47] This, however, has not prevented many of us from reliably tracking paradigmatic moral facts, such as those expressed by the moral fixed points. In fact, if what we said earlier is correct, some cases are such that an agent's having mistaken views or employing misleading models about entities of some type need not prevent him from apprehending or forming reliable beliefs about them.

Third, while I am wary of speculating about how our ancestors managed to form true moral beliefs, this last point regarding the role of mistaken views has implications for such speculations. The most important point to see is that realists need not suppose that cultural or evolutionary forces initially supplied our ancestors with an ample stock of true moral beliefs. These forces need only have supplied them with enough normative beliefs of the right sort such that, with increased understanding of the moral domain, our ancestors eliminated inconsistencies, false presuppositions, and arbitrariness in their moral views, thereby arriving at a body of more nearly reliable moral judgments. If this is right, what realism needs to explain is not how our ancestors were "guided" by cultural and evolutionary forces toward the correct moral system. What we need to offer is a decent account of how our relevant starting points in moral

47. Boyd (1988), 210–11.

thinking were not too far off (and how we have managed to progress from these starting points).[48]

How might cultural and evolutionary forces have done that? Both David Enoch and Erik Wielenberg have independently advocated what Enoch calls a third-factor explanation to account for the reliable correspondence between moral beliefs and moral facts. Enoch explains: "It is possible that the explanation of a correlation between…two factors A and B is in terms of a third factor, C, that is (roughly speaking) responsible both for A-facts and for B-facts."[49] Enoch's favored third factor is that survival or reproductive success is at least somewhat good. Wielenberg's favored third factor is certain cognitive faculties that guarantee that we have rights and that we can grasp them. If we assume either that survival is good or that we have capacities that ground rights, these philosophers claim, this would help us to explain how our relevant starting points in moral thinking were not too far off.[50]

A strategy of this sort might account for the Remarkable Coincidence.[51] In what remains, however, let me sketch a related but different strategy, which I shall call the *practice-based* strategy. A strategy of this sort does not introduce a third factor that accounts for both the existence of moral facts and the fact that we reliably track them. Rather, it directs us to identify some activity or practice P that satisfies these two conditions: first, given our needs to survive and reproduce, evolutionary mechanisms put pressure on us to participate in P; and, second, were we to participate in P, it would be unsurprising that we would, over time, reliably grasp a significant range of moral facts. That we reliably track a range of moral facts, then, is explained (in part) by our participating in the relevant practice.

48. In various ways, Copp (2008), Enoch (2011), 167, and FitzPatrick (forthcoming) make this point. In fact, Boyd made the point years ago in his classic defense of moral naturalism: "It must be possible to explain how our moral reasoning started out with a stock of relevantly approximately true beliefs so that reflective equilibrium in moral reasoning can be treated in a fashion analogous to the scientific realist's treatment of reflective equilibrium in scientific reasoning. Note that this constraint does not require that it be possible to argue that we started out with close approximations to the truth (seventeenth-century corpuscular theory was quite far from the truth). What is required is that the respects of approximation be such that it is possible to see how continued approximations would be forthcoming as a result of subsequent moral and non-moral reasoning" ((1988), 201).

49. Enoch (2010), 429.

50. Enoch (2010), 428; Wielenberg (2010), 450.

51. For reservations, see FitzPatrick (forthcoming).

Is there a practice of the relevant sort? There is: it is the practice of speaking.

Throughout our discussion, I have criticized broadly Hobbesian views of morality according to which moral facts are generated by speech acts, such as compacts. But there are components of the Hobbesian view that one can employ to flesh out the practice-based strategy, such as its appeal to prisoner dilemma-style scenarios. Take, then, a standard prisoner's dilemma-style case. In such a case, we start by assuming that the participants are endowed with self-serving but conditionally cooperative dispositions. While fundamentally self-interested, participants will cooperate with others only when they perceive it to be advantageous. According to the dominant way of thinking about such cases, in "single shot" prisoner dilemma cases—ones in which, in a single case, two parties must decide whether to cooperate or not—it is instrumentally rational for each to not cooperate. But when we iterate such cases, thereby more nearly approximating the predicaments that we face in our everyday lives, the game changes; it becomes evident that it makes sense for each participant to cooperate, unless he has evidence that the other has ceased to be cooperative. This is because cooperation raises the likelihood that with time they each can enjoy important goods that they would probably not enjoy otherwise.

Cooperation, however, requires that we do things such as communicate information reliably, coordinate our plans by working together, direct each other's actions in mutually acceptable ways, and so forth. Engaging in these activities is not as such to speak. Non-human animals can communicate information reliably and coordinate their actions in mutually beneficial ways. Yet they do not speak. But we human animals are different. We achieve these aims with a particular endowment of broadly rational and volitional capacities and within a richly structured social life. It is because we are the sorts of creatures that can, by the use of complex conventional arrangements, commit ourselves to certain states of affairs and hold each other accountable for such commitments that we can and do achieve the aims of communicating information reliably and coordinating our activities by speaking.

Suppose, then, that reflection on iterated prisoner dilemma-style cases gives us some insight into why evolutionary mechanisms might have exerted pressure on our human ancestors to cooperate in certain ways. And suppose that it would be unsurprising that cooperation for human creatures in complex social conditions such as ours would involve performing acts such as asserting, promising, requesting, commanding, declaring, and so forth. Fundamental to the Speech Act Argument is the thesis that the ways in which we can hold each other accountable are not incidental to speech. Rather, it is in virtue of altering our normative position with respect to others—putting ourselves on the normative hook by employing arrangements for speaking—that we perform illocutionary acts such as asserting and promising. Presumably, though, if it were advantageous for us to speak, then it would also be advantageous for us to be able to reliably track the conditions under which an agent can be held accountable for having performed one or another locutionary act. Score-keeping of this sort would require us to be able to reliably track various normative properties of agents such as *that I am liable to blame for having misrepresented the truth, that you are now obligated to act as you said you would,* and *that we have a right to your considering our request.* Were we unable to do this, then the aims of communication, coordination, and direction would be thwarted.

Being able to reliably track a wide range of normative features, then, is fundamental to our being able to speak. Of course, being reliable in this way is compatible with our employing normative concepts in all sorts of mistaken ways. Perhaps, for example, our ancestors assumed that promises to people other than kin and clan are malformed since only promises to kin and clan "count." Or perhaps some believed that one could not be held accountable for being dishonest to one's social inferiors. When applied in these ways, these concepts would not track the normative facts. For the pool of promisees is not limited to kin or clan; one can be held accountable for being dishonest with one's social inferiors.

Still, the mistakes made in the employments of these normative concepts could, it appears, only be of limited scope. In a world such as ours, it might be that a society could suffer something akin to a "normative inversion" in which liars were rarely held accountable for speaking falsities and promise-keepers were frequently blamed simply because they did what they said they would. For example, it might be that given certain in-group/out-group dynamics, those who belong to the relevant in-group could systematically lie to those who belong to the out-group without ever being blamed. Presumably, though, the dissembling could only go so far; were members of this in-group to lie systematically to one another and not hold each other accountable, things would not go well. Speech in that society would eventually break down—at least if we could, in a wide range of cases, reliably identify the liars and the promise-keepers. If this is so, engaging in speech requires us to employ not only a substantial repertoire of normative concepts. It also requires that we employ them in certain ways, doing such things as holding dissemblers responsible and permitting requests to be made. If this is right, the employment of these concepts would explain why participants in our practices of speech act in certain ways. It is because you take me to be liable for not intending to do what I said I would that you admonish me.

Speaking, I have claimed, requires agents to reliably track normative features of certain kinds, such as when others are liable to correction or admonition. It also requires, I have said, that agents must reliably employ normative concepts in certain ways. Would these claims establish that it would be unsurprising that, over time, we reliably grasp a significant range of moral facts?

I believe they would. For suppose the Speech Act Argument is correct: some of the normative features that count-generate speech are moral. Now take those beliefs that we form when we determine whether to hold someone accountable for not speaking the truth or not doing what he said he would. If the Speech Act Argument is correct, these beliefs concern moral facts, at least some of the time. It is, however, widely accepted that the representational contents of our beliefs determine, at least in large measure, what types of belief they are. It is also widely accepted that representational contents are themselves determined by that which they represent. The beliefs we form when score-keeping in speech, however, concern moral facts, at least some of the time. They are, then, moral beliefs. And since they reliably track those normative features that count-generate speech, they reliably track the moral facts. Admittedly, our ancestors may have had nothing like a conception of morality as we think about it. And they may have made mistakes in the ways they applied those normative concepts that denote the rights, responsibilities, and obligations of being a speaker. They might have failed to see, for example, that the obligation to tell the truth applies to human beings as such and not just to members of their clan. But this would not have prevented them from having beliefs that reliably tracked a substantial range of the moral facts.

VI Conclusion

I began our discussion by claiming that the Speech Act Argument is theoretically fecund in ways that other arguments for substantive philosophical positions are not. Among other things, I said, the argument provides non-naturalist realists with the resources to address the epistemological challenge to moral realism. This challenge, recall, hinges on the thesis that I have called:

> **The Remarkable Coincidence**: It is a remarkable coincidence that our moral beliefs reliably track the moral facts. For had we been born into a different culture, lived in a different millennium, or been the product of a different evolutionary history, we would have made very different normative judgments from the ones we now make.

Drawing upon the Speech Act Argument, I have argued that realists can say interesting and informative things to explain how our moral beliefs might reliably track the moral facts. If what I have said is correct, the explanatory roles that moral facts play in speech allow realists to say illuminating things about not only how we might apprehend these facts, but also how we might reliably track them. In this regard, the Speech Act Argument does double-duty. The argument has done the work that we asked of it.

Bibliography

Adams, Robert M. (1999). *Finite and Infinite Goods*. Oxford: Oxford University Press.

Adams, Robert M. (2006). *A Theory of Virtue*. Oxford: Oxford University Press.

Alston, William P. (1991). *Perceiving God*. Ithaca, NY: Cornell University Press.

Alston, William P. (2000). *Illocutionary Acts and Sentence Meaning*. Ithaca, NY: Cornell University Press.

Anderson, Elizabeth (2007). "If God Is Dead, Is Everything Permitted?" In Louise Antony, ed. *Philosophers without Gods*. Oxford: Oxford University Press: 215–30.

Anscombe, G. E. M. (1958). "Modern Moral Philosophy." *Philosophy* 33: 1–19.

Audi, Paul (2012). "Grounding: Toward a Theory of the *In-Virtue-of* Relation." *Journal of Philosophy* CIX: 685–711.

Austin, J. L. (1963). *How to Do Things with Words*. Oxford: Oxford University Press.

Avramides, Anita (1989). *Meaning and Mind: An Examination of the Gricean Account of Language*. Cambridge, MA: MIT Press.

Ayer, A. J. (1936). *Language, Truth, and Logic*. London: Gollancz.

Bach, Kent and Robert Harnish (1979). *Linguistic Communication and Speech Acts*. Cambridge, MA: MIT Press.

Baker, Lynne Rudder (2000). *Persons and Bodies*. Cambridge: Cambridge University Press.

Barker, Stephen (2004). *Explaining Meaning*. Oxford: Oxford University Press.

Bedke, Matthew (2009). "Intuitive Non-naturalism Meets Cosmic Coincidence." *Pacific Philosophical Quarterly* 90: 188–209.

Bengson, John (forthcoming). "Grasping the Third Realm." *Oxford Studies in Epistemology*. Oxford: Oxford University Press.

Bennett, Jonathan (1976). *Linguistic Behavior*. Cambridge: Cambridge University Press.

Bennett, Jonathan (1993). "The Necessity of Moral Judgments." *Ethics* 103: 458–73.

Blackburn, Simon (1993). *Essays in Quasi-Realism.* Oxford: Oxford University Press.

Blackburn, Simon (1998). *Ruling Passions.* Oxford: Oxford University Press.

Blackburn, Simon (1999). "Is Objective Moral Justification Possible on a Quasi-realist Foundation?" *Inquiry* 42: 213–28.

Blackburn, Simon (2001). "Reply by Simon Blackburn." *Philosophical Books* 42 (symposium on Blackburn's *Ruling Passions*): 1–32.

Blackburn, Simon (2005). "Quasi-Realism No Fictionalism." In Mark Eli Kalderon, ed. *Fictionalism in Metaphysics.* Oxford: Oxford University Press: 322–38.

Blackburn, Simon (2010). "Truth, Beauty and Goodness." In Russ Shafer-Landau, ed. *Oxford Studies in Metaethics*, vol. 5. Oxford: Oxford University Press: 295–314.

Bloomfield, Paul (2001). *Moral Reality.* Oxford: Oxford University Press.

Bloomfield, Paul (2009). "Archimedeanism and Why Metaethics Matters." In Russ Shafer-Landau, ed. *Oxford Studies in Metaethics*, vol. 5. Oxford: Oxford University Press: 283–302.

Boisvert, Daniel (2008). "Expressive-Assertivism." *Pacific Philosophical Quarterly* 89: 169–203.

Boyd, Richard (1988). "How to Be a Moral Realist." In Geoffrey Sayre-McCord, ed. *Essays on Moral Realism.* Ithaca, NY: Cornell University Press: 182–217.

Boyd, Richard (2003). "Finite Beings, Finite Goods: The Semantics, Metaphysics and Ethics of Naturalist Consequentialism, Part I." *Philosophy and Phenomenological Research* 66: 505–53.

Brandom, Robert (1994). *Making It Explicit.* Cambridge, MA: Harvard University Press.

Brandom, Robert (2000). *Articulating Reasons.* Cambridge, MA: Harvard University Press.

Brink, David (1989). *Moral Realism and the Foundations of Ethics.* Cambridge: Cambridge University Press.

Burge, Tyler (2007). *Foundations of Mind.* Oxford: Oxford University Press.

Burge, Tyler (2009). "Five Theses on De Re States and Attitudes." In Joseph Almog and Paolo Leonardi, eds. *The Philosophy of David Kaplan.* Oxford: Oxford University Press: 246–316.

Carson, Thomas (2000). *Value and the Good Life.* Notre Dame, IN: University of Notre Dame Press.

Chrisman, Matthew (2008). "Expressivism, Inferentialism, and Saving the Debate." *Philosophy and Phenomenological Research* 77: 334–56.

Chrisman, Matthew (2011). "Expressivism, Inferentialism and the Theory of Meaning." In Michael Brady, ed. *New Waves in Metaethics.* London: Palgrave: 103–25.

Clarke-Doane, Justin (2012). "Morality and Mathematics: The Evolutionary Challenge." *Ethics* 2: 313–40.

Copp, David (1995). *Morality, Normativity, and Society.* Oxford: Oxford University Press.

Copp, David (2001). "Realist-Expressivism: A Neglected Option for Moral Realism." *Social Philosophy and Policy* 18: 1–43.

Copp, David (2008). "Darwinian Skepticism about Moral Realism." *Philosophical Issues* 18: 184–204.

Cuneo, Terence (2006). "Saying What We Mean: An Argument Against Expressivism." In Russ Shafer-Landau, ed. *Oxford Studies in Metaethics*, vol. 1. Oxford: Oxford University Press: 35–71.

Cuneo, Terence (2007). *The Normative Web: An Argument for Moral Realism.* Oxford: Oxford University Press.

Cuneo, Terence. (2008). "Moral Realism, Quasi-Realism, and Skepticism." In John Greco, ed. *The Oxford Handbook of Skepticism.* Oxford: Oxford University Press: 176–99.

Cuneo, Terence (2011a). "Reidian Metaethics, Part I." *Philosophy Compass* 6: 333–40.

Cuneo, Terence (2011b). "Reidian Metaethics, Part II." *Philosophy Compass* 6: 341–9.

Cuneo, Terence (2011c). "Moral Realism." In Christian Miller, ed. *The Continuum Companion to Ethics.* London and New York: Continuum: 3–28.

Cuneo, Terence. (2012). "Moral Naturalism and Categorical Reasons." In Susanna Nuccetelli and Gary Seay, eds. *Ethical Naturalism.* Cambridge: Cambridge University Press: 110–30.

Cuneo, Terence (2013). "Properties for Nothing, Facts for Free? Expressivism's Deflationary Gambit." In Russ Shafer-Landau, ed. *Oxford Studies in Metaethcs*, vol. 8. Oxford: Oxford University Press: 223–51.

Cuneo, Terence and Sean Christy (2011). "The Myth of Moral Fictionalism." In Michael Brady, ed. *New Waves in Metaethics.* London: Palgrave: 85–102.

Cuneo, Terence and Russ Shafer-Landau (2014). "The Moral Fixed Points: New Directions for Moral Nonnaturalism." *Philosophical Studies* DOI 10.1007/s11098-013-0277-5.

Dancy, Jonathan (2004). *Ethics without Principles.* Oxford: Oxford University Press.

Darwall, Stephen (2006). *The Second-Person Standpoint.* Cambridge, MA: Harvard University Press.

Davidson, Donald (1970). *Essays on Actions and Events.* Oxford: Oxford University Press.

Donnellan, Keith (1966). "Reference and Definite Descriptions." *Philosophical Review* 75: 281–304.

Dreier, James (2004). "Meta-ethics and the Problem of Creeping Miminalism." In John Hawthorne, ed. *Philosophical Perspectives 18, Ethics.* Blackwell: 23–44.

Egan, Andy (2007). "Quasi-realism and Fundamental Moral Error." *Australasian Journal of Philosophy* 85: 205–19.

Enoch, David (2005). "Why Idealize?" *Ethics* 115: 759–87.

Enoch, David (2009a). "Can There Be a Global, Interesting, Coherent Constructivism about Practical Reason?" *Philosophical Explorations* 12: 319–39.

Enoch, David (2009b). "How is Moral Disagreement a Problem for Realism?" *The Journal of Ethics* 13: 15–50.

Enoch, David (2010). "The Epistemological Challenge to Metanormative Realism: How Best to Understand It, and How to Cope with It." *Philosophical Studies* 148: 114–38.

Enoch, David (2011). *Taking Morality Seriously*. Oxford: Oxford University Press.

Feinberg, Joel (1970). *Doing and Deserving*. Princeton, NJ: Princeton University Press.

Firth, Roderick (1952). "Ethical Absolutism and the Ideal Observer." *Philosophy and Phenomenological Research* 12: 317–45.

FitzPatrick, William (2008). "Robust Ethical Realism, Non-Naturalism, and Normativity." In Russ Shafer-Landau, ed. *Oxford Studies in Metaethics*, vol. 3. Oxford: Oxford University Press: 159–206.

FitzPatrick, William (2011). "Ethical Non-Naturalism and Normative Properties." In Michael Brady, ed. *New Waves in Metaethics*. London: Palgrave: 7–35.

FitzPatrick, William (forthcoming). "Debunking Evolutionary Debunking of Ethical Realism." *Philosophical Studies*.

Foot, Philippa (2002). *Virtues and Vices*, 2nd edn. Oxford: Oxford University Press.

Gibbard, Allan (1990). *Wise Choices, Apt Feelings*. Cambridge, MA: Harvard University Press.

Gibbard, Allan (2002). "The Reasons of a Living Being." *Proceedings of the American Philosophical Association* 62: 49–60.

Gibbard, Allan (2003). *Thinking How to Live*. Cambridge, MA: Harvard University Press.

Goldman, Alvin (1970). *A Theory of Human Action*. Princeton: Princeton University Press.

Goldman, Alvin (2007). "A Program for 'Naturalizing' Metaphysics, with Application to the Ontology of Events." *The Monist* 90: 457–79.

Green, Mitchell S. (2007). *Self-Expression*. Oxford: Oxford University Press.

Grice, H. P. (1989). *Studies in the Way of Words*. Cambridge, MA: Harvard University Press.

Habermas, Jürgen (1991). *Moral Consciousness and Communicative Action*. Cambridge, MA: MIT Press.

Hare, John (2003). *God's Call*. Grand Rapids, MI: Eerdmans.

Hare, R. M. (1952). *The Language of Morals.* Oxford: Oxford University Press.

Harman, Gilbert (1977). *The Nature of Morality.* Oxford: Oxford University Press.

Harnish, Robert (2005). "Commitments and Speech Acts." *Philosophica* 75: 11–41.

Horgan, Terry and Mark Timmons (1991). "New Wave Moral Realism Meets Moral Twin Earth." *Journal of Philosophical Research* 16: 447–65.

Horgan, Terry and Mark Timmons (2000). "Nondescriptivist Cognitivism: Framework for a New Metaethic." *Philosophical Papers* 99: 121–53.

Horgan, Terry and Mark Timmons (2006). "Morality without Moral Facts." In James Dreier, eds. *Contemporary Debates in Moral Theory.* Oxford: Blackwell: 220–38.

Horwich, Paul (1998). *Truth,* 2nd edn. Oxford: Oxford University Press.

Horwich, Paul (2010). *Truth, Meaning, Reality.* Oxford: Oxford University Press.

Jackson, Frank (1998). *From Metaphysics to Ethics.* Oxford: Oxford University Press.

Jackson, Frank and Philip Pettit (1996). "Moral Functionalism and Moral Motivation." *Philosophical Quarterly* 45: 20–40.

James, Aaron (2007). "Constructivism about Practical Reasons." *Philosophy and Phenomenological Research* 74: 302–25.

Johnston, Mark (2005). "Constitution." In Frank Jackson and Michael Smith, eds. *The Oxford Handbook of Contemporary Philosophy.* Oxford: Oxford University Press: 636–77.

Johnston, Mark (2007). "Objective Mind and the Objectivity of Our Minds." *Philosophy and Phenomenological Research* 75: 223–68.

Joyce, Richard (2001). *The Myth of Morality.* Cambridge: Cambridge University Press.

Joyce, Richard (2006). *The Evolution of Morality.* Cambridge, MA: MIT University Press.

Joyce, Richard (2007). "Moral Antirealism." *Stanford Encyclopedia of Philosophy,* available online at <http://plato.stanford.edu/entries/moral-anti-realism/>.

Joyce, Richard (2011). "The Error in 'The Error in the Error Theory.'" *Australasian Journal of Philosophy* 89: 519–34.

Joyce, Richard (2013). "Irrealism and the Genealogy of Morals." *Ratio* 26: 1–22.

Kalderon, Mark (2005). *Moral Fictionalism.* Oxford: Oxford University Press.

Kaplan, David (2012). "An Idea of Donnellan." In Joseph Almog and Paolo Leonardi, eds. *Having in Mind.* Oxford: Oxford University Press: 122–75.

Kim, Jaegwon (1993). "Noncausal Connections." In *Supervenience and Mind.* Cambridge University Press: 22–32.

Korsgaard, Christine (1996). *The Sources of Normativity.* Cambridge, MA: Harvard University Press.

Korsgaard, Christine (2008). *Self-Constitution.* Oxford: Oxford University Press.

Kripke, Saul (1977). "Speaker's Reference and Semantic Reference." *Midwest Studies in Philosophy* 2: 255–76.

Kripke, Saul (1980). *Naming and Necessity.* Cambridge, MA: Harvard University Press.

Kukla, Rebecca and Mark Lance (2009). *Yo! and Lo!* Cambridge, MA: Harvard University Press.

Lewis, David (1972). *Convention.* Oxford: Blackwell.

Lewis, David (1989). "Dispositional Theories of Value." *Proceedings of the Aristotelian Society,* Supplement 63: 113–37.

Loeb, Don (1998). "Moral Realism and the Argument from Disagreement." *Philosophical Studies* 90: 282–303.

Loeb, Don (2007). "The Argument from Moral Experience." *Ethical Theory and Moral Practice* 10: 469–84.

Loeb, Don (2008). "Moral Incoherentism: How to Pull a Metaphysical Rabbit out of a Semantic Hat." In Walter Sinnott-Armstrong, ed. *Moral Psychology,* vol.2: *The Cognitive Science of Morality: Intuition and Diversity.* Cambridge, MA: MIT Press: 355–86.

Lynch, Michael P. (2009). *Truth as One and Many.* Oxford: Oxford University Press.

Mackie, J. L. (1977). *Ethics: Inventing Right and Wrong.* New York: Penguin.

MacIntyre, Alasdair (1984). *After Virtue,* 2nd edn. Notre Dame, IN: University of Notre Dame Press.

MacIntyre, Alasdair (1999). *Rational Dependent Animals.* Chicago and La Salle, IL: Open Court.

Marmor, Andrei (2009). *Social Conventions.* Princeton, NJ: Princeton University Press.

McGinn, Colin (1993). *Problems in Philosophy.* Oxford: Blackwell.

McPherson, Tristram (2009). "Moorean Arguments and Moral Revisionism." *Journal of Ethics and Social Philosophy* 3: 1–24.

Millikan, Ruth (2005). *Language: A Biological Model.* Oxford: Oxford University Press.

Milo, Ronald (1995). "Contractarian Constructivism." *Journal of Philosophy* 92: 181–204.

Moore, G. E. (1953). *Some Main Problems of Philosophy.* London: George Allen & Unwin.

Oddie, Graham (2005). *Value, Reality, and Desire.* Oxford: Oxford University Press.

Olson, Jonas (2011a). "Getting Real about Moral Fictionalism." In Russ Shafer-Landau, ed. *Oxford Studies in Metaethics,* vol. 6. Oxford University Press: 181–204.

Olson, Jonas. (2011b). "In Defense of Moral Error Theory." In Michael Brady, ed. *New Waves in Metaethics*. London: Palgrave: 62–84.

Parfit, Derek (2011). *On What Matters*, vols. I and II. Oxford: Oxford University Press.

Railton, Peter (1986). "Moral Realism." *Philosophical Review* 95: 163–207.

Raphael, D. D., ed. (1991). *British Moralists: 1650–1800*. Indianapolis, IN: Hackett.

Rawls, John (1999). "Kantian Constructivism in Moral Theory." In his *Collected Papers*. Ed. Samuel Freeman. Cambridge, MA: Harvard University Press.

Reid, Thomas (1997). *An Inquiry into the Human Mind on the Principles of Common Sense*. Ed. Derek R. Brookes. Edinburgh: Edinburgh University Press.

Reid, Thomas (2002). *Essays on the Intellectual Powers of Man*. Ed. Derek R. Brookes. Edinburgh: Edinburgh University Press.

Reid, Thomas (2010). *Essays on the Active Powers of Man*. Ed. James Harris and Knud Haakonssen. Edinburgh: Edinburgh University Press.

Roskies, Adina (2003). "Are Ethical Judgments Instrinsically Motivational? Lessons from Acquired Sociopathy." *Philosophical Psychology* 16: 51–66.

Rosen, Gideon (1998). "Blackburn's Essays in Quasi-Realism." *Noûs* 32: 386–45.

Russell, Bertrand (1956). *Logic and Knowledge*. London: Routledge.

Scanlon, T. M. (1998). *What We Owe Each Other*. Cambridge, MA: Harvard University Press.

Schiffer, Stephen (1972). *Meaning*. Oxford: Oxford University Press.

Schroeder, Mark (2008). *Being For*. Oxford: Oxford University Press.

Schroeder, Mark (2009). "Hybrid Expressivism: Virtues and Vices." *Ethics* 119: 257–309.

Searle, John (1969). *Speech Acts*. Cambridge: Cambridge University Press.

Searle, John (2010). *Making the Social World*. Oxford: Oxford University Press.

Searle, John (n.d.). "What is Language: Some Preliminary Remarks."

Shafer-Landau, Russ (2003). *Moral Realism: A Defence*. Oxford: Oxford University Press.

Shafer-Landau, Russ (2009). "A Defence of Categorical Reasons." *Proceedings of the Aristotelian Society* 109: 189–206.

Shafer-Landau, Russ (2012). "Genealogical Critiques of Moral Realism." *Journal of Ethics and Social Philosophy* 7: 1–37.

Smith, Michael (1994). *The Moral Problem*. Oxford: Blackwell.

Strawson, P. F. (1950). "On Referring." *Mind* 59: 320–44.

Street, Sharon (2006). "A Darwinian Dilemma for Realist Theories of Value." *Philosophical Studies* 126: 109–66.

Street, Sharon (2008a). "Constructivism about Reasons." In Russ Shafer-Landau, ed. *Oxford Studies in Metaethics*, vol. 3. Oxford: Oxford University Press: 207–46.

Street, Sharon (2008b). "Reply to Copp: Naturalism, Normativity, and the Varieties of Realism Worth Worrying About." *Philosophical Issues* 18: 207–28.

Street, Sharon (2010). "What is Constructivism in Ethics and Metaethics?" *Philosophy Compass* 5: 363–84.

Street, Sharon (forthcoming). "Objectivity and Truth: You'd Better Rethink It."

Strevens, Michael (forthcoming). "Theoretical Terms Without Analytic Truths." *Philosophical Studies.*

Sturgeon, Nicholas (1984). "Moral Explanation." In David Copp and David Zimmerman, eds. *Morality, Reason and Truth.* Totawa, NJ: Rowman and Allanheld: 49–78.

Tanesini, Alessandra (2005). "A Theory of Assertives." In Heather Battaly and Michael P. Lynch, eds. *Perspectives on the Philosophy of William P. Alston.* Lanham, MD: Rowman and Littlefield: 239–50.

Thomson, Judith Jarvis (1990). *The Realm of Rights.* Cambridge, MA: Harvard University Press.

Thomson, Judith Jarvis (1996). "Moral Objectivity." In Gilbert Harman and Judith Jarvis Thomson. *Moral Relativism and Moral Objectivity.* Oxford: Blackwell.

Timmons, Mark (1999). *Morality without Foundations.* Oxford: Oxford University Press.

van Roojen, Mark (2006). "Knowing Enough to Disagree: A New Response to the Moral Twin Earth Argument." In Russ Shafer-Landau, ed. *Oxford Studies in Metaethics*, Vol. 1. Oxford: Oxford University Press: 161–94.

Wedgwood, Ralph (2007). *The Nature of Normativity.* Oxford: Oxford University Press.

Wielenberg, Erik (2010). "On the Evolutionary Debunking of Morality." *Ethics* 120: 441–64.

Williamson, Timothy (2000). *Knowledge and Its Limits.* Oxford: Oxford University Press.

Wolterstorff, Nicholas (1980). *Works and Worlds of Art.* Oxford: Oxford University Press.

Wolterstorff, Nicholas (1995). *Divine Discourse.* Cambridge: Cambridge University Press.

Wolterstorff, Nicholas (2008). *Justice: Rights and Wrongs.* Princeton, NJ: Princeton University Press.

Wright, Crispin (1992). *Truth and Objectivity.* Cambridge, MA: Harvard University Press.

Zangwill, Nick (1992). "Quietism." In Peter French, Theodore Uehling, and Howard Wettstein, eds. *Midwest Studies in Philosophy.* Minneapolis, MN: University of Minnesota Press: 17: 60–76.

Index

Printed and bound by CPI Group (UK) Ltd, Croydon, CR0 4YY